Law, Science and Experts

Law, Science and Experts
Civil and Criminal Forensics

William S. Bailey
Terence J. McAdam

Carolina Academic Press
Durham, North Carolina

Copyright © 2014
Carolina Academic Press
All Rights Reserved

Library of Congress Cataloging-in-Publication Data

Bailey, William S. (William Scherer) author
 Law, science and experts : civil and criminal forensics / William S. Bailey and Terence J. McAdam.
    p. cm.
 Includes bibliographical references and index.
 ISBN 978-1-61163-188-3 (alk. paper)
 1. Evidence, Expert—United States. 2. Forensic sciences—United States. 3. Criminal investigation—United States. I. McAdam, Terence J. author. II. Title.

 KF8961.B35 2014
 347.73'67--dc23   2014027968

Carolina Academic Press
700 Kent Street
Durham, NC 27701
Telephone (919) 489-7486
Fax (919) 493-5668
www.cap-press.com

Printed in the United States of America

I dedicate the book to my wife Sylvia. "After all these years, we're still having fun, and you're still the one."

William S. Bailey

This is for you, Elizabeth. Without your patience, understanding and gentle prodding, this book would not have been written. Thank you for always being there for me.

Terence J. McAdam

Contents

Acknowledgments

In his seminal book *Emotional Intelligence,* Daniel Goleman describes the research of the legendary Bell Labs as "beyond the capacity of any one person to tackle." The same easily can be said of Forensics, as science and technology increasingly take center stage in the resolution of legal matters. I have been the beneficiary of generously shared wisdom and insight from a broad range of outstanding judges, law professors, trial attorneys, and scientists, all of whom played a critical role in this book.

I am much in the debt of my good friend and mentor Professor John Mitchell of Seattle University School of Law, a dynamic, creative scholar and classroom teacher. John designed a Forensics course, taught it for years and then encouraged me to step up and take it over. This book never would have happened without him.

The advice, guidance and wisdom of teachers and mentors has made all the difference in my life. I owe them a huge collective debt. I am particularly grateful for the support of Justice Tom Chambers, Paul N. Luvera and Professor John J. Sullivan.

I was fortunate to have the opportunity to work with my co-author Terence J. McAdam, a skilled forensic scientist and a dynamic teacher.

Since *Daubert,* trial judges occupy the critical role of gatekeeper in the use of expert testimony. The Hon. Harry T. Edwards, Senior Circuit Judge, the Hon. Robert T. Lasnik, District Court Judge, and King County (Washington) Superior Court Judges Andrea A. Darvas, William L. Downing and Ronald Kessler provided me with keen insight into the challenges faced by trial courts in regulating expert testimony, as well as the impact it has had on jury decisions. They also helped me to understand better how this information is most effectively communicated to jurors.

My colleagues at the University of Washington School of Law have been generous in their support, guidance and encouragement. Professor Peter Nicolas planted the idea for this book. Professors Sanne Knudsen, Michael Townsend and Todd Wildermuth have a phenomenal breadth of scientific literacy, helping me to understand the relationship between law and science. Reference librarian Mary Whisner kept me up on all the latest developments in the forensic world. Dean Kellye Testy and Professors Robert Aronson, Bill Covington, Deborah Maranville and Kate O'Neill were encouraging throughout the writing process.

This book has benefitted greatly from the depth of talent and experience of some of the best trial lawyers in America. I am grateful to David Beninger, Ralph J. Brindley, John

Budlong, Erin Ehlert, C. Steven Fury, Todd W. Gardner, Ian Goodhew, Karen Koehler, Mark R. Larson, Elizabeth A. Leedom, James S. Rogers, Malcolm Ross and Michael S. Wampold. They personify the best practices of the trial bar, serving both their clients and our justice system with great distinction.

Scott Patrick Kennedy was an invaluable research assistant, creatively and methodically sorting out the trends and patterns in federal and state judicial opinions after *Daubert*. Kathy Bremner used her considerable editorial skills to improve the book, identifying corrections with pinpoint accuracy. Matthew Wurdeman transformed the Notes with his unerring sense of form and function.

A number of scientists, scholars and technical experts were very important to my understanding of this subject. I thank the following experts for their input, thought and guidance: Geoffrey Baird, MD, PhD; Robert Feldman, MD; John Fountaine, MA, CRC; Philip T. Hoffman, PhD; B.J. Oneal, PhD; Peter M. McGough, MD; Kenneth Muscatel, PhD; Denise Rodier, MS; David Stenhouse, Christina Tapia, PhD; Allan F. Tencer, PhD; Michele Triplett; and Philip J. Vogelzang, MD.

The advice, encouragement and friendship of Chicago DEA Special Agent In Charge Jack Riley has been enormously helpful to me. Sergeant Robert Vallor and Detective Alan Cruise of the Seattle Police Department Homicide Unit consistently have been very generous in providing real world information on criminal forensics.

I have had many great clients over my career, who have inspired me to do my best work. I am grateful to Roger Murray and the Philippides family for permitting me to use events from their lives.

Visualization is critical to the understanding of expert testimony. I wish to thank Duane Hoffmann for his elegant illustrations, which required enormous time and effort. I also am grateful to Kathy A. Cochran, Kevin C. Kealty, Jr., Patrick O'Neill, David Newman, Jay Syverson and Aaron Weholt for their outstanding visuals.

Keith Sipe of Carolina Academic Press is a publisher who always is open to new ideas, bringing out the best in his authors. I am grateful for his confidence in me and this book. He is backed by a top production staff, including editor Linda Lacy, production coordinator Ryland Bowman and design/layout specialist Tim Colton.

The support staff team at William Gates Hall is phenomenal, juggling as many responsibilities as air traffic controllers. Their capable assistance was a necessary ingredient to writing this book and I am much indebted to Tabitha Acosta, Dawn Bell and Laurie Carlsson.

—William S. Bailey

———————

The person who deserves the greatest acknowledgment is the love of my life Elizabeth. When I would come home after a long day at the Crime Lab or from teaching or occasionally from both, she was the one who kept me on task. Without her support I would not have completed this book.

I'd also like to thank my co-author Bill Bailey for his patience and insight. I have truly enjoyed working on this endeavor with him.

I owe a great debt to the dedicated men and women of the Washington State Patrol Crime Laboratories. Jim Tarver, the Crime Laboratory Division Commander graciously gave permission for me to work on this project. Randy Watson and Sarah Trejo from the Olympia Crime Lab produced the latent print images. Jeff Teitelbaum, from the Seattle Crime Lab, one of the best forensic librarians in the world, discovered many pertinent articles I was able to reference. Denise Rodier and Victor El Koury from the Seattle Crime Lab assisted greatly with the editing of the DNA and Evidence chapters. Kris Kern from the Crime Scene Response Team helped with the presentation of the 3-D scanner images. Melody Yu provided English translation assistance on Chinese forensic articles.

Lastly, Ray Kusumi, also from the Seattle Crime Lab, lent his photographic skills, and his talent is evident in many of the photos he provided for this book.

—Terry McAdam
Renton, WA, July 2014.

For the rational study of the law, the black-letter man may be the man of the present, but the man of the future is the man of statistics and the master of economics.
—Oliver Wendell Holmes, *The Path of the Law*,
10 HARV. L. REV. 457, 469 (1897)

It is unrealistic to expect either members of the judiciary or state officials to be well versed in the rigors of experimental or statistical technique.
—*Craig v. Boren*, 429 U.S. 190, 204 (1976)

Law, Science and Experts

Chapter 1

Introduction to Forensics

Advances in technology will continue to reach far into every sector of our economy. Future job and economic growth ... is directly related to scientific advancement.

—Christopher Bond

In the twenty-first century, science and technology increasingly dominate the way we think, communicate and live. What was once science fiction steadily has turned into everyday reality. Electronic devices now have become indispensable to both work and leisure. Our very notions of life and death have evolved as science advances. In turn, all of this is changing the character of what the law is asked to resolve, as well as the legal process itself.

The rapid change of our time can be traced back to a century ago, when the pace of scientific discovery first began to accelerate, entering public thought on a sustained basis:

> The prestige of science was colossal ... confronted on every hand by new machines and devices ... [people] were ready to believe that science could accomplish almost anything; and they were being deluged with scientific information and theory.[1]

Einstein's revolutionary theories on gravity, space and time rocked conventional wisdom, with considerable impact: "[The general theory of relativity will] overthrow the certainty of the ages, and ... require a new philosophy of the universe...."[2] By 1919, photographs during a solar eclipse conclusively proved that the force of gravity bent light, just as Einstein predicted. Thereafter, the possibilities of science seemed limitless.

The simple, steady perspective of an agricultural society shifted into a more complex one, with faith, science and law increasingly on a collision course. In 1925, John Thomas Scopes was prosecuted in Dayton, Tennessee, for teaching Darwin's theory of evolution. This was the beginning of a conflict between science and popular belief that has been with us ever since. Since the early 1980s, Gallup polling data indicates 44 percent or more of Americans still believe that God created humans in their present form.[3] Even though 97 percent of environmental scientists believe that global warming and climate change are real and caused by human activity, the Yale Project on Climate Change Communication reports that only 63 percent of Americans believe this.[4]

All the scientific information accumulated in the century since Einstein announced his general theory of relativity has created a great divide. Most of us fall on the side of not knowing much about either science or math. The technology behind the consumer products that we all use regularly is beyond us now too. As our world becomes more deeply immersed in science and technology, law increasingly is called upon to make informed decisions on scientific issues. Cases often now require special expertise that many lawyers and judges do not possess. Justice Antonin Scalia openly joked about this during oral argument in *Massachusetts v. Environmental Protection Agency*:[5]

> Mr. Milkey (for the State of Massachusetts): Respectfully, Your Honor. It is not the stratosphere. It is the troposphere.
>
> Justice Scalia: Troposphere, whatever. I told you before I'm not a scientist. (Laughter).
>
> Justice Scalia: That's why I don't want to deal with global warming, to tell you the truth.

We have reached a point in the law where willful ignorance of science and math is no longer an option. Scientific critical analysis has become just as important to client representation as legal critical analysis. Scientific debates in the courtroom now are the norm, with experts from learned disciplines routinely providing the analytical tools needed for informed decisions. In order to be effective advocates, we have to go deeper into the science behind our cases and understand how scientific hypotheses are designed, tested and modified over time.

We lawyers are supposed to be the problem solvers of our society. This now requires us to develop familiarity with scientific terms and concepts. Otherwise, we are failing in a core part of our mission, giving experts a free pass due to our own lack of competence. While we may be able to expose other kinds of witnesses trying to put their thumb on the scale, evaluating forensic experts requires concerted effort and sophisticated analysis. Are we willing and able to ask the tough questions about the assumptions made by scientific or technical experts? This requires diving into the literature, learning the hard way, and wrapping our heads around an unfamiliar methodology until we understand it.

Solving legal disputes with scientific issues is not just a simple matter of plugging in expert opinions or research studies to get the answer. Scientific certainty itself is an elusive concept, with regular disagreements about cause and effect relationships. Like any human endeavor, science is subject to error. The conclusions in a significant number of scientific peer review articles later have been found to be wrong. Even if the data itself is accurate, the interpretations given to it may not be. In the end, science is much more about probabilities than certainty, which makes it harder to use in resolving legal disputes.

Are we doing an adequate job in the law of understanding science? Do we know enough to separate out and analyze the scientific aspects of our cases? Resolving these questions inevitably involves bringing the discussion down to a simple level for the trier of fact. The ability to execute this has become a mark of what separates out the really good attorneys.

Is it a good system to try to explain complicated science to juries? Are jurors capable of making informed decisions on these issues? Is it enough just to instruct them on credibility issues, forensic and otherwise? How are they to decide on the truth, when each lawyer has experts endorsing opposite points of view? How effective are we in presenting the information a jury needs to sort out scientific truth? United States District Court Judge Robert Lasnik speaks for many of his colleagues in noting room for improvement:

> Lawyers as a group tend not to focus on the information needs of the audience in presenting experts, resulting in a battle that does not end up helping either side's case. The judge and jury end up left in never-never land, without much idea of what the experts are talking about.[6]

If the law now must find truth in a world driven by science and technology, what kind of knowledge and training do judges need in order to make intelligent rulings? In the *Daubert* trilogy, the United States Supreme Court certainly focused our attention on the question, making us more aware of the need to use expert testimony in a responsible manner. But there are other issues that the *Daubert* trilogy has not resolved.

A fundamental tension continues between what is legally admissible as relevant and what is actually good science. Prior to *Daubert,* the Federal Rules of Evidence liberalized the use of expert testimony. Relevance was given a broad definition and experts had wide latitude to render opinions within their field. The idea was that juries could sort out credibility issues, with less need for a judge to restrict admissibility. Was it realistic for the drafters of the Federal Rules to assume that the adversary system would expose bad science? Critics have responded "no" to this question, alleging that the floodgates had been opened to "junk science," "frivolous lawsuits," and bad jury decisions. *Daubert* gave tacit support to these criticisms, suggesting that the pendulum had swung too far toward anything goes. The role of trial judge as gatekeeper was resurrected to curb perceived abuses. The empirical evidence since *Daubert* suggests that this decision did change the way in which experts are used, but questions remain on whether more needs to be done.

Experience has shown us that the reliability of forensic evidence can be difficult to sort out. Beyond anecdotal and subjective assessments, we often don't know what precise impact it has had on the final result or how well jurors have applied the scientific principles to the legal issues. Expert opinions may be given more weight than they deserve. Concern has been expressed at the national level about the variable reliability and methodology in forensic disciplines. Can people without specialized training really sort out what is good science and what is not? Some fields, such as DNA analysis, are based on a solid scientific platform, with appropriately trained experts. Other disciplines are much more subjective, learned on-the-job, rather than through formal education. It can be difficult to separate real science from junk science, particularly with a persuasive expert on the witness stand. Media reports abound of experts who were believed by a jury, only to find later that the experts' opinions lacked a valid scientific basis.

The inherent manipulation of the adversarial system makes it more difficult to get at the truth. There is a temptation to try to take advantage of jurors' collective ignorance of science and math. The general public has a preference for simple stories with easy answers. Litigation pressures force us to find the experts to deliver the opinions we need to win, creating a symbiotic relationship. We adroitly use stories and analogies to create a surface appeal for the jury. Is the outcome more likely to be driven by gut reactions? Does the slickest presentation win, regardless of the relative scientific validity?

But even putting aside the manipulation issue, how do we take apart a scientific problem and present it in a way that lay people will understand? Quantitative evidence is a potential problem here. Are lawyers, judges or jurors really able to understand it? Though numbers are critical to scientific proof, the sight of them often causes many people to check out. Even among those with college degrees, liberalized curriculum requirements permit the avoidance of math and science. Under the principle of use it or lose it, what we don't use slips from our grasp.

The broad range of perspectives and life experiences on our jury panels continues to be a strong positive. We must live up to our part of the bargain, presenting competent, relevant forensic evidence. Jurors want to do the right thing and pay close attention to the testimony, scientific or otherwise. The Honorable Ronald Kessler, a veteran state trial court judge, has seen a remarkable consistency in the dedication of jurors over his long career:

> The jurors who end up serving on a panel really want to be there. I always go back into the jury room after a verdict and talk with them by myself. Every single time, they are happy about what they did. This is something that they will remember forever.[7]

The critical factor is how effective we lawyers can be in educating them. In the words of Shakespeare: "The fault, dear Brutus, is not in our stars, / But in ourselves."[8]

This is an exciting time to be a lawyer, with great possibilities before us for taking an even more prominent role in public life. Just as the computer has made legal research easier and more efficient, going deeper into science will help us to better serve our clients and the legal system as a whole. The core purpose of this book is to take an in-depth, thoughtful look at the practice and procedure surrounding the use of expert testimony in the law, both civil and criminal, giving you the tools needed to step up and handle this evidence with confidence and professionalism.

Chapter 2

The Strategic Role of Experts

All men can see these tactics whereby I conquer, but none can see the strategy out of which victory is evolved.

—Sun Tzu

Every case involves the competing opinions of scientific or technical experts woven into the narrative. The trier of fact values concreteness and accuracy in weighing the evidence and determining which side of a case should win. Both judges and juries want their decisions to be based upon solid, accurate testimony and listen carefully to the content of what experts say, determining whether or not it makes sense. They really don't get enough credit for this.

Do the areas of disagreement between the experts really make a difference to the legal standard? In this chapter, we will look at the strategic impact of experts on case outcome, whether through motion practice, settlement or trial. Little empirical research has been done on this question. We largely are left to sift through anecdotal opinions in search of the answer. Lawyers and judges vary in assessing the extent to which experts drive results, as shown in the following responses from a veteran trial judge and two highly experienced attorneys:

> The relative importance of experts depends on the case. The facts, case story and overall witness credibility usually matter more than what the experts say.[1]

Figure 2-1. Battle of experts.

Opposing experts can do permanent damage to your case, causing the jury to doubt it. If they do, you have a significant chance of losing.[2]

Experts are not usually the deciding factor in most juror decisions. But a clear standout can make a difference.[3]

Sorting Out the Variables

The variables of a case add to the complexity of sorting out the impact of experts. What are the facts and basic trial story of each party? The side closest to common sense is likely to prevail, regardless of what the experts say. What is the forum? Experts have varying degrees of latitude in state and federal courts. Who is the judge? Some regulate expert opinion more stringently than others. Who are the lawyers? Differences in skill make some better at presenting experts. What are the issues to be decided? The more technical and removed they are from everyday experience and common sense, the more important the experts become.

What is the chemistry between the experts, both opposing and on the same side? If the experts called by one side work as a team, with opinions that fit together like pieces of a puzzle, educating and assisting the trier of fact, the chances of prevailing increase. If opposing experts in the same field have résumés of equal strength, differences in charisma and emotional accessibility will impact persuasiveness. What is the makeup of the jury? Higher educational levels and sophistication will make jurors more independent, less inclined to rely on expert testimony.

Social Science Studies of Persuasion and Attitude Change

All of us have had the experience of going into a store or an automobile dealership with one kind of purchase in mind, only to find our thinking changed by a persuasive salesperson. There is no question that some people are very adept at influencing others. In *The Tipping Point*, Malcolm Gladwell studies those who launch social trends and shape thought.[4] Some of these same aptitudes apply to expert courtroom communication dynamics.

Social science long has studied the factors that go into persuasion, influencing judgment and changing attitudes. Psychologist Carl Iver Hovland of Yale University was a pioneer in this field, starting in the Second World War. He focused on how different approaches to training impacted the motivation of soldiers. Hovland and his colleagues determined that it was far more effective to present both sides of an issue even-handedly in shaping opinion than to use one-sided propaganda.[5] In the early 1950s, along with Irving Janis and Harold Kelley, Hovland examined how the prestige and reputation of a speaker affect what an audience believes.[6] The same opinion will be viewed differently, depending on who delivers it. Perceived expertise leads to a halo effect that enhances a speaker's impact. The chair of a medical department will be seen as far more persuasive than a college student.

The trustworthiness of an expert also depends on the perception of bias, which can cut for or against an opinion. Hovland and his colleagues compared the persuasive differences between high- and low-prestige information. The same message favoring an increase in penalties against juvenile offenders was attributed to both a judge and a drug pusher. The audience believed both, but for different reasons—the judge because of his prestige and expertise and the drug pusher because his opinion went against his interest as a criminal type.

Charisma is the third factor that determines the impact of an expert. Self-assured, dynamic, likeable and attractive presenters are much more likely to persuade us to their point of view. A frequently cited example of this is the matchup between John F. Kennedy and Richard M. Nixon in the first televised debate of the 1960 presidential campaign.[7] Though an experienced and articulate debater, making good, substantive points, Nixon was outclassed on the television screen by the Kennedy charm, charisma and ease.

The power of expert opinion to sway human thought was scientifically confirmed in a 2009 study led by Gregory Berns, MD, PhD, of Emory University School of Medicine.[8] The subjects in this study had to choose between a lottery and a guaranteed payment annuity while their brain activity was measured by fMRI scanning. The testing was divided into segments, some of which required these decisions to be made on their own and others where financial experts gave them advice. The results, confirmed by the fMRI findings, showed that the expert's advice had a dramatic effect on behavior: "The brain relinquishes responsibility when a trusted authority provides expertise."[9] The principal investigator, Dr. Berns, also sounded a cautionary note about the potential for abuse in this expert effect, one which is of great significance for the legal system: "The problem with this tendency is that it can work to a person's detriment if a trusted source turns out to be incompetent or corrupt."[10] The gatekeeper function of the judiciary is designed to prevent this kind of incompetent or corrupt expert from testifing in a legal proceeding.

Stripping Away Advocacy Positions

The impact experts have on case outcome is in part determined by what survives after the advocacy positions are stripped away. Judges and juries well understand the hyperbole of the adversary system, with each side overstating what it believes to be reasonable. Experts bracket the ranges of the issues in a case, giving the two extremes. Judges and juries sort through this, looking for the truth in between. However, if one expert is much better grounded in the facts of a case than another, jurors may adopt his/her opinion in its entirety:

> **Example:** In an automobile rear end collision trial, the plaintiff's treating chiropractor was of modest accomplishment. He testified that the plaintiff was in great pain, but her strong work ethic caused her to return to work right away. The defense medical expert had stellar credentials, but had only done a records review. He opined that her prompt return to work proved she had not suffered significant injury. Though his credentials were far less impressive, the jury believed the chiropractor, finding that he had much more of a feel for the plaintiff as a person and her situation.[11]

If the expert testimony is weak or even missing on an important issue, then the trier of fact will be tempted merely to substitute its own experience.

Expert Opinion — Persuasion or Rationalization?

An unanswered strategic question about the role of experts is whether they lead the trier of fact to a particular outcome, or are used as backfill to support gut reactions. Juries weigh all the human factors in a case. The side that is the most based on truth and common sense usually wins. Experts often are less important in shaping these perceptions than the underlying facts and the clients: "While less objective in some ways, the background stories of the parties matter more than what experts say on the witness stand."[12] Jurors can and often do form opinions early in a trial, with an initial leaning after opening statement. Experts can help jurors rationalize these intuitive decisions. Jurors can pick and choose among the experts' testimony, bolstering their own perception of the case, supporting the version of the facts that makes the most sense to them. In this manner, expert testimony reinforces the belief system of the jury, interpreting the facts of a case in a persuasive way:

> Jurors arrive at a result that they believe is appropriate, just and fair, using testimony which supports this outcome. Experts provide the opportunity to ascribe rationality to gut instincts.[13]

By the time key witnesses have testified, many jurors know which way they are going. Some will say later, "The expert convinced me of this," but this often can be more of a ratified gut reaction.

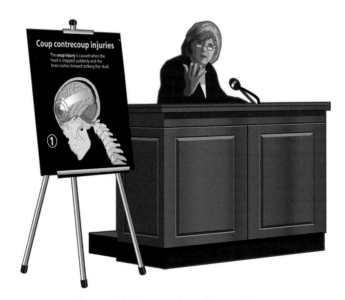

Figure 2-2. Experts shape juror opinions.

How Experts Help You Win

Experts help you win by being teachers, explaining to the jury why they should go in a particular direction. It's not about the actual opinions so much as it is the teaching, giving the jury the tools to go back and say, "This side should win because of these reasons." You seek to empower the jurors on your side, helping them advocate for the result you want. The teaching function of experts is a big part of this process, giving your jurors more power, persuasiveness and conviction during deliberations.

Do Résumés Matter?

What you may think as a lawyer about the experts in a case may be very different from how the jury will assess them. The best résumé does not necessarily determine which expert a jury will like the most. With information so readily available in today's world, people aren't as impressed by experts, titles or résumés. Who needs an expert when a quick Google search can produce all kinds of information? With ever-shorter attention spans, résumé-driven pomp and circumstance from the witness stand is a negative. There is an enormous premium in figuring out a human-interest angle in your expert's background, telling a story about it and then getting to the bottom line—the expert's opinions and why they are critical to making the right decision in your case.

Résumés can matter when there is a big difference in the quality of the experts called by each side. If your experts are much better credentialed than your opponent's, you are more likely to win.

> **Example:** In a medical malpractice case involving a child, the plaintiff called an attending orthopedist at a highly regarded children's hospital who specialized in the exact area involved. The defense called a young, well-spoken orthopedist from a Navy hospital with no pediatric expertise. The defense was worried that its expert would not measure up and ended up settling the case prior to verdict.[14]

Experts whose accomplishments make them clear standouts will rise to the top, with the potential for considerable jury influence.

> **Example:** In a medical malpractice case, the head of vascular surgery of a medical school testified for the defense. Not only was he quite accomplished in terms of his résumé, but articulate, personable and extremely charismatic. He ended up shaping the way the jury thought about the issues in the case.[15]

Experts Affect How Lawyers Feel about Their Cases

Whatever impact they ultimately may have on a jury, it is undeniable that experts can have a big effect on how we lawyers feel about our cases. A common question from opposing counsel is, "What experts do you have?" It is a great feeling when you have solid, well-respected experts to back up your case, able to deliver all the opinions you need. Powerful, credible experts with no obvious bias and strong, supported opinions are a major source of fear for opponents. They build a sense of confidence on the part of the lawyer who retains them. Conversely, shopworn experts, "the usual suspects," do not have much impact on opposing counsel. They scoff, "Is that the best you can do?"

Lawyers tend to obsess on comparing which expert has published the most in the field. It certainly is scary when the opposing expert has a volume of publications and all the right credentials, particularly when they appear to really believe what they are saying: "If the other side has a world-class expert who has written a textbook in the field or is otherwise notable, it certainly cranks up my anxiety level."[16] This is even more so if the expert has not testified frequently and cannot be easily discredited as an advocate. Jurors tend to believe experts with this profile, particularly if they seem motivated by a genuine desire to provide helpful information.

Taking Out Opposing Experts through Motions

The critical strategic importance of experts to a case can best be seen by what occurs following motion practice. This tactic is used with some frequency to limit the opinions of an opposing expert, or even to strike them entirely. The grounds used in these motions commonly fall into one or more of the following categories:

1. Based on junk science

2. Beyond his/her expertise

3. Speculation—no factual support for opinion

4. Failure to disclose opinions or background foundation in a timely manner

The court's rulings on these motions can rearrange the expert landscape in a case significantly, with some opinions stricken, or, less frequently, one or more experts excluded entirely. If this happens, a major shift in the power dynamic occurs. The lawyers on the receiving end scramble to do damage control, filling in the holes in their proof created by the court's ruling:

> **Example:** A product liability case against an auto manufacturer involved allegations of an airbag going off when it shouldn't have. The plaintiff lost vision in one eye. The defendant manufacturer's experts presented very speculative theories, concluding, "The plaintiff just hit the rearview mirror. The airbag didn't do this." These opinions were not supported by anything beyond the experts' basic qualifications and experience. The trial judge excluded both defense experts from testifying after a pre-trial motion. This left the defense without any expert support for their liability theory and they settled the case halfway through the trial.[17]

Experts in Plaintiff's Proof Sequence — Theory of the Triangle

Bearing the burden of proof, plaintiffs have an added strategic need for expert testimony in trial. Plaintiffs quickly must get their case on a very solid footing with a jury. Otherwise, they are likely to lose. Many plaintiffs' counsel orchestrate their liability cases around the theory of the triangle, in which experts often play a critical role. In this approach, the three most important parts of a trial are jury selection, opening statement and the first witness. The plaintiff's best liability expert usually fills the first witness slot, attempting to sell the theory upon which the finding of fault hinges.

In medical malpractice cases, the first witness for the plaintiff often is an expert who establishes cause and effect, destroying the defenses to causation. "Let's get that out of the way right now." This expert explains why the plaintiff's liability theory is not something goofy or obscure, disarming the defense arguments. From there, the expert gets into what the defendant did wrong. This approach also eliminates the need to attack the defendant as a bad person, instead providing the technical details of why the harm occurred. "This baby was harmed because he did not get enough oxygen in the first five minutes before he was born. He should have been delivered long before that."

Use of Rules and Standards

Experts and rules are closely linked. Every case revolves around rules and consequences. These often fix the focus of the expert debate. We need experts to interpret how these technical rules apply. What's the rule? What are the consequences if you violate it? Accident reconstruction experts start with the rules of the road. What is the speed limit? Was the defendant exceeding it? They start with the evidence and go right to the rules of the road in interpreting it. They tie them all together.

National standards are very important in this debate. People always want simple solutions and rules or guidelines can provide those. Jurors generally perceive these rules as authoritative and rely on them. If a standard or guideline helps you, use it. "Here's the rule. He either did or did not comply with it." In medical negligence cases there often is conflict over what the rule is. Plaintiff's medical experts say the rule is one thing and the defense experts disagree. How do you convince the jury that your expert's interpretation of the rule is correct? These rules are very harmful if they are against you to any extent, requiring an explanation why it doesn't apply to the facts of your case. You need to be able to point out to the jury that your opponent is misapplying and misusing the standard. The apples and oranges cliché is frequently used in these circumstances, as well as analogies to everyday life experience.

> **Sample argument:** My opponent has said a standard applies here when it doesn't. This is like using a law against speeding for a driver who goes through a stop sign. These are two entirely different things.

Technical Cases Increase an Expert's Importance

Experts are very important in technical cases, such as medical malpractice, highway design or even complex auto crashes. For example, in highway design cases, the liability battle between experts often centers on the interpretation of standards in the U.S. Department of Transportation design manual. Did the state highway department follow these? If not, how important was the deviation? Sometimes this is not addressed one way or the other in the standard. An expert's opinion often is the only means of providing the clarity needed to decide the issue.

Example: A highway car crash fatality involved the design of the pillars supporting an overpass. The defense in the case focused on the fact that a national standards body allowed the use of an earthen berm to keep cars from crashing into these pillars. The plaintiff's liability expert surveyed the scene and determined that, as built, this berm was not as high as either the national standards or the plans called for. This became the frame for the plaintiff's liability argument: "If they just had built this according to their own specs, nobody would have died or been badly hurt."[18]

Making Harmful Evidence Relevant

Sometimes experts are called for the sole purpose of trying to make harmful evidence relevant that otherwise would be kept out. The classic example is drug or alcohol use.

Example: In a serious injury case, the permanent disability status of the plaintiff was not contested. However, the defense wanted to bring in plaintiff's past issues with alcohol through a vocational expert. The defense theory was based on a broad brush "alcohol is bad" approach, that alcohol abuse shortens work-life expectancy. It was not specifically linked to the plaintiff's circumstances. The trial judge refused to allow the defense expert to testify about this, finding it too speculative and generic.[19]

Disciplines Subject to Juror Disbelief

Whether we call it junk science or not, there are some areas of expert testimony that are more open to disbelief on the part of the jury. For example, the discipline of human factors seeks to explain what people see and how they respond. Experts in this area often testify for plaintiffs in warnings or signage cases, trying to explain why the language used was inadequate, suggesting a better approach. The need to use a human factors expert generally is indicative of a weak liability case.

Opportunity to Manipulate Data Inputs

Various "black box" type computer programs have modified the traditional approach of experts, with a corresponding impact on legal strategy in a case. These programs allow for expert discretion with data inputs, which can be expressed in a range or as an estimate. The expert's use of this discretion can have a huge impact on the accuracy and outcome of an analysis. If done improperly, the results can be classic "garbage in, garbage out." Accident reconstruction is one such "black box" discipline. Though based upon valid physics principles and volumes of research, litigation experts can manipulate computer data inputs in a way that favors the party who retained them. You can't cross-examine the computer, so you have to figure out what the opposing expert did through your own expert, asking, "What were his inputs? What assumptions did he make? Are these accurate?"

Experts Can Be the Tipping Point

Social science research strongly supports that trustworthy, credible experts can have a large impact on attitude formation. While there is a range of opinion among lawyers and judges as to the importance of experts to case outcome, there is no question that all parties put enormous resources into retaining the best experts they can find and discrediting the opposing experts. Perhaps most significantly, experts have a big impact on the degree of confidence lawyers have about their cases. There is no question that a powerful synergy exists between how the trier of fact assesses the character of the parties and the opinions offered by experts.

Takeaways — The Strategic Role of Experts

1. Scientific and technical experts give competing narratives on the witness stand. The jury has to sort these out and figure out what is going on.

2. Judges and juries are very good at listening to the content of what experts say, determining whether or not it makes sense.

3. Little empirical research has been done on the impact of experts on case outcome. We largely are left to sift through anecdotal opinions in search of the answer.

4. The variables of each case add to the complexity of sorting out the impact experts have on the outcome, making it difficult to give a definitive answer.

5. There is no question that some people are adept at influencing others. For some time, social scientists have studied the factors most likely to influence judgment and change attitudes.

6. Prestige and perceived expertise have much to do with how the audience receives a message, with the potential for a halo effect that can greatly enhance the speaker's impact.

7. The trustworthiness of an expert also depends on the perception of bias, which can cut both ways. An otherwise unlikely source can be more credible if offering an opinion against interest.

8. Charisma is the third factor that determines the impact of an expert in a case. Self-assured, dynamic, likeable and attractive presenters are much more likely to persuade us.

9. Jurors understand the adversary system, knowing that each side overstates what they believe is reasonable.

10. Jurors pick and choose among the experts, depending on which direction they are leaning in the case.

11. Expert testimony often is used by jurors to reinforce their belief systems.

12. Experts help you win by being teachers, explaining to the jury why they should go in a particular direction. It's not about the actual opinions so much as it is the teaching.

13. The best résumé does not necessarily determine which expert the jury will like the most.

14. What the lawyers may think about experts may be very wrong in terms of how the jury will assess them.

15. Experts who are clear standouts can have considerable influence on the jury.

16. Whatever impact they ultimately may have on a jury, it is undeniable that experts can have a big effect on how lawyers feel about their cases.

17. Motion practice can shift the expert landscape in a case, with those on the receiving end of a ruling scrambling to fill the holes created by a judge's ruling striking all or part of an expert's testimony.

18. Experts are very important in technical cases such as medical malpractice, highway design or even complex auto crashes.

19. Every case revolves around rules and consequences. These often fix the focus of the expert debate.

20. National standards are very important in this debate. People always want simple solutions and rules or guidelines can provide those.

21. Jurors generally perceive standards as authoritative. They are very harmful if they are against you to any extent, requiring an explanation of why they don't apply.

22. Sometimes experts are called for the sole purpose of trying to make relevant some harmful piece of evidence that otherwise would be kept out.

23. Whether we call it junk science or not, there are some areas of expert testimony that are more open to disbelief on the part of the jury. Use of experts in these areas should be approached with great caution.

24. Various "black box" type computer programs have modified the traditional approach of experts. These programs allow for expert discretion with data inputs, which can be expressed in a range or as an estimate. The expert's use of this discretion can have a huge impact on the accuracy and outcome of an analysis.

Chapter 3

The Shape of the World after *Daubert*

Even a change for the better always is accompanied by drawbacks and discomforts.

—Arnold Bennett

Ever since the United States Supreme Court's landmark 1993 decision in *Daubert v. Merrell Dow Pharmaceuticals*,[1] the practical impact of the case has been widely debated. A fundamental ambiguity in the decision itself invites this. On the surface, it appeared that the plaintiff had won, as the language of the opinion purported to relax and lower the threshold for admitting expert testimony.[2] Yet the standards set forth in the opinion arguably raised the bar, going beyond the long established *Frye* criteria of general acceptance in the scientific community. Others have maintained that *Daubert* has had little or no practical effect at the trial court level compared to *Frye*.

Regardless of who is correct, practitioners and judges alike have struggled to apply *Daubert* at trial: How can the judge's role as "gatekeeper" be squared with the jury's role as fact-finder? Which factors should be considered in a reliability assessment, and what weight should each receive? Where is the line between admissible and inadmissible expertise? Surveying the most heavily cited empirical studies, appellate decisions,

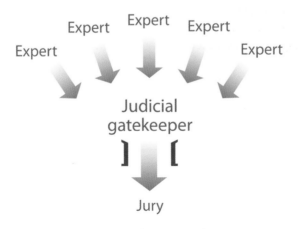

Figure 3-1. Judges are gatekeepers.

and scholarly perspectives on *Daubert* show distinct patterns, revealing the opinion's legacy.

Social Science Attempts to Measure *Daubert*

It was inevitable that the uncertainty that followed *Daubert* would attract the attention of social scientists, excavating the layers of scholarly debate to find out what really is going on. Beginning in 2001, and most recently in 2013, several large research studies have compiled data on *Daubert's* legacy in the court system. These studies fall into two categories: broad surveys of judges and attorneys, and examination of reported opinions. Both types of studies convey a mixed message, ranging from little apparent effect to judicial embrace of a more stringent standard. Some of the disagreement is due to differing methodologies. However, the bottom line of all the research is that *Daubert* resulted in a permanent change in the pretrial landscape, with significant consequences for the use of experts. While the actual rates of testimony exclusion are not significantly higher than pre-*Daubert*, the case has had a strong influence on the perceptions of lawyers and led to a variety of conflicting interpretations among trial judges.

Quantitative Studies

Several studies since 2000 have looked for trends in reported judicial opinions. The earliest and most influential of these was the RAND study in 2001.[3] Hundreds of reported federal opinions following *Daubert* were compared with those before. The RAND study was among the first to conclude that, contrary to the Supreme Court's apparent intent, *Daubert* did not relax the admission standard. Judges took their new role as "gatekeepers" to heart, finding evidence unreliable at a significantly higher rate after 1993.[4] After 1997, however, these rates declined again. The authors hypothesized that this may have been due to litigants and judges adjusting to the new standard. Finally, the study also noted the increasing focus on challenging engineering, technology, health care, and medical evidence.

Research from the second decade of *Daubert* is even more instructive. In 2011, a PricewaterhouseCoopers study focused primarily on challenges to financial experts, though its results were not limited to this.[5] The study found that, from 2000 to 2010, the number of challenges to all kinds of experts had risen a staggering 347% before seeing a modest decline in 2011. The success rate of those challenges remained stable, hovering around 45%. Therefore, while an expert's odds of surviving a challenge remain stable, the popularity of the so-called "*Daubert* motion" has continued to increase into the standard's second decade.

A 2013 study by Andrew Jurs and Scott DeVitto paints yet another picture.[6] Building on a prior study,[7] their research analyzed removal rates in a database of four million cases. After carefully isolating the *Daubert* standard as the key variable, they found that civil defendants facing adverse expert testimony are significantly more likely to remove their case to federal court from non-*Daubert* jurisdictions. These numbers show that civil defendants consider the *Daubert* standard more favorable for their cases, actively seeking its shelter. Regardless of whether the *Daubert* standard *actually* is more defendant-friendly, this data offers strong evidence of the *perception* that this is true.

Survey Studies

The Federal Judicial Center conducted the first major survey on the impact of *Daubert* in 2000.[8] Several hundred judges and attorneys were asked about their experiences with expert testimony. These answers were compared with a similar set from 1991 (two years before *Daubert*). The study indicated that judges were scrutinizing the evidence more carefully after *Daubert*: while they permitted expert testimony without restrictions 75% of the time in 1991, this had dropped to 59% in 2000. And reliability—the key concept flowing from *Daubert*—was specifically a factor in exclusion about 18% of the time. These numbers may have underreported the trend because they tracked *trial* exclusions, not pre-trial exclusions.

Interestingly, although the data showed that judges' behaviors *had* changed, the majority of judges (60%) felt that their behavior had *not* changed.[9] The authors hypothesized that the other 40% of judges might possibly have accounted for the statistical difference entirely on their own. However, it is also possible that judges' perceptions of their post-*Daubert* behavior were simply out of line with the reality. Regardless, it suggests some disagreement in the judiciary.

The second major survey study by Sofia Gatowski was published in 2001 and showed still more discord. A majority (60%) of judges were proponents of a stronger role for themselves as gatekeepers in the expert admissibility analysis. However, the judges surveyed were almost evenly divided in several camps: some felt that *Daubert* had raised the threshold for admissibility, others that it intended to lower it, and still others that it intended neither. And 11% of judges were simply unsure.[10] Confusion and disagreement continue to define *Daubert's* legacy.

Key Lessons from the Research

At first glance, the empirical research seems discordant and confusing. But both the RAND and PricewaterhouseCoopers studies demonstrate that it is unlikely that today's rate of expert exclusions differs significantly from before 1993. It would seem that the commentary to the 2000 amendment to Federal Rule of Evidence 702 is correct: "Case law after *Daubert* shows that the rejection of expert testimony is the exception rather than the rule."[11]

However, those seeking admission of expert testimony should not be too quick to take comfort. First, while the *success rate* of motions to exclude expert testimony may be stable and commensurate with pre-1993 levels, the *frequency* of those challenges has climbed steeply since *Daubert*.[12] So while the odds of surviving a *Daubert* motion once it's brought remain stable, the odds of facing a challenge in the first place have increased a great deal. The judges' differing interpretations of *Daubert* in the survey studies should give further pause. The level of scrutiny experts face may vary widely by court. Finally, civil defendants' removal rate to *Daubert* jurisdictions may be a concern in its own right. Plaintiffs' worry about removal and defendants' perceptions of a stricter standard under *Daubert* give evidence to a reality beyond the reach of the quantitative studies.

Making and Defending a *Daubert* Motion

Since 1993, both subsequent jurisprudence and codification in FRE 702 have helped to clarify *Daubert*. Most notably, the Supreme Court has since held that trial court *Daubert* analyses are reviewed under the abuse of discretion standard,[13] and that *Daubert's* gatekeeping function applies to all forms of expert testimony, not just science.[14] Nonetheless, confusion about *Daubert's* proper application persists. Ambiguities in the doctrine have led to disparate interpretations across jurisdictions and substantive areas.

There are practice standards for making or defending *Daubert* motions. Most of the time, the best strategy will depend entirely on the forum and the expertise at issue. Nonetheless, case law and commentary from the last decade furnish several key considerations.

The Judge's Role: Gatekeeping vs. Deferring to the Jury

Daubert famously described trial judges as "gatekeepers" assigned with keeping unreliable expertise out of court. Nonetheless, juries remain the fact-finders charged with weighing the available evidence, imperfections and all. The tension between these two concepts has been a prime source of friction among *Daubert's* interpreters. However, there are indications that, since the initial spike in *Daubert* exclusions after 1993, the pendulum has been swinging back in the direction of judges granting more deference to the jury.

First, a recent 2011 addition to the influential Reference Manual on Scientific Litigation warns that overzealous gatekeepers may have misinterpreted *Daubert*:

> [T]here are serious concerns about whether the guidelines enunciated by the [Supreme] Court have been interpreted … to limit, rather than respect, the discretion of trial judges to manage their complex cases, whether the guidelines conflict with the preference for admissibility contained in both the Federal Rules of Evidence and *Daubert* itself, and whether the guidelines have resulted in trial judges encroaching on the province of the jury to decide highly contested factual issues and to judge the overall credibility of expert witnesses and their scientific theories.[15]

The comments accompanying the 2000 amendments to FRE 702 also convey the need for restraint in gatekeeping, emphasizing that judges assess only the reliability of an expert's methodology and not the correctness of their conclusions.[16] These perspectives serve to reanimate the Supreme Court's own words in *Daubert*, which purport to liberalize, and not restrict, the admission of expert evidence.[17]

The circuit courts have also emphasized both the limited nature of the gatekeeping role and respect for the province of the jury. "*Daubert* neither requires nor empowers trial courts to determine which of several competing scientific theories has the best provenance."[18] Additionally, "[t]he reliability requirement ... should not be applied too strictly. Helpfulness to the trier of fact remains the ultimate touchstone of admissibility."[19] Ultimately, litigants merely have to show by a preponderance of the evidence that their experts' opinions are reliable—not that they are correct.[20]

The Importance of Peer-Review Literature to Judges

However, gatekeeping under *Daubert* does sometimes call for judges to assess the science where novel or emerging theories are at issue. As several critics have argued, this can put judges—many of whom are no better qualified to assess scientific merit than jurors—in an uncomfortable position.[21]

Nonetheless, as courts have embraced this role, several instructive patterns have emerged. While actual scientific publications are somewhat cumbersome and difficult as trial evidence, reported opinions have made clear that the presence and quality of published literature frequently makes all the difference in a *Daubert* hearing.[22] In *Wells v. SmithKline Beecham Corp.*, for instance, the Fifth Circuit carefully scrutinized all the literature supporting the plaintiff's expert's claim that the defendant's Parkinson's treatment caused a gambling addiction—examining statistical significance, peer review, and causality—before excluding it all as unreliable.[23] And while inadequate literature supporting a given claim may be picked apart, the complete absence of any published support for a novel claim can mean its swift rejection in a *Daubert* contest.[24] As one commentator has argued, *Daubert* has increasingly moved courts toward an epistemological approach to determining admissibility, forcing them to probe more deeply into a theory's truth and merit than they would have under *Frye* (which would have pushed them merely to accept the judgment of their peers and ancestors).[25]

Epidemiological studies, in particular, often occupy the main battleground—especially in toxic tort cases. While they are not required, they are generally the best possible evidence of disease causation,[26] and many *Daubert* motions turn on them. Cases involving the drug bromocriptine are illustrative. In *Rider v. Sandoz Pharm. Corp.*, the Eleventh Circuit sorted through six categories of evidence purporting to show a link between the drug and hemorrhagic stroke.[27] Among these were epidemiological reports that failed to rise to a level of statistical significance. While the court noted that such studies were not strictly essential to proving causation, it nonetheless held plaintiff's body of scientific evidence to be unreliable given their absence.[28] Similarly, in *Glastetter v. Novartis Pharmaceuticals Corp.*, the Eighth Circuit affirmed the exclusion of a plaintiff's evidence purporting to show that bromocriptine causes hemorrhagic stroke.[29] As in *Rider*, the court noted that epidemiological studies are not required, but the plaintiff failed to persuade the court without them.[30]

Disproportionality: *Daubert*'s Lack of Impact on Criminal Cases

Daubert has done much less to encourage judicial scrutiny of the science behind criminal expertise. Several commentators have noted, with bewilderment, that *Daubert* has had almost no effect on criminal litigation.[31] Traditional forms of forensic identification, such as through hair, fingerprint, handwriting, and bite mark analysis, have been anointed as time-honored, tried-and-true reliable by courts after *Daubert*, simply bypassing the type of rigorous methodological scrutiny seen in toxic tort and other areas.[32] Prosecutorial evidence, in particular, seems to be immune from scrutiny: the National Academy of Sciences' landmark 2009 report noted that "the vast majority of the *reported* opinions in criminal cases indicate that trial judges rarely exclude or restrict expert testimony offered by prosecutors."[33] The empirical data also reinforces these perspectives: a large systematic study of appellate criminal decisions found "no change in the overall rate of admission for all types of expert evidence."[34]

Cases involving fingerprint analysis illustrate this reality well. Some courts, including the Ninth Circuit, have essentially waived the *Daubert* hearing in this context, concluding in short passages that the methodology is obviously reliable.[35] Others have admitted it as tried-and-true, simply referring to the long history of respect for fingerprint identification in a brief analysis.[36]

What Triggers Exclusion?

The slight scrutiny given to criminal experts shows that the degree to which courts apply *Daubert* standards varies with the subject area.[37] A plaintiff alleging a causal connection between product and disease may face a more exacting burden than a prosecutor trying to identify a criminal defendant. The line between exclusion and admission also appears to move depending upon the judge and circuit.

As the survey studies discussed earlier reveal, there is broad disagreement among judges as to the proper interpretation of *Daubert*. Some judges feel that *Daubert* liberalized the admission of forensic evidence, others that it restricted it, and still others that it did neither.[38] While this may be a disquieting reality for litigants considering a *Daubert* hearing, ironically, it is in line with the Supreme Court's original description of the standard as a "flexible" one.[39] As with many other standards that grant a trial court broad discretion, judges are free to bend the standard according to their own inclinations.

Zooming out from the level of individual trial judges, variability is an issue between jurisdictions as well: different districts and circuits apply the standard differently.[40] For instance, the Ninth and Eleventh Circuits have been especially strict in their interpretations of *Daubert* and are perceived to be defendant friendly.[41] By contrast, the Eighth Circuit has held that expertise should be excluded only after a strong showing that it is of no assistance whatsoever to the jury.[42] Practitioners must know their own locality in order to understand the line between admission and exclusion.[43] Given the ambiguities of the *Daubert* doctrine, there are very few national patterns.

In any *Daubert* jurisdiction, however, litigants must be familiar with the reliability factors, as they are crucial to exclusion. These also vary. As the Supreme Court emphasized in *Kumho Tire*, the original factors listed in *Daubert* are non-exhaustive, and they will not apply in every case.[44] In addition to the five original factors (testing, peer review, known error rate, existence of standards, and general acceptance), courts have considered at least five others:

(1) Whether experts are "proposing to testify about matters growing naturally and directly out of research they have conducted independent of the litigation, or whether they have developed their opinions expressly for purposes of testifying." *Daubert v. Merrell Dow Pharmaceuticals, Inc.*, 43 F.3d 1311, 1317 (9th Cir. 1995).

(2) Whether the expert has unjustifiably extrapolated from an accepted premise to an unfounded conclusion. *See General Elec. Co. v. Joiner*, 522 U.S. 136, 146 (1997)....

(3) Whether the expert has adequately accounted for obvious alternative explanations. *See Claar v. Burlington N.R.R.*, 29 F.3d 499 (9th Cir. 1994) (testimony excluded where the expert failed to consider other obvious causes for the plaintiff's condition)....

(4) Whether the expert "is being as careful as he would be in his regular professional work outside his paid litigation consulting." *Sheehan v. Daily Racing Form, Inc.*, 104 F.3d 940, 942 (7th Cir. 1997)....

(5) Whether the field of expertise claimed by the expert is known to reach reliable results for the type of opinion the expert would give.... *See Moore v. Ashland Chemical, Inc.*, 151 F.3d 269 (5th Cir. 1998) (en banc) (clinical doctor was properly precluded from testifying to the toxicological cause of the plaintiff's respiratory problem, where the opinion was not sufficiently grounded in scientific methodology)....[45]

One of the original five factors—the presence of testing in the methodology—is often seen as the most important and is most frequently the basis for exclusion.[46] But the reported opinions make clear that a court has broad discretion to analyze any and all of these factors when assessing reliability.

State Court Realities

The variability flowing from *Daubert* is reflected in the differences between states on the admission of expert testimony. Since 1993, 25 states have adopted *Daubert* or a similar test, 15 and the District of Columbia still retain *Frye*, six have not officially abandoned *Frye* but have begun using the *Daubert* factors, and four have developed their own tests.[47] Any practitioner must carefully research the details of his or her own state's standards and find relevant cases.[48]

The range of state court approaches brings us back to our initial question: Is there a practical difference between the *Frye* and *Daubert* standards? Even if *Daubert* did make a significant change, there is evidence that the remaining *Frye* jurisdictions have been gradually evolving to converge with *Daubert* jurisprudence.[49]

The Bottom Line

Empirical research from the last decade suggests that exclusion rates under *Daubert* have remained stable since about 1997 and are comparable with their pre-1993 levels. However, it also suggests that the *Daubert* motion—a common and growing tactic— has nonetheless remade the pretrial landscape like few developments since the *Celotex* trilogy. And practitioners perceive a real difference between *Daubert* and *Frye* jurisdictions, whether or not it's real.

Unfortunately, judges, forums, and circuits disagree as to the proper interpretation of *Daubert*, and it is applied differently in different substantive areas. Regardless of whether the *Daubert* standard has significantly changed the use of experts, you need to be able to dance to the new music. Preparation for a *Daubert* motion requires the use of published research to back up an expert's opinions. You must consider how that research relates to the *Daubert* and post-*Daubert* factors, and discourage your experts from speaking conjecturally or hypothetically in depositions.

Takeaways—The Shape of the World after Daubert

1. The practical impact of *Daubert* has been widely debated ever since the case was handed down in 1993.

2. Practitioners and judges alike have struggled to apply *Daubert* at trial: How can the judge's role as "gatekeeper" be squared with the jury's role as fact-finder?

3. Research studies have compiled data on *Daubert*'s legacy in the court system. These studies fall into two categories: broad surveys of judges and attorneys, and examination of reported opinions.

4. Both types of studies have conveyed a mixed message, ranging from little apparent effect to judicial embrace of a more stringent standard.

5. The bottom line emerging from all the research is a permanent change in the pretrial landscape, carrying significant consequences for the use of expert witnesses.

6. While the actual rates of testimony exclusion are not significantly higher than pre-*Daubert*, the case has had a strong influence on the perceptions of lawyers and led to a variety of conflicting interpretations among trial judges.

7. The RAND study was among the first to conclude that, contrary to the Supreme Court's apparent intent, *Daubert* did not relax the admission standard. Judges took their new role as "gatekeepers" to heart.

8. The RAND study also noted that challenges had increasingly focused on evidence involving engineering, technology, health care, and medicine.

9. The PricewaterhouseCoopers study found that, from 2000 to 2010, the number of challenges to all kinds of experts had risen a staggering 347% before seeing a modest decline in 2011. The success rate of those challenges remained stable, hovering around 45%.

10. Civil defendants facing adverse expert testimony are significantly more likely to remove their case to federal court from non-*Daubert* jurisdictions. These numbers show that civil defendants consider the *Daubert* standard more favorable for their cases.

11. The Federal Judicial Center study indicated that judges were scrutinizing the evidence more carefully after *Daubert*. They permitted expert testimony without restrictions 75% of the time in 1991, but this had dropped to 59% in 2000. And reliability—the key concept flowing from *Daubert*—was specifically a factor in exclusion about 18% of the time.

12. Although the Federal Judicial Center data showed that judges' behaviors *had* changed, the majority of judges (60%) felt that their behavior had *not* changed.

13. Confusion and disagreement is a theme that continues to define *Daubert*'s legacy.

14. The commentary to the 2000 amendment to FRE 702 appears correct: "Case law after *Daubert* shows that the rejection of expert testimony is the exception rather than the rule."

15. While the *success rate* of motions to exclude expert testimony may be stable and commensurate with pre-1993 levels, the *frequency* of those challenges has climbed steeply since *Daubert*.

16. There are indications that, since the initial spike in *Daubert* exclusions after 1993, the pendulum has been swinging back in the direction of judges granting more deference to the jury.

17. While actual scientific publications are somewhat cumbersome and difficult as trial evidence, reported opinions have made clear that the presence and quality of published literature frequently makes all the difference in a *Daubert* hearing.

18. *Daubert* has increasingly moved courts toward an epistemological approach to determining admissibility, forcing them to probe more deeply into a theory's truth and merit than they would have under *Frye*.

19. Epidemiological studies, in particular, often occupy the main battleground—especially in toxic tort cases.

20. *Daubert* has done much less to encourage judicial scrutiny of the science behind criminal expertise. Several commentators have noted, with bewilderment, that *Daubert* has had almost no effect on criminal litigation.

21. The degree to which courts apply *Daubert* standards varies with the subject area.

22. There is broad disagreement among judges as to the proper interpretation of *Daubert*. Some feel that *Daubert* liberalized the admission of forensic evidence, others that it restricted it, and still others that it did neither.

23. Variability is an issue between jurisdictions, with different districts and circuits applying the standard differently.

24. It is crucial for practitioners to know their own locality in order to gain a better understanding of the line between admission and exclusion.

25. The original factors listed in *Daubert* are non-exhaustive, and they will not apply in every case. In addition to the five original factors (testing, peer review, known error rate, existence of standards, and general acceptance), courts have considered at least five others.

26. One of the original five factors—the presence of testing in the methodology—is often seen as the most important and is most frequently the basis for exclusion.

27. The variability flowing from *Daubert* may be the most notable in different states. Since 1993, 25 states have adopted *Daubert* or a similar test, 15 and the District of Columbia still retain *Frye*, six have not officially abandoned *Frye* but have begun using the *Daubert* factors, and four have developed their own tests.

28. Regardless of whether the *Daubert* standard has significantly changed matters since its adoption, you need to understand how to dance to the new music.

29. Preparation for a *Daubert* motion requires the use of published research to back up an expert's opinions.

30. Discourage your experts from speaking conjecturally or hypothetically in rendering their opinions.

Chapter 4

The Scientific Enterprise

Science is a way of thinking much more than a body of knowledge.

—Carl Sagan

Science is an unusual enterprise that seeks greater understanding of our world and beyond. It is driven by curiosity, the joy of discovery and the desire to improve the quality of human life. Scientific research is guided by first principles, simple, basic statements of truth and falsity. These are the reference points that help to make sure that new research findings will be valid and accepted.

Science assumes that a real world independent of humans exists and looks to explain the underlying forces that shape it. A descriptive discipline, science strives to pursue this knowledge with scrupulous neutrality, looking for yes or no answers that prove or disprove a hypothesis. The end goal of scientific research is to come up with accurate descriptions of cause and effect.

Scientific Method Basics

In theory, science is straightforward and works well. It begins by asking a question, which is refined into a hypothesis, seeking to explain natural phenomena. An experiment is designed to test the hypothesis, generating data, which is collected and analyzed, searching for patterns and causal relationships. University of Washington Zoology Professor Robert T. Paine describes the core purpose of all scientific research: "Experimental manipulation is ... getting results you can interpret. If you test an idea—that's what science is all about."[1]

Science focuses first on developing data that is accurate and reliable, then shifting to interpreting it: "We let the data do the talking in science. Hopefully our experimental designs will be well thought out, permitting us to draw valid conclusions from the data they generate."[2] The essential question is, "Does the data prove, disprove or modify the hypothesis?"

Most scientists in any field will agree on certain core principles. For example, in physics, this includes basic calculations of force and mass. The degree of consensus varies from one discipline to another. For example, somewhat more agreement on the

Figure 4-1. Science tests the validity of hypotheses.

basics exists in physics than in medicine. In any field, the level of scientific debate increases as the subject matter goes beyond the area of core agreement.

Consensus, Competition and Change

In *The Structure of Scientific Revolutions*, Thomas Kuhn introduced the idea that most science comes from a consensus, based on accepted bodies of truth. There is a certain amount of accumulated evidence that is necessary before things are accepted as being so. Though Kuhn coined the phrase "paradigm shift" to describe the momentous change that can occur in scientific thought, the typical progression is more linear and gradual. Like everything else in the universe, science is evolving. Later information can disprove what had initially been accepted as true. Lord Kelvin used physical principles to estimate that Earth was 100 million years old, relying on measurements of our planet's temperature. He assumed in his calculations that the Earth loses heat continuously. Subsequent analysis by scientist John Perry modified Kelvin's work, adding a new heat transport mechanism. The subsequent discovery of radioactivity put the final piece of the puzzle in place, supporting the present day estimate of the Earth's age at 4.5 billion years.

Nobel Prize winner Linus Pauling's work focused on analyzing the molecular structure of proteins. He developed a triple helix model of DNA. This was the catalyst for later analysis by James Watson and Francis Crick. They figured out that Pauling's model was flawed. The true structure of DNA was a double helix, turned inside out from the way Pauling had it. Sir Issac Newton's scientific observations provided the foundation for our basic understanding of the world and the universe. He developed the field of classical mechanics, explaining the motion of bodies and how different forces act to produce this, describing the process in mathematical terms. Several centuries later, Albert Einstein extended Newton's work into the whole new dimension of quantum mechanics, the classic progression of one scientist building upon the work of another.

However, challenge to the work of colleagues does not occur nearly to the extent claimed by the scientific community. There is a tendency by scientists to give too much credence to major new published findings of colleagues, not questioning the basic premise. A shocking 2012 article in *Nature* concluded that out of 53 landmark cancer studies, only 6 had reproducible data.[3] This has caused some to question the integrity of the research design process: "A claim is not likely to be disproved by an experiment that takes that claim as its starting point."[4]

Challenges to Colleagues

Personalities, egos, rivalries and different schools of thought exist in science, just as in any other field of human endeavor. Scientists can line up on one side of an opinion or another, critical of the other point of view. For example, in the mid-1950s, Dr. Jonas Salk was one of the great medical heroes of the world, developing the first effective vaccine against polio, an inactivated or "killed" form of the virus. Dr. Albert Sabin had a different approach, perfecting an orally administered weakened "live" virus shortly after Salk's was launched. Sabin was very blunt in stating that his method of inoculation against polio was superior to Salk's "pure kitchen chemistry." Nuclear scientists J. Robert Oppenheimer and Edward Teller clashed frequently over issues related to fusion, fission and research priorities during the creation of the first atomic bomb in the Manhattan Project during World War II. Teller infamously testified against Oppenheimer in the latter's security clearance hearing in 1954, actively criticizing his scientific decisions, which Teller believed hindered thermonuclear weapon development.

While they may be geographically distant at widely scattered institutions, scientists are keenly aware of the work of others with similar research interests. They go to the same professional conferences and read the same influential journals, staying up on the latest developments. This leads to a defined community of interest in specialty areas, part of which includes checking the validity of colleagues' work. In fact, a more accurate way to describe the scientific method is cooperative competition, where colleagues continually challenge and reassess the ideas of one another to get at the truth. Under the principle of publish or perish, prestige in science is directly related to the quality and quantity of articles produced. Reflecting this, medical journals alone publish a staggering amount of information, with the results of 75 clinical trials coming out every day.[5] When new findings appear in the literature, other scientists do follow-up studies to test their validity. The heavy reliance on research grants reinforces the tendency of scientists to verify the accuracy of conclusions reached by others. Proposed research that focuses on validating the truth of published work also has a better chance of getting funded.

Disagreements are inevitable when new research findings depart from what previously had been accepted as true. For example, Katherine Flegal is a senior scientist at the Centers for Disease Control and Prevention. She was the lead author in a 2012 article which analyzed 100 studies, concluding that a large group of people categorized as overweight had less of a risk of dying than people of normal weight. This built upon a 2005 study by Flegal suggesting that those of normal weight had a slightly higher risk of dying than those who were overweight. Dr. Flegal's findings were contrary to the accepted notion that overweight people are less healthy and her research subsequently faced criticism by other scientists. A key focus of her detractors was on the criteria she used to select people of normal weight. For example, smokers and people with pre-existing illnesses were included. Biostatistician Donald Berry remarked: "Some portion of those thin people are actually sick, and sick people tend to die sooner."[6] Dr. Walter Willett of the Harvard School of Public Health was more brutally direct in his assessment of the validity of this research: "This is an even greater pile of rubbish [than the earlier study in 2005]."[7] It is inevitable that new research findings like Flegal's will need to be replicated in further studies before being adopted by the scientific mainstream.

Resistance to Changes in Conventional Wisdom

It is human nature to get invested in particular outcomes and scientists are no exception. The desire to prove the truth of a particular hypothesis can result in bias and flawed analysis. Research has to be examined objectively and the close scrutiny by colleagues after publication helps to build integrity and accountability.

Scientific objectivity can tilt in favor of the status quo, just as in any other field. Scientists can be strongly committed to a traditional position, particularly those whose reputations and research are tied to it. Archaeologist Carl Gustafson was subjected to this bias following a new discovery at a dig on the Olympic Peninsula near Sequim, Washington. He found a 13,800-year-old mastodon bone with what appeared to be a spear point embedded in it. This was 800 years before the Clovis people were thought to have migrated from Asia over the Bering Sea land bridge. Unfortunately for Gustafson, since the 1930s, the academic community in archaeology had embraced the Clovis-first position. It was believed that no humans populated the Americas prior to this migration. Though certain that he had proof to the contrary, Gustafson was either dismissed or ignored over the next 35 years.

The development of DNA sequencing led to a re-examination of Gustafson's find in 2011, causing a complete about-face of interpretation. In fact, a spear point made from another mastodon bone was embedded in Gustafson's find, exactly as he claimed. In addition, the role of human hands in fashioning this spear point was confirmed by CT scan. With this new information, the Clovis-first position was no longer sustainable.[8] Though the acceptance of a new position like Professor Gustafson's can be delayed, when the conventional wisdom is proved to be wrong by irrefutable evidence, scientists with contrary opinions are forced to change. "We once thought this was so, but now we know it is not."

Manipulation and Bias

Smart though they may be, scientists are fallible human beings. They can make mistakes and manipulate outcomes just like the rest of us. While science is committed to honest, open and objective inquiry, even celebrated researchers have changed their results. In his book *The Great Betrayal: Fraud in Science*, Horace Freeland Judson recounts how historians examining Louis Pasteur's notebooks in 1971 discovered that he had faked data in support of the effectiveness of his rabies vaccine. Animals with the vaccine died at the same rate as those without. While it turned out that Pasteur was right in his ideas about immunitization, his methods in proving it were not exemplary. The same can be said of pioneering 19th-century geneticist Gregor Mendel, who altered data from the study of the hybridization of pea plants to get the outcome he wanted.

Beyond outright falsification of data, scientists are subject to the more subtle influence of confirmation bias, paying more attention to the data that supports their hypothesis, ignoring that which is inconsistent. Robert Millikan was a celebrated physicist who won the Nobel Prize in 1923 for his work measuring the elementary electronic charge of particles and the photoelectric effect. His laboratory notebooks at the time of his famous 1909 oil drop experiment show a selective reporting of data. As time went on, the results got more and more consistent, as contrary data was pushed aside.

External factors also can create experimental bias. Scientists may have the prospect of personal financial gain from the outcome of a research project. This can cloud the objective analysis of research data. Research outcomes have tremendous economic consequences for drug companies, determining whether or not a drug gets FDA approval. In these circumstances, it is not a neutral question to ask, "How effective is this drug?" Drug company scientists want studies to show the effectiveness of their proprietary products, as blockbuster drugs mean huge profits. Physicians who prescribe drugs may not receive all the information on their effectiveness due to publication bias. Studies that are favorable to a new drug often are published while those that are unfavorable may not be. For example, while drug companies seeking FDA approval for eight antipsychotic drugs performed 24 studies of their effectiveness, the four of this group that were unflattering never found their way into professional journals. Three of these showed that the new drug tested was no better than a placebo and the fourth demonstrated that less expensive drugs were more effective. Dr. Erick Turner, a psychiatrist at Oregon Health Sciences University, remarked that physicians are "living in this highly censored environment." [9]

These various biases in science show it to be all too human, subject to the same frailties as less quantitative disciplines:

> The textbook "scientific method" of dispassionately testing a hypothesis is not how science really works. We often have a clear idea of what we want the results to be before we run an experiment.... [S]cience as a lived, human process is different from our preconception of it. [10]

Implementation of Research Findings

Scientists test cause and effect relationships, often not directly involved in what happens after that. The ultimate use to which research is put goes beyond the purview of science. If a substance is proved to be carcinogenic, the steps taken thereafter are a matter for government and industry action. This can be delayed by political considerations that have nothing to do with the science. Certain subjects seem to require many years of research. For example, though the U.S. Surgeon General linked smoking and lung disease in 1964, this subject continues to be examined, with the effects of secondhand smoke still debated in some circles.

The resistance of policy makers to implementation is one reason for the repetition in research studies. For example, while it has been long established that fatigue leads to impaired judgment, the medical establishment has resisted limiting the hours that interns and residents work. It was only in 2008 that the Institute of Medicine issued guidelines limiting shifts to 16 consecutive hours. The reason for the delay was sheer business-as-usual reflex. Time and time again Harvard sleep expert Dr. Charles Czeisler has encountered resistance to his findings in this area: "They use the same argument over and over, even when we've tested it. It drives me up the wall … I can't believe we have to do this extra study."[11]

In and Out of the Laboratory

Though we tend to think of all scientists in a laboratory setting, this is not always so. Sir Issac Newton still is considered one of the most influential scientists of all time, even though research laboratories did not exist in his 17th and 18th centuries. Newton's scientific observations focused on the natural world around him, seeking to explain why things occurred in a particular way, as well as the background forces involved. Most of us are familiar with the true story of how Newton formulated the law of gravity after watching an apple fall to the ground. (It did not hit him on the head, as some popular versions would have it.)

While scientists and mathematicians in our modern world continue to do theoretical work outside the confines of a laboratory, the bulk of scientific research now revolves around the testing of a hypothesis under controlled conditions. The near-universal form for this is the randomized clinical trial, often abbreviated as an RCT. Dr. Hal Barron, chief medical officer of Roche and Genetech, describes how this fits into the classic scientific method:

> When you do any kind of trial, you're really trying to answer a question about truth in the universe. And, of course, we can't know that. So we try to design an experiment on a subpopulation of the world that we think is generalizable to the overall universe.[12]

An RCT is a research design in which the outcomes of two or more groups are compared to determine cause and effect relationships. A common form of RCT measures and compares the consequences of using a particular drug or medical treatment. The subjects in an RCT are chosen for certain specific characteristics, such as having a medical condition like cancer, for which the experimental drug is thought to have therapeutic potential. It is ideal to have the group as similar as possible at the start of the study, which forms the baseline against which changes are measured. The participants in an RCT are broken up into two or more groups, assigned on a totally random basis. This is the equivalent of placement through the flip of a coin, though it typically is done through the use of a computer program. All research subjects have the same chance of ending up in one group or the other. The experimental groups get the medical intervention and the control group does not, receiving a placebo, conventional treatment or nothing at all.

The end goal of all RCTs is quantification. The health of subjects is monitored over time, measuring important vital signs repeatedly. Differences between the experimental and control groups are studied to determine whether the medical intervention has had any impact on the outcome. Are the two populations different from each other? How so? What is the level of significance? The close similarity between the comparison groups at the beginning of the study makes it easier to sort this out. Comparisons between the groups can be complicated by the placebo effect. Some subjects in the control group improve simply because of their belief that they are being treated effectively.

Any valid scientific conclusions that emerge from an RCT should be reproducible. If the data is reliable and objective, the results should be consistent when experiments are repeated by others. Scientists want and expect other researchers to test the validity of their conclusions. If new research findings truly are important, others in the field will try to replicate and expand upon them. If subsequent experiments have the same outcome, general agreement on the truth of the proposition develops, becoming a stepping-stone to the next level.

There are limits to what an RCT can be expected to prove. One area that has proved elusive to this form of research is the relationship between diet and health. In the l960s when the intake of dietary fat and the prevalence of heart disease became a medical concern, it was determined that doing long-term trials would be too expensive. This would require studying what people eat and the illnesses they get over decades, drawing a link between diet and disease. Even then, there is no way to establish a causal relationship between the two. This kind of RCT is just as likely to lead to a wrong answer. As a result, nutritionists have learned to adapt to a lower standard of proof, doing animal studies and trying to extrapolate to humans.[13]

Proving Causal Relationships

The scrutiny of other researchers may identify flaws in the methods or conclusions of an initial study, throwing the validity into doubt. For example, the Fred Hutchinson Cancer Research Center in Seattle followed 2,763 older women in the Puget Sound area of Washington state between 2000 and 2008 to learn if the use of a common class of high-blood-pressure drugs increased their risk of breast cancer. Those who had been taking these drugs experienced breast cancer at twice the level of those who had not.

Despite the apparent correlation, the Fred Hutchinson study was not sufficient to prove a causal link. Past studies on the effects of this same drug were in conflict. The research design of the study also was criticized, with the majority of the subjects white and wealthy, not reflective of the multicultural general population. The lack of women of other races was significant as this demographic can have a major impact on the effects of medication. In the end, despite years of effort by a highly respected medical research facility, there was not enough proof of a cause and effect relationship between blood pressure medication and the development of breast cancer. Lead researcher

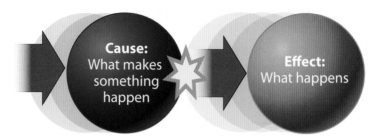

Cause and effect explains relationships.

Christopher Li acknowledged this: "These are some intriguing findings, but we do not think they should change current clinical practice in any way."[14] Dr. Keith Ferdinand, a prominent cardiologist, agreed, remarking that while the results were "provocative," associations in observational studies like this frequently fall apart when subjected to randomized trials.[15]

Junk Science

Though he did not coin the term, Peter Huber inserted "junk science" into the national debate on forensic evidence with the 1991 publication of his widely quoted and cited book, *"Galileo's Revenge, Junk Science in the Courtroom."* In 1997, Justice John Paul Stevens was the first member of the United States Supreme Court to use it in an opinion in *General Electric v. Joiner*,[16] referencing the 18th- and 19th-century practice of phrenology, which held that the personality and behavior of an individual could be predicted by the shape and configuration of their skull and facial features.

Junk science has become a term used by media commentators to criticize the use of experts in court. It refers to data or research that is inaccurate, improperly gathered, influenced by ulterior motives or based on reasoning inconsistent with the scientific method. Corporations and industry often accuse civil plaintiff lawyers of using junk science to prove the harmful effects of exposures to substances or damage to patients from the use of pharmaceuticals. The plaintiff's bar responds that industry minimizes public health concerns for the sake of profit.

Big Data on the Rise — The *Moneyball* Effect

Government agencies and research institutions now collect massive amounts of data. The development of advanced computer algorithms raises the new research option of big data analysis. Best-selling author Michael Lewis examined this approach in the small world of professional sports in his book *Moneyball*. Faced with the limited player talent budget of a smaller market baseball team, front office executive Billy Beane of the Oakland Athletics figured out a statistical method to identify overlooked bargain players who could be successfully combined into a winning team. This data driven method confounded the conventional wisdom of relying on the subjective analysis of scouting reports.

The *Moneyball* approach now is used in many different fields, including commerce, politics and science. For example, in the 2012 presidential election campaign, a computer "geek squad" was an important part of President Barack Obama's team's strategic plan, identifying groups of voters throughout the United States who were the most critical to the president's re-election. Thereafter, targeted messages were sent to these voters. Governor Mitt Romney's campaign did not do nearly as well on this dimension. The difference between the two campaigns in the use of big data made a difference in the outcome.

Making sense of big data often is beyond the capacity of any one human being, or even a group. This is not a problem for computers though. The more data fed into them, the smarter they get. As a result, scientific analysis increasingly relies on computers, rather than human judgment. The artificial intelligence revolution in computer science is aided by natural language processing, pattern recognition and machine learning. Gary King of Harvard's Institute for Quantitative Social Science has said: "It's a revolution.… There is no area that is going to be untouched."[17] However, certain negative attitudes toward big data analysis persist among some scientists and academicians. Though he believes in the great value of big data, Nobel Prize-winning economist Robert Shiller notes ambivalence toward it among colleagues:

> There's an attitude.… That it's like janitor work; it would dirty our hands. There's social climbing in academia … some of the best theorizing comes after collecting data because then you become aware of another reality.[18]

There is no question that data driven artificial intelligence is taking an increasing role in sorting out research data. Health management decisions have been improved through big data analysis, even without knowing the precise cause and effect mechanism involved. The fact that scientists may only be able to speculate as to the cause does not negate the validity of the connection.

A study by the Fred Hutchinson Cancer Research Center in Seattle focused on the possible side effects of taking fish oil supplements on prostate cancer. The initial results in 2011 associated fish oil with significantly increased incidence and severity of prostate cancer. Epidemiologist Alan Kristal and his team were astonished at this data: "To be honest, I didn't believe it. It was striking enough to get it into the literature just to see if anyone would repeat it."[19] A subsequent study by the Fred Hutchinson team confirmed that men who had the highest level of omega-3 fatty acids, the kind found in fish oil, had a 43 percent increase in the risk of prostate cancer generally and a 71 percent increase for the most serious form of this disease. Despite this strong statistical link, researchers could not come up with a biological mechanism to explain it.

Big data is likely to play an even greater role in future scientific research as larger amounts of data are collected and computers get more sophisticated in analyzing it. But the precise mechanism or causal relationship involved in an outcome may be left hanging. In this way, big data complicates the traditional method of establishing causation. Scientists always want to understand why something occurs. But researchers now don't necessarily have to have an underlying theory driving the process. They can set up a computer algorithm without understanding why.

Differences between Research Facilities

Beyond differences in research emphasis, the setting where the work is done can make a difference. A university setting has a certain cachet, particularly if the institution is well known. Some industrial research laboratories have equal impact, such as the legendary Bell Labs in New Jersey or the Xerox PARC facility in California, both of which produced many important technological advances. Major pharmaceutical companies have highly specialized research departments. Scientific entrepreneurs also have the option of getting venture capital to start new companies, such as in the bio-tech field. Each one of these work settings has implications for the scope of the research, funding, staffing and the respect that will be given to the outcome.

Differences of Approach between Branches of Science

Though good scientific practices have equal application to all fields, each branch has differences in culture and tradition. Engineers work in the physical world, keeping planes in the sky and bridges from falling down. They are less prone to warring schools of thought, guided by a number of well-established tools and principles, such as the work of Newton. Engineers like the quantification of hard science, using data and math to resolve structural issues. They are heavily focused on the quantitative and objective data, always wanting to see the numbers: "What are the weights?" "What are the speeds?" If the data is accurate, the calculations and interpretation should come out the same. They have an analytic and experimental side. The analysis comes first, often formulated with the use of a computer model, followed by specific testing to verify the validity of the analysis. While engineers can and do disagree, the range is more narrow than in other disciplines.

As an applied science, drawing upon biology and chemistry, there is more variation and disagreement in medicine than engineering. There always seem to be differences of opinion in the medical literature on a given subject. Some ideas remain accepted as absolute fact while others have been disproved by subsequent research.

Evidence-Based Medicine

Traditional medical training was not evidence-based, largely shaped by faculty mentors through word of mouth: "This is true, based on my years of clinical experience." The head of a department would literally write down, "Here is what I expect you to do in specific cases. This is the best practice." This was top-down management, using top-down guidelines. Anybody who deviated from the department chair's guidelines would be called out in front of their peers.

Applied research has shifted medicine away from subjective clinical judgment. Over time, the heavy reliance on the opinions of faculty mentors was questioned, as it may not have a valid scientific basis. In fact, it may actually harm the patient, completely turning the world on its head. For example, hormone replacement therapy for post-menopausal women once was commonly prescribed until research showed an increased incidence of cancer for these patients. A similar development changed the once common practice of inducing labor at 37 weeks, rather than waiting for the full 39-week term of pregnancy. A series of studies showed more breathing, temperature regulation and blood sugar problems for babies born through elective inductions than full-term births. A Danish study of thousands of 10-year-olds who were born prior to the completion of the 39-week gestation period showed greater cognitive problems than those who were full-term.[20] All this medical evidence resulted in the practice of elective inductions being severely curtailed.

Evidence-based medicine applies the body of scientific research to patient care in a very structured manner. The most experienced and knowledgeable clinicians have met in their professional groups and used the research to codify the best practices, replacing unsupported opinion. As a result, there are many more scientific standards in medicine now, supported by more evidence.

The Outsized Impact of DNA Analysis on Criminal Forensics

The use of DNA laboratory analysis of crime-scene evidence is clearly scientific, backed up by decades of high-level research since the structure of the DNA molecule was identified by Watson and Crick in 1953. DNA analysis can show with a high probability that the defendant touched or loaded a weapon, or committed a sexual assault. When samples are properly obtained from a crime scene and tested in the lab, it is expected that the resulting probabilities will be accurate, with the jury drawing the right conclusions.

The 2009 report by the National Academy of Sciences was highly critical of other criminal forensics though, finding widespread use of questionable techniques and experts in both federal and state trial courts.[21] These problems come at the next level down from DNA, where disciplines like fingerprint identification have some of the characteristics of science, but are more prone to subjective interpretation. These other fields often were developed in crime labs rather than in research settings and their overall reliability does not measure up to forensic DNA analysis. A big part of this difference is that scientists developed DNA analysis first. Only much later did the legal system start converting it to use in questions of guilt or innocence.

There are criminal forensic disciplines that have some of the characteristics of science, but are more subjective. Prosecutors continue to use these, as noted in the NAS Report in 2009. Bite-mark analysis is one such. Fingerprint analysis is another. The limitations of the latter were discussed at length by the news media following the wrongful arrest of Oregon lawyer Brandon Mayfield in 2003 for the Madrid train bombing. Though Mayfield was not at the scene and did not commit this crime, multiple certified examiners said that the fingerprint was his. Though no longer touted as "100%" reliable since the Mayfield case, fingerprint analysis remains an enormously useful investigation tool, despite its greater subjectivity.

Takeaways — The Scientific Enterprise

1. Scientific research is guided by first principles, which are simple basic statements of truth and falsity.

2. Science seeks to be a neutral descriptive discipline that assumes that a real world exists independent of human beings.

3. The scientific method consists of a hypothesis, tested by an experiment in which data is generated and then analyzed for cause and effect relationships.

4. The challenge of science is to come up with accurate statements of cause and effect.

5. Science is built on consensus, resulting in accepted bodies of truth.

6. Every field has core concepts that are agreed upon by nearly all, but the relative degree of this depends on the culture and tradition within a particular branch of science.

7. Scientific truth is subject to change as our knowledge base expands.

8. There are personalities, rivalries and egos in science, just like everywhere else.

9. Regularly checking the validity of colleagues' work in a cooperative competition is a critical element of science.

10. The heavy reliance on research grants reinforces the tendency of scientists to verify the accuracy of conclusions reached by colleagues. When new findings are published in the literature, scientists at other institutions do follow-up studies to test their validity.

11. Reproducibility is very important. If research findings are valid, others should be able to replicate them.

12. There are frequent disagreements between scientists on the validity of research findings, particularly when these depart from what had been accepted as true previously.

13. While grounded in objectivity, there can be a bias in favor of the status quo in science, just as in any other field. Scientists in any field can be strongly committed to a particular position, especially if it long has been accepted.

14. Even science is subject to bias from external factors, which can change the scientific opinion, introducing experimental bias. If a scientist has a personal stake in the

outcome of a research project with a big commercial payoff, it may be harder for him/her to be objective.

15. The scientific focus is on whether or not there is a cause and effect relationship, not on what should happen after that. The uitimate use to which research is put goes beyond the purview of science.

16. A randomized clinical trial is a research design in which the outcomes of two or more groups are compared to determine cause and effect relationships.

17. The scrutiny of other researchers may identify flaws in the methods or conclusions of an initial study, throwing the validity into doubt.

18. While junk science is more a term used by media commentators about the use of experts in court than to describe scientific practices, the basic core revolves around the use of data or research that is inaccurate, improperly gathered, influenced by ulterior motives and based on reasoning inconsistent with the scientific method.

19. The development of the massive data generated today plus advanced computer algorithms raises the new research alternative of big data analysis.

20. Big data is likely to play an even greater role in future scientific research as computers get more sophisticated in analyzing it, but questions about causation may be left hanging, unexplained.

21. There are differences of culture and tradition among the various branches of science, which must be taken into account.

22. Evidence-based medicine has replaced the prior nonscientific method that relied heavily on subjective clinical judgment.

23. The use of scientific techniques in criminal cases has led to increasing questions and concerns, with a debate over what constitutes true forensic science.

24. DNA analysis in criminal cases sets a standard for reliability and accuracy that seldom is achieved by the other forms of criminal forensic science.

25. Non-DNA forensic evidence, such as fingerprint analysis, has many of the same characteristics as science, but allows for more subjectivity.

Chapter 5

Science and Law —
When Worlds Collide

I think mistakes are the essence of science and law. It's impossible to conceive of either scientific progress or legal progress without understanding the important role of being wrong and of mistakes.

—Alan Dershowitz

Science focuses on the world of natural phenomena, while the law is a human construct for resolving disputes and protecting society. Law covers the whole gamut of relationships. When disputes cannot be resolved by agreement, the law provides a forum and process for resolution. Law and science are drawn together when case facts require expert interpretation and analysis. Scientific and technical experts can help both criminal and civil lawyers sort things out with a wide array of tools.

Criminal activity harms society and the courts are responsible for protecting citizens through deterrence and accountability, deciding questions of innocence, guilt and punishment. Evidence is gathered by the police at a crime scene and examined by experts in a laboratory. Where relevant, a scientific analysis is made of evidence such as DNA traces, ballistics and blood chemistry. The goal is to determine a particular defendant's culpability. On the civil side, business deals fall apart, marriages dissolve and heirs fight over estates. Experts analyze the elements of who deserves to win or the damages to be awarded.

Law and science search for the truth in different places. Judges look backward to legal precedent. Scientists are more forward thinking, starting out with agreed upon first principles, then trying to extend them to new situations. In this search for the truth among competing narratives, the law seeks to use science in a pragmatic manner to answer the questions created.

The legal system is at its best when looking at individual cases and trying to be neutral, rather than trying to make global assessments like scientists do. The trier of fact, judge or jury, must determine what is really true, sorting out all the conflicting information presented by the parties. If the respective positions in a case are totally inconsistent, only one can prevail. The danger always exists for the biggest, strongest and most audacious to prevail by sheer power.

Unlike science, law is normative and outcome oriented, without the same sense of distance between the lawyer and what is being analyzed. The social constructs the law focuses on cover a broad spectrum of opinion, lacking the independent external reality of science. It often is difficult to come up with a set of accepted starting points.

Two Completely Different Methods of Searching for the Truth

Both science and law search for the truth, but by two completely different methods. Scientists generally work together in a more cooperative fashion, trying to analyze and explain reality in an objective manner. The adversary system is much more of a winner take all process, searching for the truth among competing narratives. Though the legal system strives for scrupulous fairness, unlike science, the process is not neutral. Lawyers work against one another, focusing on a particular result, each claiming to have a monopoly on the truth. As advocates, we must spin the case in the way most favorable to our clients, discrediting opposing points of view. Savvy clients do not want us to say, "We are going to get to the truth here, even if it hurts us." Litigation is all about winning. Each party has a preconceived idea of the outcome they want, looking for supporting scientific data, critically attacking anything else.

Something of the purity that science strives for is lost in the translation, as we lawyers look primarily for tactical advantage, not objectivity. Truth is relative, driven by our need to win. We want to skew any scientific interpretation in our client's favor. Anything to the contrary is attacked. Distortions are inevitable. Longtime state and federal trial Judge Robert S. Lasnik notes the difficulty this imposes on science: "The winner take all world of the courtroom is not a great place for developing objective scientific opinion."[1]

A true expert is not an advocate, relying instead on science to support his/her analysis. There are real reputation risks for scientists who get involved in litigation or policy decision-making, as they may present the science in a way that is not purely descriptive. The minute a scientist becomes an advocate or a policymaker, he or she crosses a line and is compromised. Good scientists don't want take the chance of being put in this position. In addition to the inevitable distortions of legal advocacy, applying science on a

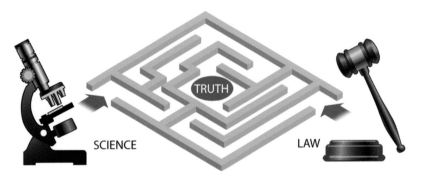

Figure 5-1. Law and science take different paths to truth.

case-by-case basis does not allow the opportunity to see the big picture. Legal cases try to find truth from pieces of a puzzle rather than looking for patterns in a large field of information. At best, the incorporation of research into legal cases is erratic and uncertain. For example, in the late 1970s, Dr. Elizabeth Loftus conducted important research on the unreliability of eyewitness identification.[2] However, despite appearing in respected peer review journals, expert testimony based on the Loftus research, that eyewitness identification was suspect, largely was excluded from criminal trials. The basis usually given for this was that the credibility of eyewitness testimony was within the exclusive province of the jury and a matter of common sense, not science.

However, in the face of continued research exposing the paradox of eyewitness testimony, the least reliable yet the most believed by jurors, some state supreme courts, such as New Jersey,[3] now have required it. Jurors need to know how the mind and memory work, as well as how eyewitness identification can be tainted. But it took decades for this to be accepted in criminal trials. Countless defendants were convicted on the basis of eyewitness identification without the benefit of expert testimony on its inherent unreliability.

Why did it take the courts so long to take notice of the well-documented unreliability of eyewitness identification? Is this indicative of a bias against forensic evidence on behalf of an accused, or simply an ingrained judicial skepticism against new forms of expert testimony? If this research had favored the prosecution, would the use of experts in this field have taken as long? Many questions like this remain unanswered, as little study has been made of decisions made at the trial court level, where all the action is.

Questions about the Trier of Fact's Capacity

How capable is a lay jury of sorting out conflicting scientific evidence to make an informed decision? The simplistic representation of science in popular culture and the math phobia of the general population raise questions about the ability of jurors to apply science in solving contested legal issues. There is no way to make the background science simple in certain types of cases, such as DNA analysis, toxic torts or environmental cases. Can juries be trusted to understand and sort through conflicting scientific interpretations, particularly when statistics are involved? TV shows such as "CSI" create unrealistic expectations about what science can prove, with the general public believing that "DNA always finds the guilty person." As much as we would like it to, science can't always provide us with conclusive evidence to solve the problem. What happens then?

Juries are free to accept or reject expert testimony, alternately relying on gut instinct or giving up, if the conflicting evidence just seems too complicated. If the scientists themselves can't agree, how can we realistically expect lay jurors, or even judges, to settle the question? Will they be more susceptible to experts trying to create doubt on causation? The default position always is a finding of no liability because "We can't figure it out." The difficulty of understanding science is not limited to juries. Judges reviewing agency decisions can say, "This is a very complicated issue, I am going to defer to the experts inside the agency."

What can we realistically expect scientific evidence to prove? Do we need different causation standards to accommodate the difficulties of proof in science-based cases?

Do we let all the relevant science come in and then let the judge or jury decide? With latent injuries, alternate theories of causation often create considerable doubt. Does something have to be a significant contributing factor in order for liability to attach? What is the minimum threshold? Courts often struggle with these questions.

Policymaking and Science

Beyond its use in litigation, science shapes the formation of legislation, on the theory that it is a neutral and objective basis for public policy. As Thomas McGarity and Wendy Wagner observe in "*Bending Science*,"[4] the usual lines get blurred when science is put in the middle of policymaking. Scientists are somewhat uncomfortable in this role, preferring to focus on gathering descriptive information and establishing causal relationships. Things like risk and exposure levels depend on policy judgments by others, often in government agencies. Past scientific debates over whether or not to ban lead as a gasoline additive or the use of DDT to control insects have resulted in legislative action. Cause and effect relationships must be defined by descriptive analysis in order to come up with regulatory standards. How many parts per million of a substance can be injurious to human health? How much dioxin does it take to cause cancer in a 70 kg white male?

There is a basic divide between normative (law) and descriptive (science). When we use science in legal disputes, we're trying to get it to take a side in the fight, to define the "therefore what?" "Therefore we should set dioxin levels lower." That is the role of the policy makers and advocates, not scientists.

Differences in Access to Information

Truth seeking in science is aided by open communication between scientists and the peer review process. The benefits of openness are presumed. The adversarial nature and competitiveness of legal disputes tightly control the facts and opinions that can be used. Unlike science, where colleagues at different institutions share information, lawyers are secretive and proprietary. In big commercial cases, experts often are quarantined into litigation and non-litigation camps, not allowed to talk to one another.

Lawyers worry about what information is discoverable by the other side: "What do I have to turn over?" "At what point in the process?" "What kind of advantage might this give them?" This is not a question of cover-up, conspiracy or making things up that aren't true, just litigation strategy. We don't require lawyers to turn over everything they know in discovery, protecting the confidentiality of their work product. Typically, the contracts between scientists and law firms specify nondisclosure. For example, Exxon privately retained a number of scientists to refute the magnitude of the injuries in the wake of the spill in Prince William Sound, not all of whom publicly offered opinions.

True scientists have a single-minded focus on their work, concerned with getting it right. It often just is not worth their while to get involved as a forensic expert. The perceived hostility of the legal process is not nearly as important as the loss of time for things not directly related to their field.

Corrupting Influence and Bias

Expert work also can bring corrupting influences and implications of bias, of which money is the most significant. A scientist's reputation for impartiality can suffer. Hired experts tend to take extreme positions for one side or the other. In looking for experts, our foremost criterion is, "Here is a reliable player who will testify for our side." For example, medical experts retained by big tobacco companies testified for many years that cigarette smoking was not linked to lung cancer, despite considerable research proving that it was.

The claimed science behind an expert's opinion has to be looked at by the judge and jury in a very detached way. This does not always happen. The adversary system is not set up to test the validity of scientific opinion in any systematic way and surface appearance may be enough to prevail. A certain cynicism has attached to the big business of expert testimony. When Toyota faced considerable potential legal difficulty as a result of injuries and deaths due to sticking accelerator pedals, they hired Exponent, one of the main sources of expert testimony for manufacturers embroiled in product liability litigation. Judge Robert Lasnik sees the big challenge lawyers face in confronting well-paid experts who are advocates for a particular position:

> There are experts you can trust and others you know are liars. But they have credentials and can come into court and testify. You have a difficult task sometimes to point out to the jury what liars they are.[5]

Cumulatively, the hired guns make millions of dollars per year testifying for a particular side in litigation. The side with the most money sometimes can wear the opponent down in a war of attrition. Resources sometimes can allow a litigant to perpetuate what is essentially a scientific fraud longer than they should. One side can be bought off or overwhelmed. This is part of the backdrop in the cautionary tales from real-life cases in books or movies, such as *A Civil Action* or *Erin Brockovich*. This is not a science problem so much as it is a matter of ethics. Experts who should know better become wedded to a theory for financial gain, conveniently ignoring what the real science is. This is seen in the legislative process too, where experts testify for one side or another in hearings or in the news media.

Questions about Prosecution Experts

In criminal cases, both questions of bias and adequacy of credentials sometimes have been raised about prosecution experts. Testifying for money is not the issue here, but rather, the tendency of the law-enforcement community to hang together. A lab can be told by the prosecutor that a match is needed to get a conviction. Or before a photo montage is shown to the victim, a detective can be affected by the knowledge that, "We really don't have a case if we don't get an identification here."

A *New Science* survey of forensic scientists in England showed just how widespread these pressures are, with nearly 30% of those in police laboratories agreeing that this happens "sometimes."[6] This is made even worse by the workload, with 85% reporting that they have insufficient time to do what is asked of them "sometimes." Though 85% of the survey group stated that these advocacy and time pressures "never" affect their results, concerns are raised, particularly with the great weight given by judges and jurors to expert testimony about laboratory tests.

Studies have shown that some government crime labs have not always followed best practices.[7] The problem here often is not the science itself, but how the labs are run. The affiliation of crime labs with other law-enforcement agencies can compromise their independence, lacking sufficient checks and balances. Unproven forensic techniques sometimes have been used. People from crime labs have been allowed to testify as experts on the basis that they have looked at similar evidence for a long time and have valid opinions about what it shows. Experience alone, without a volume of corroborating data, does not meet the standards of scientific rigor. While it only is possible to determine ethnicity from a hair sample, in the past, some prosecution witnesses have offered opinions that it proved the perpetrator's actual identity. The same kind of overextension has characterized testimony on bite marks and handwriting exemplars. Even without proof that their findings are scientifically valid, based on reproducibility, prosecution witnesses tend to be believed by judges and jurors.

Even with fingerprint testimony, which has a well-established database and agreed-upon set of identification criteria, there can be a question of how good the print is that was lifted at the scene. Some expert fingerprint opinions have been offered on the basis of a smudge. Perhaps the most well-known and often repeated example of this is the Mayfield case in Oregon in 2003, where a lawyer was identified incorrectly as the perpetrator of the Madrid, Spain, train bombing on the basis of a partial fingerprint.[8]

What Quality of Experts Do We End Up Getting?

The aversion of most scientists to the legal system and the potential corrupting influences of the advocacy process raise "Why you?" questions about experts who self-select and agree to testify. Who are we left with? Are they the best, or simply available? Are they even still active in their field? Some experts do legal consultations for the income as they phase out of active work in their fields. Are they continuing to do things consistent with true expertise?

Science continues to move forward. Is a medical consultant continuing to treat patients in his/her specialty? Any expert who has stepped out of his/her field and primarily offers opinions to lawyers has less institutional structure and enforced discipline for staying current. While retired experts still are eligible to testify, legitimate questions can be raised about the validity of their opinions. Reduced activity in the field is a red flag.

Differences between Legal and Scientific Standards of Proof

Even under the best of circumstances, there are basic differences between law and science. We cannot pretend otherwise, as the culture of each is separate and distinct. This is most evident in the clash between legal standards of proof and scientific ones. Scientific certainty is expressed through quantification and confidence intervals. When scientists say something is so, it must be with a high degree of certainty. It is tricky to translate this into legal standards that are expressed in terms of "more probable than not." This standard often puzzles scientists, who have trouble grasping or agreeing to it. They often conclude, "I don't understand this. It is not relevant to me or my work."

Can law and science even talk to one another with two fundamentally different standards of proof? Where does a 95% confidence interval in a scientific study fit into the legal standard of proof? Can these ever translate straight across? Scientists often feel uncomfortable and ill-used when forced to use the legal standard. Alex B. Berezow, a scientist with a PhD in microbiology, wrote a guest editorial on his negative experience as a juror, focusing on how lax the legal standard of proof seemed in comparison to science:

> The case for which I was selected involved a traffic accident…. Because this was a civil case, nothing had to be proved "beyond a reasonable doubt." The standard, instead, was a "preponderance of evidence."

> 51%? That's barely better than a coin toss. In science, we are rarely allowed to publish data or state conclusions unless we are at least 95% confident. Granted, the legal system does not require absolute certainty to reach a verdict, but 51%? … Preposterous.

> When asked whether anyone objected to this standard, my hand shot up. I insisted that as a scientist, I needed more evidence…. I was the first person booted from the jury pool.

> As I left the courthouse, I was struck by the clash of civilizations: The World of Law and the World of Science use different systems of logic and speak different languages…. From the World of Law the message sent that day was crystal clear: "Scientists, go home."[9]

Even though allowed a large amount of wiggle room, scientists often are uncomfortable with expressing opinions on the competing narratives of a case. We lawyers must always work to educate our scientific experts on legal probability. Thereafter, the trier of fact has to figure out, "What's going on here? Are they just quibbling about the margins?" Do the areas of disagreement between the experts really make any difference to the legal standard? Is it the kind of doubt that really matters or just showmanship?

Takeaways—Science and Law: When Worlds Collide

1. Law is a social construct centered on human relationships, while science looks to explain natural phenomena in the real world.

2. Legal cases increasingly involve questions that require scientific input and interpretation.

3. Science and law both involve a search for the truth, but go about it in very different ways.

4. The scientific method emphasizes neutrality in gathering and interpreting information.

5. The adversary system has a strong effect on how science is used in legal cases.

6. Unlike science, law is normative and outcome oriented. It just doesn't have the same feeling as science.

7. A true expert is not an advocate, relying instead on science to support his/her analysis.

8. In the search for truth among competing narratives, the law uses science in a pragmatic manner to help answer the questions created.

9. The law looks backward at precedent to solve problems, while science is more forward looking in its orientation.

10. The case-by-case approach has not proved the best way to test the validity of scientific methods in a legal setting.

11. Something of the purity that science strives for is lost in the translation, as we lawyers look primarily for tactical advantage, not objectivity.

12. Though the legal system strives for scrupulous fairness, the process is advocacy driven, not neutral.

13. Each side to a legal dispute selectively presents information favoring its point of view, attacking everything to the contrary.

14. In addition to the inevitable distortions of legal advocacy, applying science on a case-by-case basis often does not allow the opportunity to see the big picture.

15. Law is at its best in looking at individual cases, not trying to make global assessments.

16. Causation is a critical issue in many legal cases that requires scientific input.

17. Juries usually do not have a scientific background or mathematical proficiency. For this reason, understanding scientific experts often is challenging for jurors.

18. Jurors are free to accept or reject expert testimony, alternately relying on gut instinct or defaulting, if the conflicting evidence just seems too complicated.

19. True science focuses on determining causal relationships, not policymaking. However, the cause and effect relationships created by descriptive scientific analysis are the basis of legislative regulatory standards.

20. Truth seeking in science is aided by open communication between scientists and the peer review process. The benefits of openness are presumed.

21. The adversary system in law allows the parties to withhold work product, reflecting the competitive nature of the process.

22. Top scientists have a single-minded focus on their work, concerned with getting it right. This makes them reluctant to get involved in legal cases, which does not benefit their work.

23. Respected scientific experts rely on research data to support their analysis.

24. Expert witness work can bring corrupting influences and implications of bias with it, of which money is the most significant. A scientist's reputation for impartiality can suffer, as hired experts tend to take extreme positions for one side or the other.

25. In criminal cases, both questions of bias and adequacy of credentials sometimes are raised about prosecution experts. Testifying for money is not the issue here, but rather, the tendency of the law-enforcement community to hang together.

26. The combined aversion of most scientists toward getting involved in legal issues and potential corrupting influences of the advocacy process raises "Why you?" questions about testifying experts.

27. The standard of proof in law is much more vague and general than that of science, which focuses on quantification.

28. Competitive pressures of the adversary system have caused unevenness in the quality of scientific information presented to judges and juries in both criminal and civil cases.

Chapter 6

Hard and Soft Science

Science is the father of knowledge, but opinion breeds ignorance.

—Hippocrates

Credibility Implications

Forensics requires a closer look at the divide between hard and soft science, as this has significant credibility and persuasion implications. The general public tends to view science in a binary manner, either hard or soft. The natural sciences of biology, chemistry and physics fall into the "hard" category and social sciences like history, sociology or cultural anthropology are "soft." A definite value judgment goes along with the label, with public opinion generally viewing hard science as more credible than its soft counterparts.

Even if most people cannot understand the specifics of hard science, the associated quantitative data makes it trustworthy. Everything in hard science is thought to be neat and orderly, with precisely measured tolerances, temperatures and differences. A hypothesis can be objectively verified as true or false through carefully controlled research experiments. There is nothing fuzzy about this in the public mind, with the very term "hard science" implying rigorous laboratory conditions with brainy, otherworldly Albert Einstein types in white lab coats.

Focusing on human behavior, soft science has to fight through a much less orderly thicket of emotion, contradiction and paradox to reach conclusions. Social scientists

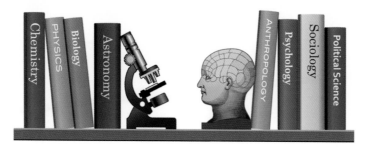

Figure 6-1. Genuine differences exist between scientific fields.

often do not have the luxury of working in a tightly controlled laboratory bubble world. This makes precise measurement much more difficult, with multiple variables to account for. These include social class, money, education, religion and personality type. The less quantifiable nature of social science leads the general public to conclude that it is not as credible.

There is no question that many in the soft sciences feel stung by the suggestion that their work somehow is inferior to hard science, perhaps not even science at all:

> I get annoyed when people suggest [these] disciplines are less valid.... It's a shame that there is a hierarchy within the sciences.... I so often have to battle my way through conversations ... to convince [others] anthropology is equally as important to the development of human thought as any other science.[1]

The perceived second-class citizenship of soft science has resulted in diminished interest in the humanities among college students. Funding of soft science has declined as well, with mounting attention and resources lavished on science, technology, engineering and mathematics. Reflecting on this trend, Princeton University history professor Anthony Grafton describes himself as "a newspaper comic strip character whose face is getting smaller and smaller."[2]

Move towards Greater Quantification

The prestige associated with hard science has triggered a perceptible shift toward greater quantification in other academic disciplines. For example, digital databases increasingly are a part of college English. Critical text mining is used for identifying patterns of literary development.[3] Harvard English professor Louis Menand explains why:

> In the scholarly world, cognitive science has everybody's ear right now, and everybody is thinking about how to relate to it. How many people do you know who've read a book by an English professor in the past year? But everybody's reading science books.[4]

The boundaries between soft and hard science are constantly shifting in our modern data driven world. Fields that once were thought of as soft science increasingly have focused on hard data. Psychology is a good example of this trend. The public identifies psychology in legal cases with experts who attempt to explain criminal behavior. The defendant's state of mind or competence is often at issue, with divergent points of view from the experts called by each side.

However, there is no question that many branches of psychology are hard science. Controlled psychology research experiments measure the development of learning skills, response to stimuli and the effectiveness of behavioral modification. Cognitive psychology is heavily quantitative, studying information processing and human performance characteristics. Research psychologists seek to tie behavioral conditions to specific causes, such as autism.

Genuine Differences between Hard and Soft Science

Setting aside the reflexive public categorization of science into simple hard and soft categories, genuine differences do exist between the various fields of science. Though many lay people think of biology as a hard science, physicists and chemists tend to regard it as softer. Biologists do experiments and try to replicate results, but face a greater level of uncertainty in the outcomes than in either physics or chemistry.

Hard sciences generally are less prone to warring schools of thought, with more agreement on basic principles and analytical tools. If the data is accurate, different scientists in the same discipline should reach the same conclusion. For example, theoretical physics is highly quantitative, capable of clear predictions. Scientists can calculate the altitude necessary for a stationary satellite to be able to send TV signals over a defined geographic area. Engineering also is calculation driven, designing planes and bridges to withstand defined stresses and loads: "I always like to see the numbers, what are the weights, the speeds? Those are quantitative and objective."[5] While scientists in these quantitative fields can and do disagree, the range is narrower, due to greater consensus on the fundamentals.

Willingness to Tackle Tough Scientific Questions

A basic question for us to answer in approaching hard science in legal cases is, "What are we willing and able to be critical of?" Can we ask the tough questions on the background assumptions being made? There is not a real appetite among lawyers for learning the hard way, diving into the articles, trying to get our heads wrapped around an unfamiliar methodology:

> The bottom line is that science is hard. If you want to be intellectually honest about this, the number of people who really understand forensic science is incredibly small. So much so, that if you insisted on using only those capable of understanding the science, nothing would ever get done.[6]

The capacity of a lawyer to competently analyze and/or challenge hard science has major implications for the ultimate outcome of a case. Most jurors have no gut level capacity to gauge the credibility of hard scientists, as this is beyond the realm of common knowledge. There is a reflexive deference to testimony based on numbers. Truth is assumed with hard scientists, who are seen as objective, credible and formula-bound. "Chemistry is chemistry, you can't change the outcome." This poses major potential difficulties for lawyers, who must ask, "How do I build up the science on my side and tear it down on my opponent's?"

The second-class citizenship of soft science definitely plays out in the power dynamics of the courtroom, a potential source of juror skepticism. For this reason, lawyers in civil practice tend to be wary of soft science experts:

> The testimony is mostly basic common sense. I am reluctant to use them, as too often, they end up looking like hired guns. You run the risk of losing your credibility if you call them. Even psychology can be a risk.[7]

The Impact of Hard Science on Criminal Cases

The application of DNA analysis and other laboratory techniques has pushed crim-inal forensic evidence strongly into hard science. The influence of television crime shows like "Bones" and "CSI" reinforce this in the public mind. Prosecutors build their cases around evidence gathered at the scene that is analyzed and interpreted in the crime lab.

DNA analysis sets a standard for scientific objectivity that other forms of forensic proof have trouble matching. "This guy loaded the gun, the touch DNA tells us that." In most criminal cases where it is used, DNA evidence bolsters other testimony, such as eyewitness identification, making guilt more or less probable. The laboratory tech-niques surrounding DNA analysis are so sophisticated now, not much of a sample is re-quired to get a valid profile. This shifts the equation from conjecture and speculation to relative certainty. The same applies to certain other laboratory tests, such as the iden-tification of illegal drugs seized from a defendant. Is this heroin? The answer is a straight-forward yes or no.

Defense Challenges to DNA Evidence

If the prosecution has DNA evidence in a criminal case, most defense lawyers will hire their own expert to review it. If the prosecution knows that a DNA sample is too small and is going to be consumed in the testing process, defense counsel is notified in advance. The defense has the option of hiring its own DNA expert to observe. If a DNA sample has not been consumed in the testing process and is big enough, the defense ex-pert can have it independently tested. Presumably, if the testing is done incorrectly, the defense can call its expert at trial. This almost never happens.[8]

The defense usually does not challenge the crime lab's analysis of DNA in a direct way. Rather, defense experts discuss the general subject of flawed DNA testing and interpreta-tion. This can take the form of contamination and chain of custody type arguments. The bottom line is not, "This is not the defendant's DNA," but rather "They haven't proved that it is beyond a reasonable doubt." In closing arguments, the science of DNA itself is not attacked, but rather the methodology of the police and crime lab. This approach was used by the defense team in the O.J. Simpson murder trial in Los Angeles in 1995. The issue isn't proving the prosecution evidence wrong so much as it is establishing reasonable doubt.[9]

Other Prosecution Forensic Tools

Though the public generally believes that fingerprint analysis is an objective hard science, the claims once made of 100% certainty in fingerprint comparisons have been muted in recent years. Similar to DNA evidence, defense fingerprint experts typically do not come out and say, "This is not a match." Rather, their approach is, "The method-ology of the crime lab is flawed." This is particularly true when there is only a partial print found at the scene.

It is now common for the prosecution to use cell phone data to track the defendant's whereabouts during the commission of a crime. Since most people now carry smart phones, cell phone tracking evidence has become a routine part of felony cases. Judges frequently are called upon to sign search warrants, ordering cell phone providers to give information to law enforcement. Sometimes the defense requests this information too. The prosecution can put together a credible case based on where the defendant's phone was. With three cell towers, a defendant's presence can be narrowed down to within a very small area, allowing the prosecution to say, "The defendant was at the scene." It also has the side effect of satisfying the CSI effect for the jurors. "Now we're doing scientific evidence."

The hard disk on the defendant's computer is another common form of electronic evidence used by the prosecution and law enforcement. This is low hanging fruit, given how many peer-to-peer exchanges occur now. It is easy for the police to break into these exchanges and get the IP address. The police then can get a search warrant and find out the details of computer ownership from the service provider. This foundation leads to a search warrant of the house where the computer is. The police then seize it and examine the hard disk. Searching the defendant's computer often is conclusive evidence in cases like child pornography.

The police and prosecution know that the defense will raise chain of custody and alteration issues, so they make a mirror image of the defendant's hard disk and give it to defense. Though the defense usually hires its own computer expert, this effort often does not result in exculpatory evidence. The typical defense to computer evidence is based on reasonable doubt. "Somebody else put this on there. This cannot be traced to the defendant."[10]

The Bottom Line: Forensic Evidence Makes Criminal Cases Tougher to Defend

Scientific forensic evidence makes the defense of criminal cases much tougher now than it used to be. For example, in the 1970s, the state-of-the-art for prosecuting rape cases was the acid phosphatase test, which determined the presence of semen. All this test showed was that somebody's semen was present, not connecting it with any particular individual. Now, the prosecution can prove conclusively whose semen it is. This is a huge difference, dramatically reducing the chances of defense counsel introducing reasonable doubt in these cases.

Direct challenges to the scientific validity of the prosecution experts now are rare:

> My colleagues on the criminal bench and I are not seeing much sustained debate on hard scientific evidence. This only comes in isolated fits and starts. After the National Science Foundation severely criticized the way that crime labs compared fingerprints, we noticed some upsurge in the challenges to fingerprint evidence. The defense jumped on this and said that it completely debunked fingerprint evidence, to the point where it no longer was accepted in the scientific community. *Frye* motions were brought that this all should be

suppressed. The judges didn't go that far and buy this argument. That was pretty much the end of it.[11]

The typical approach of the defense is to talk in a general way about the flaws that can occur with the kinds of scientific evidence relied upon by the prosecutor, bringing in experts to testify about this. It is often external factors that drive whether criminal cases go to trial, rather than any controversies over the scientific evidence itself: "We don't have that many whodunits in federal court. Most of the time, scientific tests are stipulated to in the criminal cases that come before me."[12]

Some defense attorneys will go so far as to get drugs retested, but this rarely turns up any promising evidence for them. Crime labs usually do not err in identifying what type of drug is involved in a case. The defense arguments tend to focus not on what drug is involved, but who did what when. "It wasn't me, he's lying, I didn't drop this envelope of cocaine."

Scientific evidence fundamentally has changed how criminal cases go through the system, slowing them down. Lawyers have to cope with all this and it takes time. There are a small number of criminal defense experts available to testify. This alone causes delay, which in turn keeps people in jail longer awaiting trial. Scientific evidence has a less obvious impact on caseloads. Public defenders are in court every day, working very hard. They only can try so many cases and none of them is easy anymore. The unintended consequence of prosecutors filing more drug and theft cases as misdemeanors is that the remaining felonies have serious consequences and are very difficult to defend. The caseloads of prosecutors are far more complex as well.

Questions Left Unanswered by Hard Science

Hard criminal forensic evidence like DNA does not address the ultimate question of guilt or innocence, as this usually includes a combination of elements. Some common issues in criminal cases remain relatively unaffected by hard science. For example, you don't ask DNA experts, "What was the defendant's state of mind?" For questions like this, scientific certainty starts to fall off. The mental state of a defendant is a much fuzzier concept.

Softer science does address ultimate legal questions, along with making a determination of the requisite mental state. The quality of the advocacy by the expert and the lawyer then becomes far more important. The defense may bring in a psychologist to testify about the defendant's state of mind. When the science involved in a legal case shifts more to making sanity decisions, the foundation becomes more tenuous. What qualifies an expert to offer opinions on the question of whether someone knows right from wrong?

The various theories of personality are vague enough to allow a certain amount of wiggle room in addressing legal questions of state of mind. The answers often are not nearly so black and white as in hard science. Reasonable minds may differ. As a result, psychological issues are among the most common battlegrounds in criminal cases. Did the defendant have the intent to kill? Was it premeditated? Does he meet the definition of insanity? Where do you draw the line? A sociopath saying "I don't care about the consequences of my actions" is not the same as the inability to tell the difference between right and wrong.

The softest parts of forensic psychological testimony raise a number of issues. How quantitative is the research on which this opinion is based? Is it based on the studies of one case? Were the psychological tests designed for one purpose and used for another? Is knowing right from wrong a valid scientific question? Jurors often feel in as good a position to answer these questions as an expert.

Self-defense is another facet of the state of mind defense, centering around the reasonableness of the defendant's conduct. Was there a perception of harm that justified his response? This has been the focus of considerable comment in so-called "stand your ground" states, where defendants can establish their subjective fear as a justification for the use of lethal force.

Diminished capacity is essentially the "no defense" defense, when there is nothing else. It can involve the nullification of criminal intent by intoxication or use of drugs. Logically, this defense is easy for the prosecution to defeat: "This is goal directed activity by the defendant. He had to intend the act. Maybe he was really drunk and wouldn't have done it if he was sober, but it still is goal directed behavior."

Use of Soft Science in Plea Bargaining

The defense approach in criminal cases now tends toward the use of soft sciences experts to support plea-bargains. For example, defense lawyers will bring a forensic psychologist to argue diminished capacity. The general public is not aware of the extent of this. Judges often have a very narrow sentencing range, the result of legislation establishing matrices. This requires the defense to focus on persuading the prosecutor to reduce the charge.

The path of least resistance is for the defense to get a diminished capacity evaluation of some kind. Certain forensic mental health professionals tend to find diminished capacity as a matter of course. The defense then will take this report to the prosecutor. With far more cases than they can try, a defense psychological evaluation can serve the prosecutor's ends too, giving them an excuse to plea-bargain the case down. At times, a deal will be cut on this basis, even though the report may not be particularly credible. The victim can be told, "We have to reduce this charge to a lower one, because of this report. We might lose."

Eyewitness Identification and False Confessions

Eyewitness identification and false confessions are soft science issues that are based on a body of respected research. These come up regularly in criminal cases. There is a small group of defense experts who testify on these subjects. As with many forms of forensic testimony, it is common for this testimony to be scripted. "Ask these questions in this sequence." Variations can be required, depending on the specific facts, such as cross-racial identification, weapon use, photomontage or a show up.

There is a concerted effort by the prosecution to exclude experts on eyewitness identification. The usual arguments are: "It is intuitive, the jury doesn't need an expert for this." "What they are testifying about isn't really accepted in the relevant community." There is a knee-jerk, pro forma quality to these prosecution responses, as these soft science experts are not generally a serious threat to getting a conviction:

> These experts are a self-selecting group who market themselves to the defense legal community. They don't really hurt our cases. It only takes a passing acquaintance with the subject matter to impeach them. They usually have nothing to say that is specific to the case before the court. Most of the points they make are of the sound-bite nature: "You should be cautious about making these kind of nuances." "Who really knows what?" We don't really fear it on the prosecution side. It's not the kind of thing that the jury is going to make a decision based on.[13]

Personality Testing: How Objective?

Psychological experts have suggested that personality testing is hard science, more objective than a clinical assessment. Originally formulated out of research that started in the late 1930s, the Minnesota Multiphasic Personality Inventory (MMPI) is one of the most common personality tests. The norms of this test originally were based on a population of people in Minnesota. The MMPI has objectivity because it is consistently administered and the reading of it is done in a blind fashion, consistent from one set of test results to another. Individual MMPI results are reported in profile form, based on the responses to hundreds of true or false questions.

However, the consequences of psychological predictions from personality testing can be severe. "Here's someone with a personality type that makes them more likely to reoffend." If this opinion is believed, what will the lifelong consequence be for this person? Questions have been raised about this. Was the test used to render an opinion that the test was not designed for? Does it have any validity or prediction value in a litigation setting? Some judges are concerned about the forensic use of personality testing. It is easy for jurors to hang their hat on a convenient profile that says people with a certain personality type are more likely to engage in particular conduct:

> After having been in the system for 40 years as a prosecutor and a judge, I am skeptical of the claims made for personality tests. The personality testing data overall is less impressive than with well-founded clinical assessments. A clinical impression based on repeated interviews will carry some weight. It is very dangerous to suggest that personality can be defined on the basis of a test alone. For the jurors looking for a handle they can hang onto to justify gut feelings, these personality tests can fulfill this need. "The experts said that this person is more likely to engage in risk seeking behavior. He is prone to violent outbursts."[14]

While there are validity scales used with personality tests, there is a potential for the subject to manipulate the outcome by trying to present in a particular way.

> **Example:** In a capital murder case, opposing experts testified on the question of the defendant's sanity. The defendant took two MMPI tests, one shortly after he was arrested, and another much later, closer to trial. When he was first arrested, the defendant was saying "I did it, I shouldn't have, I feel terrible about killing these children, I should die for what I did, I want to plead guilty." By the time we went to trial, the defendant had changed his tune. He didn't want to die.
>
> The defendant answered some of the same questions on the two tests differently. Some of the questions were inane, such as, "Do you have difficulty starting a urine stream?" When the defendant was first arrested, he said "No." In April of the following year, when he's going to trial, he says "Yes." There was the same inconsistency on the question, "Do you have flashes in your head where you see visions?" The answer was "no" on the first examination and "yes" on the second.[15]

Juries Try to Base Their Decisions on the Facts

At the end of the day, juries try to make decisions based on facts, guided by the gestalt of "What really happened here?" To the extent that this can be influenced by forensic evidence, hard science has a definite advantage. In that soft science offers opinions on subjects that can be decided on the basis of common sense, jurors tend to be more skeptical of it. This is particularly true in fields such as psychology. Jurors typically go beyond the opinions of these experts, making their own assessments about the defendant's behavior.

> **Example:** An armed defendant went to the offices of a Jewish philanthropic organization and shot a number of people who worked there, killing one and seriously injuring others. His first murder trial ended in a hung jury on the question of whether the defendant was mentally competent to form the requisite intent. The first trial took weeks, with lengthy expert testimony on the sanity issue. The jurors said later that the defendant looked mentally ill, just sitting there in the courtroom. He did not take the stand so they did not hear him talk.
>
> The prosecution team had a planning meeting before the second trial, ripping their case apart. "How can we do this better next time? How can we narrow down the elements of his mental state?" They had volumes of tape recordings of the defendant. All of his interviews with the experts were recorded, as well as a large volume of jail calls.
>
> In the second trial, the prosecution used these tape recordings to give the jurors direct experience with how the defendant sounded, rather than having their experts interpret and filter this information: "I asked the defendant this and he said that."

The prosecution played the actual responses of the defendant to questions for the jurors. The prosecution linked them to a PowerPoint, so when the experts said, "I asked the defendant this," the prosecutor clicked to the PowerPoint and the jury heard his answer: "I walked down the hall and took my gun out." Beyond this interview material, the prosecution selectively played the calls the defendant made leading up to and following the shootings, explaining to his mother and father why he did it.

The second jury found the defendant's own words to be really powerful evidence of his mental state, and returned a verdict that he was guilty as charged. All the prosecution needed to do was give the jurors a direct connection to the defendant's thought process to get them to form their own opinion of his sanity. The days of testimony from the psychology experts in support of the insanity defense or diminished capacity were not persuasive in the face of this.[16]

Takeaways — Hard and Soft Science

1. Forensics requires a closer look at the hard and soft science divide.

2. The general public tends to view science in a binary manner, either hard or soft.

3. There is a definite value judgment that goes along with the hard and soft labels. Public opinion generally regards hard science as more credible.

4. Even if people cannot understand the specifics of hard science, the close association with quantitative data causes them to trust it.

5. The numbers in hard sciences are intimidating to most lay people and may cause them to defer.

6. Hard sciences are less prone to warring schools of thought, with a number of agreed upon tools and principles.

7. Even within the hard sciences, there are differences in approach and potential for quantification.

8. In that soft science offers opinions on subjects that can be decided on the basis of common sense, jurors tend to be more skeptical of it.

9. The soft sciences feel stung by the suggestion that their work somehow is inferior or less credible than hard science.

10. Fields that once were thought of as soft science increasingly have focused on hard data.

11. The fundamental question for lawyers on hard science issues is what are we willing and able to be critical of? Can we ask the tough questions?

12. Forensic evidence now is an essential element in how prosecutors build criminal cases.

13. Hard forensic evidence like DNA analysis does not address the ultimate question of whether or not the person is guilty, which usually includes a combination of elements.

14. If the state has DNA evidence in a criminal case, most defense lawyers will hire their own scientific experts to review it.

15. Criminal defense lawyers usually do not challenge the crime lab's analysis of DNA in a direct way. Rather, their expert will discuss generally the accuracy problems labs can have.

16. This typically takes the form of contamination and chain of custody type arguments.

17. In drug cases, the defense arguments tend to focus not on what drug is involved, but who did what when.

18. Scientific evidence has slowed down the speed with which criminal cases go through the system.

19. Though less obvious from the outside, scientific evidence requires criminal lawyers to do more work in handling their cases.

20. A limited pool of experts shows up frequently in criminal cases. Civil attorneys have a greater number of choices of experts.

21. It is now common for the prosecution to use cell phone data to track the defendant.

22. Law-enforcement personnel routinely examine the hard disk on a defendant's computer.

23. Criminal defense lawyers often use soft science experts to support their plea-bargaining attempts.

24. Diminished capacity is essentially the "no defense" defense, used when there is nothing else. It is not clear that knowing right from wrong is a scientific question.

25. Other regular soft science issues in criminal cases are eyewitness identification and false confessions.

26. While the prosecutors routinely move to exclude defense soft science experts, they are not considered a significant barrier to getting a conviction.

27. Psychological experts have suggested that personality testing is hard science, more objective than a clinical assessment. There is some concern about the use of these in criminal cases.

28. Jury decisions are driven by the facts, trying to answer the question of "What really happened here?" Hard forensic evidence is much more likely to influence the outcome than soft science.

Chapter 7

Criminal Forensic Science

I am in blood / Stepp'd in so far, that, should I wade no more, / Returning were as tedious as go o'er.

—William Shakespeare, *Macbeth* (Act III, Scene IV)

Definition and Scope

Forensic science in its simplest form can be defined as any science used for the purposes of the law. The list of forensic disciplines that exist under the name of forensic science is long and constantly growing. Traditional forensic science, sometimes termed core forensics analysis, is most often encountered in a crime laboratory setting. It embraces such diverse areas of study as fingerprints, firearms and toolmarks, trace evidence, chemistry, DNA, document examination, and toxicology. Each of these disciplines has many subdisciplines. Trace evidence analysis, for example, involves analyzing shoeprint impressions, hair, fibers, paint, glass, soil, metals, fire debris samples, and explosives residues, as well as many other materials.

Other forensic disciplines encountered outside the crime lab whose study often impacts court proceedings include forensic pathology, forensic archaeology, forensic anthropology, forensic nursing, forensic engineering, forensic entomology, forensic odontology, forensic psychology, forensic psychiatry, and computer forensics.

Crime scene investigation combines many of the forensic disciplines above in addition to bloodstain pattern interpretation and crime scene reconstruction.

Obviously not all of these areas of forensic study can be covered in this book but traditional forensic science and crime scene investigation, and in particular the significance of the conclusions that can (or cannot) be drawn from the numerous evidence types, will be emphasized.

History and Development

Forensic science was first applied in China. "Feng Zhen Shi" is an ancient Chinese system of autopsy.[1] "Feng" means seizure; "Zhen" means investigation examination, and testing; "Shi" refers to the standard implementation of government-defined "process."

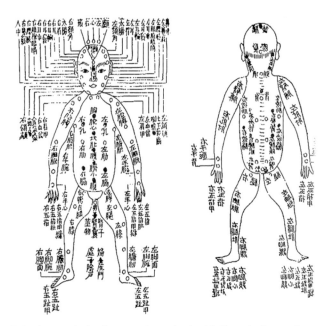

Figure 7-1. Anatomical reference charts in the *His Yuan Lu* for use by coroners.

The Feng Zhen Shi was found in a group of legal documents carved on bamboo slips in the tomb of Emperor Qin Shi Huang, in Hubei province, Yunmeng county, in 1975. It is estimated that the find dates from approximately 200 B.C. It is considered to be the earliest judicial inspection system in Chinese history. The bamboo slips include cited cases with the illustration of the exams and diagnostics which followed the "Shi." There are examples for all officials at all levels to follow according to this official process.

Another very influential Chinese document is the "*His Yuan Lu*" or "*Instructions to Coroners.*"[2] The *His Yuan Lu* (translated literally as "the Washing Away of Wrongs"), written by Song Ci, dates from the reign of Shun Yu of the Sung dynasty, A.D. 1241–1253. It was eventually translated into English, German, Japanese, French and other languages. It provides instructions on general examination of the deceased for wounds and for estimating the time of death, before dealing at length with wounds to the body and artifacts from everything from a knife fight to a bludgeoning, from burned bones to death by strangulation. Diagrams such as that shown in Figure 7-1 were used to standardize notations for the coroners.

Limited research facilities and poor manufacturing practices often meant that many years went by between scientific discovery and its exploitation. In 1590, two Dutch eyeglass makers, Zaccharias Janssen and son Hans Janssen, experimented with multiple lenses placed in a tube. The Janssens observed that viewed objects in front of the tube appeared greatly enlarged, creating both the forerunner of the compound microscope and the telescope. It was not until the work of English physicist Robert Hooke and Dutch microscopist Anton van Leeuwenhoek, almost 80 years later, that scientists were able to examine blood, cells, insects, bacteria and other microscopic objects.

Although fingerprints have existed since the arrival of mankind, it was in 1687 that the Italian physiologist Marcello Malpighi published "Concerning the External Tactile Organs" in which the function, form, and structure of the friction ridge skin, which makes up fingerprints and footprints, was discussed. Malpighi is credited with being the first to use the newly invented microscope for medical studies. In his treatise, Malpighi noted that ridged skin increases friction between an object and the skin's surface; friction ridge skin thus enhances traction for walking and grasping.[3] In the 19th century many researchers studied fingerprints. In a letter dated February 16, 1880, to the famed naturalist Charles Darwin, Henry Faulds wrote that friction ridges were unique and classifiable, and alluded to their permanence. Subsequently Faulds was the first person to publish in a journal the value of friction ridge skin for individualization, especially its use as evidence.[4]

About the same time, French scientist Alphonse Bertillon began to apply his system of anthropometrical identification to one of the greatest problems in criminal investigation, identifying individual perpetrators.[5] This procedure involved the recording of numerous body measurements of individuals (see Figure 7-2).

The Bertillon system became very successful throughout the world and for more than 20 years was the most accurate method of personal identification. However this dominance was challenged when a man was arrested in 1903 and brought to the Leav-

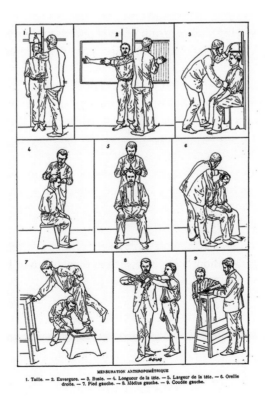

MENSURATION ANTHROPOMÉTRIQUE
1. Taille. — 2. Envergure. — 3. Buste. — 4. Longueur de la tête. — 5. Largeur de la tête. — 6. Oreille droite. — 7. Pied gauche. — 8. Médius gauche. — 9. Coudée gauche.

Figure 7-2. Bertillon's system of body measurements.

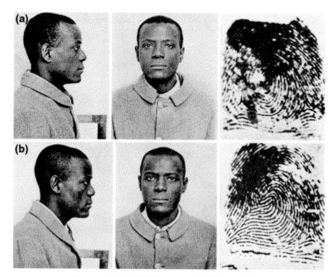

Figure 7-3. Will West and William West.

enworth prison in Kansas. The man claimed that his name was Will West and that he had never been previously arrested. Prison personnel took the man's Bertillon measurements and his photograph to facilitate a prison records check. The records showed that a man named William West, with very similar anthropometric measurements and a striking resemblance to the new inmate, was already incarcerated in Leavenworth prison (see Figure 7-3).

Guards sent to check William West's cell may have suspected they were dealing with an escapee; instead, they found William West asleep in his bed. After comparing records of both men, prison personnel seemed unable to tell the men apart. Upon taking and comparing the fingerprints of both prisoners, it was clear that the fingerprint method of identification could distinguish between the two men.[6] Later information indicated that William and Will West both corresponded with the same family members, and thus were probably related. Both men had almost identical anthropometric measurements yet easily differentiated fingerprints. Fingerprints as a unique identifier of individuals supplanted anthropometry soon after.

In the early 20th century advances in forensic science occurred simultaneously on many fronts. Dr. Karl Landsteiner discovered that blood could be differentiated into A, B, AB, and O groups. Albert S. Osborn published "Questioned Documents" which became a widely consulted reference for document examiners. In 1912, the first official police crime laboratory in the world was opened in Lyon, France, by Dr. Edmond Locard. This laboratory became the model for similar laboratories throughout the world.

Locard published more than 40 works in many languages including the seven volumes of the *Traité de Criminalistique* (Treatise on Criminalistics), published between 1931 and 1935. Locard advanced forensic science in many areas. However his most important and lasting contribution to forensic science is the Locard Exchange Principle. Locard stated, *"Toute action de l'homme, et a fortiori, l'action violent qu'est un crime, ne*

Figure 7-4. Dr. Edmond Locard (1877–1966).

peut pas se dérouler sans laisser quelque marquee," which translates as "any human action, and particularly if that violent action is a crime, cannot take place without leaving a trace." Today that has been shortened to "Every contact leaves a trace."

It is inevitable that the transfer of traces takes place, even if someone—the criminal or an "official" visitor to the scene—does not mean for it to. To illustrate this consider a person wearing blue cotton jeans who is sitting on a red nylon upholstered chair. Blue cotton fibers will be transferred from the jeans to the red nylon chair; simultaneously, red nylon fibers will be transferred to the blue jeans. The person, when they leave, has acquired red nylon fibers on their blue jeans, leaving behind blue cotton fibers on the red seat. Another example is if a white vehicle strikes a black vehicle. The damaged area of the white vehicle will have transfers of black paint and the damaged area of the black car will have transfers of white paint. In addition, there will be broken light lenses, tire marks, broken plastic vehicle parts and other materials at the site of the collision. It is safe to say that essentially all evidence is transfer evidence and the form of evidence relates to what can be said about the transfer.[7]

The scientific advances in chemistry, physics, biology, and manufacturing during, and following, the Second World War that led to an expansion in the capabilities in forensic science, were propelled by the advent of accessible computer technology in the mid-20th century. Techniques familiar in crime laboratories today, such as gas chromatography, mass spectrometry, scanning electron microscopy, and electrophoresis, all followed.

The greatest advance in forensic science since fingerprint analysis is undoubtedly the 1984 discovery of DNA typing for solving crimes and the subsequent improvement of the technique. In the world of advertising hyperbole that we inhabit today, it is not an overstatement to say that DNA typing has revolutionized the entire application of forensic science.

In considering the development of forensic science it is notable that the use of fingerprints to uniquely identify an individual only occurred just over 100 years ago and that the first DNA profiling was less than 30 years ago.

Functions of a Criminal Forensic Scientist

TV notoriety not only causes unrealistic public expectations about the capabilities of forensic science but also generates interest in these jobs. The typical crime laboratory director now fields multiple calls/emails per week asking, "How do I become a forensic scientist?" Most of these come from junior or senior high school students who have watched *CSI*-type shows on TV. When asked why this is attractive, their reply often is "because it would be so cool." Ten years ago, an announcement of a job as a forensic scientist in a state crime laboratory might elicit 10–20 applicants. Today the number might be over 100, a number of which acknowledge, "I really got into this watching *CSI*."

The typical applicants will use Google or Bing and ask "What does a forensic scientist do?" and get back several hundred thousand hits. The American Academy of Forensic Scientists (AAFS) is one of the first sites available, which states:

> The work of the forensic scientist may reduce the number of cases entering the overloaded court system by assisting the decision-makers before a case reaches the court. The facts developed by forensic scientists, based on scientific investigation, not circumstantial evidence or the sometimes unreliable testimony of witnesses, may convince prosecuting or defense attorneys, a grand jury, or a judge that an issue does not merit a court hearing.[8]

This is all true but what really does a forensic scientist do? There are more than 12,000 forensic scientists in the United States.[9] Most work a minimum of 40 hours per week in local or state government. The people who collect the evidence are rarely those who analyze it. Unlike TV, they are specialists, not generalists; a scientist who works in DNA does not analyze firearms evidence. All forensic scientists who work in accredited laboratories must have a minimum of a four-year college degree. Many have master's or doctorates.

A tremendous amount of a forensic scientist's time is spent in running samples to ensure quality control. This is particularly true in DNA where the quality standards are so rigorous. A large amount of time is also spent on verifying and calibrating instruments. An airline pilot before every flight runs through a checklist to verify that the airplane is safe to fly; similarly the forensic scientist would never consider running a case sample on an instrument without first verifying that an instrument is operating according to specifications.

CSI—Myth vs. Reality

Consider the following statements:

> Thanks to the enormously popular various *CSI* shows, not only does forensic science play a role in most criminal cases, it also is now part of mainstream American culture. Prosecutors are faced with jurors who expect forensic evidence to be as clear-cut as it is on television, where it is easy to understand, interesting, and 100 percent accurate. Jurors faced with lengthy expert testimony

discussing complex scientific principles may disbelieve the evidence, holding prosecutors to an impossible standard. At the same time, it also is possible that given their familiarity with some forensic science terms, jurors may believe the evidence to be more accurate than it really is, aligning it with their television experiences in which the evidence is always infallible. As a result, lawyers on both sides of cases are faced with the daunting task of convincing jurors that art does not always imitate life.[10]

This is what is called the "*CSI* Effect."

Forensic scientists always find it amusing how they are portrayed on TV. They do not do *any* of the following while at work; fly helicopters, drive Hummers, wear leather pants and designer clothes to crime scenes, interview suspects, work in semi-darkness with only pink or pale blue mood lighting for illumination, have instruments that provide all results within 10 seconds, or solve all crimes in one hour (with commercial breaks). This is what the public perceives, and as a result a forensic scientist is often asked to begin their testimony by explaining how their job is *not* like *CSI*.

Application of Scientific Method to Criminal Forensics

Forensic science starts with a search for evidence and other relevant information. Once collected, these materials are carefully analyzed as each data source provides an opportunity for a deeper understanding of the case.

The goal of applying the scientific method to the facts and evidence of a legal case is to sort out the data and to evaluate its significance, promoting a deeper understanding of what happened. At an early stage in the review of material, one or more hypotheses may be formed. Later, a prevailing hypothesis may emerge that fits the facts and best explains the overall case. This is then tested, sometimes using specialized forensic or laboratory methodologies and procedures. The results may or may not validate the hypothesis. Finally, the testing methods, procedures, results, and their corresponding conclusions are conveyed in an oral or written report.

Lawyers and Criminal Forensic Science

Law is concerned with what facts are admitted into evidence; forensic science is concerned with the facts of the case. The lawyer on each side wants the scientist to say what favors their client, but scientists are uncomfortable with questions that involve speculation without hard facts. They do not personally favor either party in their testimony. Scientists only testify to what the evidence tells them. Truth is considered a loyalty to what really is, as far as can be determined at that time.

Scientists who testify for the prosecution do not look to the prosecutor for help if the defense is subjecting them to rigorous cross examination. Lawyers who ask a scientist a question beginning with "in your expert opinion" and followed by scenarios involving several hypotheticals, are likely to be disappointed. The scientist often answers by exposing the unconnected nature of the scenarios, stating that there are insufficient facts to render an opinion. This is not evasion but a reflection of the psyche of most scientists, who, when they are unsure of their data, are reluctant to speculate.

It's difficult to teach science to nonscientists. Most jury members haven't had a class in science since high school. Most attorneys (and judges) have a liberal-arts background. A trial is a very poor environment for a jury member to learn enough about a complex subject to make a determination. How hard will it be if you are a jury member? There will be no course outline. You will not be allowed to do any background reading. You won't even be able to discuss the material with any of your fellow students (or anyone else) until the course is completed. Finally, you will have two teachers, who will each present a conflicting view about the science itself.

In 2005 the United Kingdom House of Commons Science and Technology Select Committee stated that "forensic science is now central to the detection and deterrence of crime, conviction of the guilty and exculpation of the innocent. Moreover, the significance of forensic science to the criminal justice system can be expected to intensify in years to come."[11] As the Committee concluded, "it is of great concern that there is currently no mandatory training for lawyers in this area."[12]

Compare this to forensic science labs where heavy emphasis is placed on scientists not only learning the science, but also the legal context. A forensic scientist without a foundation in the law would be rightly considered lacking. In training, forensic scientists learn about courtroom etiquette and present their scientific findings as expert witnesses, using a real crime scenario. They are robustly cross-examined by experienced forensic scientists, who themselves have acted as experts at court.

Science can quickly become very complex. No matter which adversarial position is taken, the science needs to be explained by the scientist without bias. How it is explained is critical to the understanding of the listener. As it most cases, it is best to use the KISS (keep it simple stupid) approach. Explain it the way you would to a group of intelligent 12-year-olds—by the way, this is the same group who can reprogram your computer or cell phone in seconds! Use analogies, use simple terms that are easily understood, use diagrams. Avoid acronyms, avoid complex polysyllabic words.

As an example, to analyze a sample such as rock cocaine the scientist often uses a gas chromatograph mass spectrometer, a very complex instrument that costs approximately $100,000.

The following illustrates how this might be explained to a jury.

> Q. "To analyze the material you said you used a gas chromatograph mass spectrometer (and I hope I said that right). How does it work?"

> A. "As the name gas chromatograph mass spectrometer is such a mouthful, we abbreviate it to GCMS. [*If you have to use an acronym, explain the reason why.*] A GCMS is really two instruments joined together. The first instrument, the GC, consists of an oven and a coiled glass column, which if stretched out, is the length of a football field. [*The standard column is 100 meters long—a football field in length is easier to understand, particularly in the U.S. where the knowledge of the metric system is minimal.*]

Figure 7-5. Gas chromatograph mass spectrometer.

"We begin by dissolving the material in methanol and then injecting it into the glass column. Gas is pumped through this column to move the injected material along. The inside of the glass column has a coating that reacts with whatever material is injected into it. This coating separates whatever is in the material into its components based upon the time it takes the components to move through the column.

"So now you have what was present in the mixture separated out into its components. How do you identify what the components are made of? [*Steer the jury by asking the question for them.*] We use the second part of the GCMS—the MS.

"In the MS the components are blasted with an electronic beam that breaks up the molecules into fragments. [*Use of language—"blasted with an electron beam" is better than "the molecule is irradiated with a collimated beam of electrons."*] Now this is the crucial part. [*Clue in the jury that this is the time to pay attention.*] Each molecule, depending upon its structure, breaks into a number and type of fragments that are unique to each molecule. So like apples and oranges are both fruit but are very different, so the molecules of heroin and cocaine each always break into fragments whose differences can be detected.

"We use computers to categorize what fragments are produced with known materials and we then compare the fragments that the unknown sample produces to those known materials.

"So to recap [*always add a summary for technical testimony*], a GCMS is two instruments joined together. The first instrument separates the components in a material. The second part detects what each of those components is made of."

A Gas Chromatograph Mass Spectrometer is a good example, for many thick books have been written about the theory and techniques involved. The above description of how it works may appear very oversimplified to a practicing scientist but explaining it in detail would take hours, and subject the jury to excruciating tedium. Worse still, being too technical could mean that the jury loses interest and dismisses the evidence involved as being unworthy of consideration.

Strengthening Forensic Science

In 2009, the National Research Council (NRC) issued a 350-page report titled *Strengthening Forensic Science in the United States: A Path Forward.*[13] The report begins with:

> Recognizing that significant improvements are needed in forensic science, Congress directed the National Academy of Sciences to undertake the study that led to this report. There are scores of talented and dedicated people in the forensic science community, and the work that they perform is vitally important. They are often strapped in their work, however, for lack of adequate resources, sound policies, and national support. It is clear that change and advancements, both systemic and scientific, are needed in a number of forensic science disciplines—to ensure the reliability of the disciplines, establish enforceable standards, and promote best practices and their consistent application.

Not unexpectedly the report was initially controversial with forensic practitioners, who saw the report of a committee, which was composed almost exclusively of attorneys and heads of university science programs, as critical and self-serving. However time has led forensic scientists to study the criticisms and led to a better understanding of what needs to be done to improve forensic science.

The main issues identified by the NRC are as follows:
- Disparity in the forensic community
- Laboratory accreditation and personal certification are not mandatory
- Forensic laboratories are under-resourced and under-staffed
- Forensic science research is not well supported
- Lack of strong governing body
- To increase the confidence in the testing results presented in litigation, each of the multiple forensic disciplines and subdisciplines needs to be evaluated as to the question of whether there is or is not *science* in that field of study.

The NRC provided 13 recommendations, chief of which was that Congress should establish and appropriate funds for an independent federal entity, the National Institute of Forensic Science (NIFS). Of course with the recent economy woes and lack of meaningful bipartisanship this entity still does not exist, so there has been little progress on the issues identified by the NRC. However a discussion still bears merit.

There are disparities in the forensic community with respect to funding, access to analytical instrumentation, the availability of skilled and well-trained personnel, certification, accreditation, and oversight. The driver for most of these issues is funding, especially since the recession of 2008.

The NRC sees laboratory accreditation as one of the essentials of improving the forensic community. A laboratory is awarded a certificate of accreditation when an assessment of the laboratory's operations shows it has successfully met the internationally recognized ISO 17025 standards for testing laboratories. Accreditation for laboratories is not mandatory, except for the notable exceptions of the states of New York and Texas. If a lab is accredited it certainly inspires confidence that the laboratory is using a good model for its operations. However this does not ensure that individual scientists are personally certified. There are programs for forensic science certification but again they are not mandatory.

Existing data suggests that forensic laboratories are under resourced and under staffed, which contributes to case backlogs and likely makes it difficult for laboratories to do as much as they could to (a) inform investigations, (b) provide strong evidence for prosecutions, and (c) avoid errors that could lead to imperfect justice. Being under resourced also means that the tools of forensic science—and the knowledge base that underpins the analysis and interpretation of evidence—are not as strong as they could be, thus hindering the ability of the forensic science disciplines to excel at informing investigations, providing strong evidence, and avoiding errors in important ways.[14]

Forensic science research is not well supported, and there is no unified strategy for developing a forensic science research plan across federal agencies. Relative to other areas of science, the forensic disciplines have extremely limited opportunities for research funding.

Although the Federal Bureau of Investigation and the National Institute of Justice have supported some research in forensic science, the level of support has been well short of what is necessary for the forensic science community to establish strong links with a broad base of research universities.

Another statement from the report opines, "The law's greatest dilemma in its heavy reliance on forensic evidence, however, concerns the question of whether—and to what extent—there is *science* in any given forensic science discipline."[15] In later sections of this section on forensic science, the scientific basis for selected forensic disciplines will be discussed.

Takeaways — Criminal Forensic Science

1. Forensic science in its simplest form can be defined as any science used for the purposes of the law. The list of disciplines that exists under the name of forensic science is long and constantly growing.

2. Forensic science was first used in China, possibly as far back as 200 B.C.

3. In 1896 French scientist Alphonse Bertillon began to apply his system of anthropometrical identification to one of the greatest problems in criminal investigation,

namely to uniquely identify individual criminals (Bertillon 1896). This procedure involved the recording of numerous body measurements of individuals.

4. William and Will West, who were both incarcerated at the same time in Leavenworth, Kansas, in 1903, had almost identical anthropometric measurements yet easily differentiated fingerprints. Fingerprints as a unique identifier of individuals supplanted anthropometry soon after.

5. Dr. Edmond Locard's most important and lasting contribution to forensic science is the Locard Exchange Principle, which today is summarized as "every contact leaves a trace."

6. The greatest advance in forensic science since fingerprint analysis is undoubtedly the discovery in 1984 and the subsequent improvement of DNA typing for solving crimes.

7. For a criminal forensic scientist, case analysis and the formulation of opinions generally follow the principles of the scientific method.

8. In 2009, the National Research Council (NRC) issued a 350-page report titled *Strengthening Forensic Science in the United States: A Path Forward.*

9. Forensic science research is not well supported, and there is no unified strategy for developing a forensic science research plan across federal agencies. Relative to other areas of science, the forensic disciplines have extremely limited opportunities for research funding.

Chapter 8

The Crime Laboratory

It is a capital mistake to theorize before you have all the evidence. It biases the judgment.

—Sherlock Holmes, *A Study in Scarlet*

In 2009, the nation's 411 publicly funded crime laboratories received an estimated 4.1 million requests for forensic services. Of these, 8 out of 10 were for the screening or DNA analysis of biological evidence (i.e., forensic biology) (34%), controlled substance analysis (33%), or toxicology (15%). During the same year, 83% of publicly funded crime labs were accredited by a professional forensic science organization compared to 71% in 2002. Between 2002 and 2009, the overall accreditation rate increased across state (80% to 92%), county (66% to 75%), municipal (45% to 62%), and federal (67% to 79%) labs.[1]

No two crime labs are alike. They range in size from huge facilities like the FBI crime lab in Quantico, Virginia, that employs over 500 forensic scientists, to small two-person labs in the basement of a rural police station. The services they offer may be everything from a lab that analyzes only drug evidence to full-service labs that offer expertise in most forensic core disciplines. The labs can be operated by city, county, medical examiner, coroner, or state authorities. In addition to the differences above, disparities exist in the forensic community with respect to funding, access to analytical instrumentation, the availability of skilled and well-trained personnel, certification, and accreditation.[2]

What follows is a general description of the workflow and evidence analyzed in a larger full-service crime laboratory. The specifics of the analysis of the major forensic disciplines and the strength of the conclusions that can be drawn from that analysis will be dealt with in depth in later chapters.

Evidence Unit

The first section is the Evidence Receipt Unit. Here all evidence is received either in person or by mail. It is initially surprising to many people when they learn that most forensic evidence today is delivered and dispatched to crime labs using the U.S. Postal Service or private carriers such as UPS or FedEx. However, when you consider that people are able to track the cool shoes they have bought online, using software on their smartphones, the idea seems less unusual.

The evidence is usually physically accompanied by a Request for Laboratory Examination Form (RFLE) or an electronic version of the same request form that is attached in an email from the submitting agency. This form lists the vital information for the suspect, the victim, the date of the offense, the nature of the offense, the agency case number, the contact information for the submitting detective, and a list of the evidence items submitted for analysis. This latter evidence list will designate each item by a unique exhibit number, e.g., item TMcA-1: Black woolen jacket from John A. Smith, TMcA-2: Blue denim jeans from John A. Smith, and so on, for each of the items.

Every item of evidence must list the individual or the exact location where it was collected. A cardboard box labeled as "containing rape kit from victim" would not be accepted.

In addition to being uniquely identified, each evidence item must be separately packaged (if possible) and sealed to avoid contamination. The seal on the evidence packaging is typically marked with a case number, item number, the date when sealed, and the sealer's initials.

Evidence packages are properly sealed if the evidence inside is protected from loss or contamination and any attempt to enter the package would be easily noticed. Staples on envelopes or paper bags do not constitute proper seals; staples also present the possibility of puncturing or otherwise damaging the evidence inside the packaging. The open flaps of envelopes must be sealed with tape and each strip of tape must be initialed. Bottles and jars must be capped tightly to avoid leakage and then sealed with tape. The tape must extend across the top of the lid and down both sides of the body of the container.[3]

The laboratory property and evidence custodian (P&EC) or evidence officer verifies that all the evidence listed on the RFLE is present, and that each piece of evidence is properly sealed. Most labs then affix a computer generated bar code that assigns a

Figure 8-1. Typical evidence room.

sequential number to each case with all associated evidence items. This begins the chain of custody for each item in the case. Using a bar-code scanner, the P&EC enters a description of the packaging for each item and the details of the RFLE into the lab evidence system. Using the evidence system computer he or she then assigns a location in the evidence vault where the items in the case are physically stored. The lab evidence system automatically records the time of this transaction. The items stay in that location until they are requested by the forensic scientist who will perform the analysis of the evidence items. At the time the P&EC retrieves the items, he or she scans them over to the scientist using a bar-code scanner. The forensic scientist enters a unique personal identification number (PIN) to indicate they have received all the items. Again each transaction is automatically timed. The scientist then takes them to the bench where they stay until the analysis is complete. Upon completion of analysis the scientist brings them back to the P&EC where the process of barcode scanning and PIN entry is repeated. Similarly the P&EC then places the items in a specific vault location where they remain until they are ready to be shipped out to the police agency that submitted them.

Using a typical laboratory evidence recording system such as that described above ensures an unbroken chain of custody of evidence for each separate piece of evidence from the time it was received into the laboratory until the time it is shipped out. Depending on the laboratory P&EC's may perform other duties such as verifying that submitted guns are unloaded and that drug syringes do not have attached needles.

DNA Unit

The DNA unit also includes the traditional biology or serology unit. This section identifies and then obtains DNA profiles on dried body fluids. These dried fluids are encountered as reference sample swabs from suspects or victims, as stains that have dried on objects such as an individual's clothing, or as stains that have been collected from crime scenes.

This unit usually analyzes cases involving crimes against persons such as homicides, sexual assaults, assaults, and some burglaries and or robberies. They examine evidence items in order to determine: the presence and identity of body fluids on an item, and whether DNA profiles associated with evidence items match DNA profiles of suspects or victims. DNA analysis has radically changed the way items are analyzed in a laboratory. Often evidence items have to be analyzed by more than one unit.

An example is a gun that must be examined for latent prints, DNA and firearms evidence. The maximum amount of information must be extracted from the gun. Depending on the condition of the item, the nature of the tests to be performed on the item, and the circumstances of the case, the order in which each discipline gets to analyze the item is critical. Typically for a gun it is processed by the latents section first, then by the DNA section, and lastly by the firearms section. At any time in the testing of the gun, the finding of unexpected evidence, such as hairs or fibers, may cause a reevaluation of the order of testing.

DNA instrumentation and analysis procedures are so sensitive today that the slightest amount of DNA may show up in a profile. This explains the rigorous lengths to which DNA sections go to prevent contamination. The introduction of foreign DNA through coughing, sneezing, or even prolonged talking in the vicinity of evidence during testing can be minimized by wearing a facemask. Similarly the use of latex gloves and head covers is mandatory. All laboratory implements such as forceps must be sterile or disposable. Swabs used to collect biological stains are sterile and individually wrapped. Surfaces where items are to be examined are cleaned with a bleach solution then covered with clean paper. After the items are examined the paper is removed and the surface cleaned again. If after all these precautions, the DNA of the forensic scientist shows up in the DNA profile generated from the DNA analysis of items from the crime, the laboratory appoints a senior forensic scientist to investigate the circumstances of this contamination. At the end of the investigation, if necessary the scientist who contributed his or her DNA may be suspended from casework and have to successfully undergo remedial training before being permitted to analyze evidence again.

Firearms Unit

The firearms section examines firearms, cartridge cases, discharged bullets, clothing to detect gunshot residue and thereby obtain information about muzzle-to-target distance, and any item of evidence associated with the discharge of a firearm. They perform these examinations to determine if the bullet removed from the victim at autopsy was fired from the suspect's gun or to determine if the cartridge case found at the scene of a drive-by shooting was fired through the same gun that was used to commit a double homicide. Clothing may be examined to detect gunshot residue and thereby obtain information about muzzle-to-target distance. Each weapon leaves char-

Figure 8-2. Cartridge case under microscope.

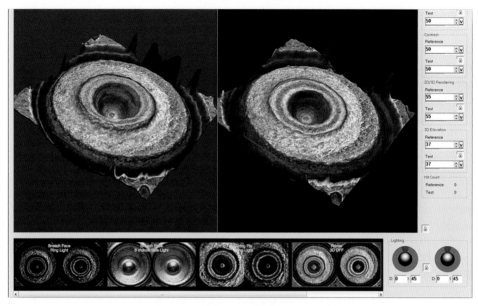

Figure 8-3. BrassTrax NIBIN screen image.

acteristic marks on ammunition components as they are cycled through the weapon. Bullets acquire lands, grooves, and striations as they travel through the barrel. Cartridge cases are an ammunition component that is familiar to movie goers as the brass casings that produce the characteristic tinkle noise when they land on a hard surface after they have been ejected from a semi-automatic or automatic weapon. The cartridge case acquires unique marks as it is struck by the firing pin of the gun, then makes hard contact with the breech of the gun, before being extracted and ejected from the breech.

Today firearms examiners use the National Integrated Ballistics Information Network (NIBIN) database as a screening tool to capture and compare digital images of the unique markings on the base of cartridge cases. If the database suggests a similarity between the markings on cartridge cases from different shooting incidents, the evidence from those two incidents must be resubmitted and examined by a firearms examiner who will make the confirmation as to whether the two cartridges cases from the different incidents were fired in the same gun.

Latent Fingerprint Unit

Latent print examiners collect and preserve latent physical evidence in the lab, at crime scenes and from a wide variety of materials using technical procedures to obtain fingerprints, palm prints, and footprints from various surfaces and materials. Once a print is obtained the examiner then classifies and identifies the print which often requires comparing the print with computerized identification systems or comparing it manually with other recovered prints.

Fingerprints are a reproduction of the pattern of ridges and valleys present on the friction skin found on the palm side of fingers and thumbs. They are classified into three main classes of pattern called loops, arches and whorls. Each of these classes has many subclasses. For example, arches can be plain or tented. With the advent of the widespread use of computers in the 1970s the classification systems and identification began to be influenced by automated fingerprint identification systems (AFIS).

In 1999 the FBI introduced the Integrated Automated Fingerprint Identification System (IAFIS), which links local AFISs to the FBI fingerprint database. Fingerprints can be scanned and digitally encoded facilitating rapid searching of the database for possible matching reference fingerprints. IAFIS includes not only fingerprints, but corresponding criminal histories; mug shots; scars and tattoo photos; physical characteristics like height, weight, and hair and eye color; and aliases. The system also includes civil fingerprints, mostly of individuals who have served or are serving in the U.S. military or have been or are employed by the federal government. The fingerprints and criminal history information are submitted voluntarily by state, local, and federal law-enforcement agencies.

IAFIS is the largest biometric database in the world, housing the fingerprints and criminal histories for more than 70 million subjects in the criminal master file, along with more than 34 million civil prints.[4] As mentioned above the fingerprints unit works closely with the other crime lab units to maximize the information that can be obtained from an item of evidence.

Trace Evidence Unit

Depending on the laboratory, the Trace Evidence Unit may be called the Materials Analysis Unit, the Microanalysis Unit, or the Physical Evidence Unit. Forensic scientists who work in this unit use many different types of microscope, chemical tests and instrumental methods to analyze materials including, but not limited to, hair, fibers, paint, glass, explosives, fire debris, soils, botanicals, drugs, poisons, and unknowns. Compared to the units described above the Materials Analysis Unit requires a diverse knowledge base to include physics, chemistry, geology, and expanding to incorporate knowledge of instrumentation, and advanced computer skills.

Given the issue of widespread drug abuse in our society with its attendant problems of assault, robbery, and homicides, it is not unsurprising that drug cases provide the bulk of all samples that are submitted to crime laboratories. The vast majority of these drug cases are analyzed using instruments such as a gas chromatography mass spectrometer or an infrared spectrometer, many of which are programmed for automated analysis sequences that run 24 hours a day, 365 days a year.

In addition to the instruments mentioned above, this unit utilizes stereomicroscopes, comparison microscopes, polarized microscopes, microspectrophotometers, scanning electron microscopes, and X-ray fluorescence spectrometers to characterize, compare and occasionally identify materials. As will be expanded upon in later chapters, most of the work of this unit involves a comparison of the various properties of reference materials to materials found at the scene.

Crime Scene Investigation Unit

More crime labs are beginning to use crime scene units staffed by dedicated forensic scientists for the collection of evidence from major crimes rather than the model whereby police officers pick up what they think may be relevant, package it, label it, and send it to the lab for "processing." This newer approach has many advantages for the crime lab. Police officers today are trained to recognize significant evidence but not to the extent of trained forensic scientists.

When the evidence is submitted to the lab, the scientists have a much better picture of how each evidence item is related. Forensic scientists also receive much more in-depth training on specialized topics such as blood stain pattern interpretation and bullet trajectory analysis. Knowing what procedures will be subsequently used in the lab enables the scientist to better package and preserve the evidence they collect. Crime laboratories spend a tremendous amount of time interacting with police agencies who submit evidence. Often the collection of the evidence is not confined to items that are germane to the case but also includes many items that are collected "just in case they are needed."

A forensic scientist who attends a crime scene speaks the same language as the forensic scientist who handles that evidence and consequently the analysis is more focused. Police agencies excel at the collection of evidence from burglaries that involve a large number of incidents coupled with a limited time at the scene. The crime lab must be careful to limit their crime scene unit to major crimes against persons, where the specialized skills of the forensic scientist will have the greatest impact.

Forensic scientists who attend crime scenes must have extensive ongoing training in the core forensic disciplines. It is advisable for them to have worked in the crime lab for several years learning their craft before they are considered for the crime scene unit. Lastly they must be physically fit. It may not seem like it on television, but crime scene investigation is very demanding work, both physically and mentally. Spending long hours wearing a Tyvek suit can lead to dehydration, especially in summer. Crawling into confined spaces, ripping up carpet to look for blood, or cutting walls to find bullets can all lead to fatigue as well as safety hazards. Adequate water and rest breaks must be built into the crime scene procedures.

Crime scene documentation involves multiple measurements, tests, and observations, all of which are scrutinized for the smallest mistake by other experts later, sometimes years later. Decisions are constantly being made about which stain to test, which fingerprint to collect, how many photos to take, and which reagent to use to develop the latent blood. "Getting it right the first time" is very tiring mentally. The team must have adequate rest if mistakes are to be kept to a minimum.[5]

Takeaways — Crime Laboratory

1. In 2009, the nation's 411 publicly funded crime laboratories received an estimated 4.1 million requests for forensic services. Of these, 8 out of 10 were for the screening or DNA analysis of biological evidence (i.e., forensic biology) (34%), controlled substance analysis (33%), or toxicology (15%).

2. Most crime labs are organized into sections based on type of examination.

3. Typically these are the evidence section, DNA section, firearms section, drug section, trace evidence section, latent prints section, and crime scene investigation section.

Chapter 9

Crime Scene

Murder is always a mistake—one should never do anything one cannot talk about after dinner.

—Oscar Wilde

The crime scene is where all forensic science begins. Crime scene investigation presents many challenges. Crimes scenes are dynamic, not static events. Physical evidence created during the commission of the crime is constantly being removed, and added to, during the course of the investigation. Physical evidence to be collected at a crime scene can be anything from an engine block dropped on a victim's head (think Wile E. Coy-

Figure 9-1. Uncovering the buried body of one of the Green River homicides victims.

Figure 9-2. (left) Investigators searching for the remains of a Green River homicides victim.
Figure 9-3. (right) Seattle Police Department CSI investigator searching for evidence.

ote and the falling anvil) to invisible traces of DNA. How do investigators know what to collect? In what order do they collect the evidence? How do they preserve the evidence? Mistakes made at the crime scene cannot be undone.

In comparison with other branches of forensic science, crime scene investigation has only recently been deemed worthy of study and research. Traditionally crime scene investigation was performed by detectives or evidence officers with only basic training. Complex forensic techniques such as blood stain pattern analysis or bullet trajectories were performed by just a few practitioners. To a certain extent, before and certainly in the aftermath of the O.J. Simpson investigation, police agencies became preoccupied with not missing any critical piece of evidence. This led to "garbage truck forensics,"[1] which occurred when police agencies at a crime scene collected every possible item of potential evidence, and submitted it to the crime lab to sort out what was important and what was not. This inevitably led to long delays in processing and analyzing evidence, and in producing a written report.

Circular arguments arose wherein crime labs were asked by the police agencies, "Why don't the scientists, who seem to know so much, come out and collect the evidence at the crime scene?" To which the scientists replied, "We can't because we have so much evidence to analyze." Eventually an arrangement was arrived at where many crime labs in the U.S. sent forensic scientists with specialized training to assist police agencies with major crimes such as homicide, assault, and rape. This led to an increase in the quality of the evidence collected and submitted to the crime labs and allowed the police agencies to concentrate on burglaries and other high-volume crimes.

The processes employed to collect and preserve evidence that is germane to the investigation can follow the following sequence, first described over 40 years ago:

- Protecting the scene(s)
- Documentation of the location, scene, and evidence

- Collection of the potential evidence
- Preservation of the evidence
- Labeling of evidence and related materials
- Chain of custody considerations
- Letter of transmittal (to the custodial agency or laboratory)
- Collection of reference materials (known as samples of comparison)[2]

Protecting the Scene

Before any forensic investigation can begin, the first officer on the scene must render physical aid if necessary to any injured parties, then secure the scene. The priority of the first officer then shifts to protecting the scene, thereby preventing the destruction or diminishment of the utility of the evidence present.

The phrase "protecting the scene" begs the question "from whom?" This begins with persons at the scene, injured or otherwise, known or unknown. An ambulatory injured person should be prevented from wandering about the crime scene. Family members present should be removed from the scene as soon as possible. Family members outside the scene who want to enter the scene to check on the welfare of their loved ones or to retrieve wallets, purses, clothing, etc., must be prevented from doing so. Let's not forgot the assailant who might want to come back to finish the job. Human beings are naturally inquisitive. Think of how many traffic jams are caused by "rubberneckers" at the scene of an accident.

If a crime occurs and the police have cordoned off the area then usually a crowd of onlookers quickly forms. Members of the crowd aren't sure what they will see but know they want to see "something." Putting up yellow tape doesn't have the same effect as a force field in "Star Trek." People will always want to get closer to the action and police agencies have to be vigilant. This phenomenon is not limited to the public. In a homicide in a department where such events are rare, not only the responding officer and the lead detective will be in attendance at the scene but many other members of the department will find an excuse to be there. This extends to the captains and the chief of the department, who may turn up just to see what is going on.

Another major interested player is the media. Typing "journalists versus police" into any search engine will return thousands of entries highlighting the problems each group has with the other. Journalists will want to know answers to "What happened? How does this event affect the public? What is the police agency doing to restore order?" Members of the media feel that they have a right to know, whereas police agencies, who also feed on information, disperse it only on a need-to-know basis. Many police agencies have formed media relations units that interact with the media, providing contact and what the media feeds on—information.

Figure 9-4. (left) Seattle P.D. CSI investigator dusting for latent fingerprints.
Figure 9-5. (right) Seattle P.D. CSI investigator locating evidence using a portable metal detector.

Documentation of the Location, Scene and Evidence

The dream of every crime scene investigator (CSI) is to walk into the crime scene, press the button on a clock, and have time stand still, "freezing" the scene until it is completely and properly processed.[3] As we have stated above crime scenes are dynamic not static events. The weather, availability of daylight or personnel, access to witnesses' statements, and many other factors may hamper the investigation but time is the constant enemy of the documentation of the scene. Investigators have only a limited amount of time to work a crime site in its untouched state. The opportunity to permanently record the scene in its original state must not be lost. Such records will not only prove useful during the subsequent investigation but are also required for presentation at a trial in order to document the condition of the crime site and to delineate the location of physical evidence.

Every step of the investigation should be documented thoroughly with an appropriate method. A scene can be documented in many ways but detailed notes, photography, video, and sketches are the principal methods used.[4] Obviously these activities cannot take place at once, so a plan on how to completely document the scene must be formulated as soon as possible.

Note taking must be a constant activity throughout the processing of the crime scene. These notes must include a detailed written description of the scene with the location of items of physical evidence recovered. They must identify: The time an item of physical evidence was discovered, by whom it was discovered, how and by whom it was packaged and marked, and the disposition of the item after it was collected. Notes must be detailed, chronological, complete, specific, legible, and permanent. The note taker has to keep in mind that this written record may be the only source of information for refreshing one's memory. It is not an exaggeration to say that note taking may be the most important task at a crime scene for all investigators if a successful prosecution of the culprit(s) is the desired outcome.

Less than 10 years ago, 35 millimeter (mm) photography was the preferred format. The advent of digital cameras has revolutionized crime scene photography. Where digital photography really outshines 35 mm photography is in its ability to integrate with other technologies and media and share images cheaply, quickly, and repeatedly. Digital cameras can integrate with GPS systems to apply a location tag to each image. When the images are downloaded to a computer that can be easily linked to TV monitors or projectors, they are ideal for courtroom displays. Images can be wirelessly transmitted to printers for direct printing. When loaded onto a computer, it is a simple matter to share images via email or on CD to other investigators or attorneys. Another important property of digital images is the ability, by use of mathematical algorithms, to perform photo enhancement. This permits cropping, magnifying, brightening, darkening, adjusting the color balance, and making many other enhancements to the image. To perform such image manipulations with 35 mm film, a chemical darkroom is needed.[5]

Nearly everyone today has access to a digital camera and most cell phones come with a camera feature. Although the image output of these devices is adequate, it is not of the quality required for crime scene documentation. A high-quality camera with good optics and extensive programmable features, made by a reputable camera manufacturer, is essential.

Unless there are injured parties involved, items of physical evidence must not be moved until they have been photographed. The order in which these items are photographed to show their position and location relative to the entire scene is: Long range establishment shot; medium range; close-up, with and without measurement scale. The close-up images must be captured from all necessary angles.

Videotape provides a unique perspective on the crime scene layout. It is good at demonstrating the layout of the crime scene and how the evidence items relate to the crime. Formerly, police agencies recorded the scene with video to show the scene before processing began. However, it is better to assess the scene to learn what the crime is about and then formulate a plan of what to videotape. The key to good videotaping is slow camera movement; this is why slow panning of an area is necessary. Overuse of zoom or wide-angle features on the video camera when focusing on items of interest can cause viewers of such footage to quickly experience an unsettling visual effect and the importance of such items may be lost.

Once photographs are taken, the CSI will sketch the scene. Sketches can be of several types. A rough sketch, which is a draft representation of all essential information and measurements at a crime scene, is drawn at the crime scene. It shows all recovered items of physical evidence, as well as other important features of the crime scene. A finished sketch, which is a precise rendering of the crime scene, is usually drawn to scale. This type is not normally completed at the crime scene. Unlike the rough sketch, the finished sketch is drawn with care and concern for aesthetic appearance.

Acquiring measurements at a crime scene provides quantitative information to back up other types of visual documentation. With computer software these measurements can be transformed into two-dimensional, and three-dimensional representations of the crime scene.

3-D laser scanners are becoming more common (see Figure 9-6). They use a scanner to exhaustively cover all three dimensions of the crime scene in a quick and detailed manner, collecting a huge quantity of data (see Figures 9-7 and 9-9). The raw data is known as a point cloud. Once laser scanned, any angle or measurement can be

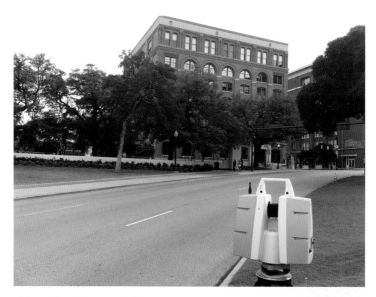

Figure 9-6. A Leica ScanStation 3-D laser scanner imaging the former Texas Book Depository at Dealey Plaza, Dallas, Texas.

Figure 9-7. The infamous grassy knoll in Dealey Plaza as captured by the Leica ScanStation.

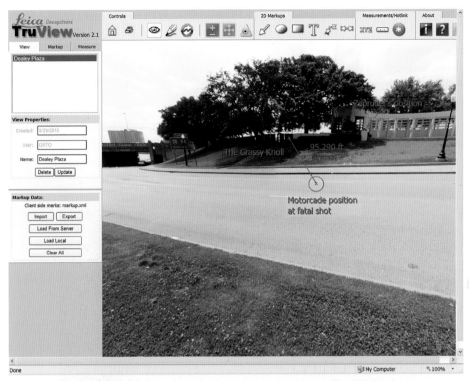

Figure 9-8. Once laser scanned, any angle or measurement can be extracted using free software.

Figure 9-9. 360° laser scan of Dealey Plaza.

extracted, forever. Free viewing software such as Leica Truview can be used to explore the scene (see Figure 9-8). 3-D laser scanners allow the recording of the entire crime scene, locating all potential pieces of evidence at once, at the very beginning of the investigation. Even the best investigators cannot measure everything or predict what might become significant after a crime scene has been released and new facts develop.

In contrast, a laser scanner is objective about what gets documented, protecting investigators from overlooking key evidence. It impartially and comprehensively captures everything in its line of sight and within its range, even areas surrounding the main crime scene that may later come into play.[6] It is a complementary resource to the traditional crime scene photographer, not a replacement.

Collection and Preservation of the Potential Evidence

Many books have been written on the subjects of the collection and preservation of evidence at crime scenes. Given that evidence can be anything from a fiber to an automobile, decisions on what is relevant to collect and preserve can be daunting. Before you can collect any evidence, you first have to be able to recognize it. The senses of sight, hearing and smell are the best tools available to the crime scene investigator to detect evidence. Today, touch is rarely, if ever, used because of contamination potential, and the idea, as seen on TV, of sticking your finger into a bag of white powder then tasting it to identify cocaine seems quaint and amusing to the modern CSI.

Through interview the relationship of the victim to potential suspect(s) can be established. This will have an effect on what evidence is collected. For example, if a woman is raped by a man in her own car, then the presence of his semen in that vehicle is of much greater significance than if it were found in a vehicle owned by the suspect.

If a CSI is unsure of what evidence is present then a systematic search must be undertaken. Typical methods include strip or lane search, grid search, spiral search, or trail

Figure 9-10. Green River homicides investigators searching for bone fragments.

Figure 9-11. Discovery of human bone fragment.

search. Which search method is used will depend on the crime scene and the availability of personnel. Before any searching can proceed the CSI must ensure that he or she has obtained legal permission to conduct the search. In addition to the right to search considerations, the methods used to collect and preserve the evidence must be scientifically valid. Non-destructive methods of detection are used preferentially over destructive chemical detection methods.

The search for physical evidence must extend beyond the homicide crime scene to the autopsy room of a deceased victim. Here, the medical examiner or coroner will carefully examine the victim to establish a cause and manner of death. As a matter of routine, tissues and organs will be retained for pathological and toxicological examination. At the same time, arrangements must be made between the examiner and investigator to secure a variety of items that may be obtainable from the body for laboratory examination.

Contamination at a crime scene can begin immediately after the scene is discovered. The necessary actions of rendering aid and securing the scene by police officers and emergency medical technicians will contaminate the scene. Such contamination cannot be avoided but everyone else who enters the scene must minimize any subsequent contamination. Contamination minimization procedures include the use of disposable gloves, coveralls, and evidence collection supplies; and the use of a unique path (different from that used by the fleeing suspect) to enter and leave the crime scene. The identification of everyone who entered the scene is necessary if any shoeprint impression or DNA elimination samples are needed later in the investigation.

Whenever evidence is collected, consideration must be given to the collection of reference or "known" samples. For example, when paint evidence is collected from the damaged area of a vehicle which has been struck by another unknown vehicle, a sample of paint from an undamaged area of the victim vehicle, adjacent to the damaged area, must be collected. In a rape case where victim and suspect are known, known reference DNA samples must be obtained from both individuals.

The procedures for the preservation of evidence depend on the nature of that evidence. Some evidence is transitory (such as a shoeprint on wet glass) and may have to be collected as soon as possible. Objects such as guns or other weapons are collected and packaged using suitable materials after they have been adequately photographed. Biological samples, such as dried blood and semen, can be collected in their entirety if deposited on clothing, or on a moistened swab if on a surface such as the wall of a room where a homicide was committed. Each different item or similar items collected at different locations must be placed in separate containers. Packaging evidence separately prevents damage through contact and prevents cross-contamination.

The well-prepared evidence collector will arrive at a crime scene with a large assortment of packaging materials and tools ready to encounter any type of situation. The type of packaging will be determined by the nature of the evidence but paper packaging is preferred for most types of evidence. Ziploc bags are convenient for sandwiches, and sometimes goldfish, but they do not permit biological evidence to breathe, and bacteria will form that may destroy or diminish the usefulness of the DNA. They are also not suitable for fire debris evidence because conversely, the vapors from accelerants, such as gasoline, can escape through the pores in the plastic material, leading to contamination. Metal cans or nylon (not plastic) bags must be used for fire debris evidence.

Chain of Custody Considerations

The chain of custody can be defined as "the witnessed, unbroken, written chronological history of who had the evidence from the time of collection until it is presented as evidence in court."[7] Every item of evidence collected at a crime scene must have an associated chain of custody that is unbroken. This begins with the proper labeling of the item as to the contents, source, date, time, item number, agency case number, and the name or initials of the collector. Today most police agencies and crime labs use an electronic chain of custody which has been generated by a bar-code scanner system. If needed for court, a paper chain of custody document for each item can be printed from the electronic chain of custody.

Takeaways — Crime Scene

1. The crime scene is where all forensic science begins.

2. Crimes scenes are dynamic, not static events.

3. After rendering physical aid to any injured parties and securing the scene, the priority of the first officer then shifts to protecting the scene, thereby preventing the destruction or diminishment of the utility of the evidence present.

4. The opportunity to permanently record the scene in its original state must not be lost.

5. It is not an exaggeration to say that note taking may be the most important task at a crime scene for all investigators if a successful prosecution of the culprit(s) is the desired outcome.

6. A high-quality camera with good optics and extensive programmable features, made by a reputable camera manufacturer, is essential for crime scene documentation.

7. 3-D laser scanners exhaustively cover all three dimensions of the crime scene in a quick and detailed manner, collecting a huge quantity of data. The raw data is known as a point cloud. Once laser scanned any angle or measurement can be extracted, forever.

8. Before any searching can proceed the CSI must ensure that he or she has obtained legal permission to conduct the search.

Chapter 10

Physical Evidence

I didn't invent forensic science and medicine. I just was one of the first people to recognize how interesting it is.

—Patricia Cornwell

Physical evidence is examined by forensic scientists to either identify a material or to compare one material to another. Drug evidence is almost exclusively submitted to crime labs for identification. The vast majority of other evidence is submitted for comparison, for example to show if there is any association between the fibers from a suspect's clothing and the foreign fibers found on a victim's clothing, or to compare the bullet recovered from an autopsy to a test fired bullet from a suspect's weapon, or to compare the paint from the clothing of a victim of a fatal hit-and-run to the paint from a damaged vehicle.

Identification

The object of an identification is to determine the physical or chemical identity of a material to the exclusion of all others with as near absolute certainty as existing analytical techniques will permit. Tests must be devised that give characteristic results for specific standard materials. Once these characteristic test results have been established, they may used repeatedly to prove the identity of suspect materials.

The legal profession is interested in the answer to the question of what constitutes certainty. A common line of questioning by newer attorneys in trials involving drugs is "How certain are you that the material you tested was cocaine? Are you 100% certain, 99% certain, or 95% certain?" The scientist needs to be confident that their tests identified cocaine to the exclusion of all other materials. If not, the attorney has been handed the gift of reasonable doubt.

Comparison

A comparative analysis determines whether or not a suspect item and a standard/reference specimen could have a common origin. The suspect item and the standard/

reference item are subjected to the same tests and examinations. Any differences in the results between the two materials means they do not have the same origin. If the two materials give the same results for the tests the scientist must decide whether to discontinue the testing or to continue testing to see if significant differences arise. To aid in this decision we need to discuss probability which, depending on the type of evidence, can give rise to many questions.

Consider a paint comparison involving paint from a damaged blue car and blue smears that are present on a damaged white car. An obvious comparison test would be color. If they appear the same color of blue, most people would agree that you would need to do more testing to establish that the blue car is the origin of the blue paint smears. Say you examine the paint under a microscope and discover that the blue paint on the white car consists of four layers that has a sequence of clear coat over blue, over light grey, over dark grey. You would then look at the paint from the blue car. If you find that the paint from the blue car has the same paint layer sequence you would say that the probability that the blue car is the origin of the blue paint smears has increased. If you then discover that the blue vehicle is a 2012 Ford Fusion and that Ford painted that model and year with the same layer sequence, again you might say the probability that the blue car is the origin of the blue paint smears has increased. You might wonder if the chemical composition of the paint that is used by Ford for each individual layer is the same as that for each layer of the blue car, and the blue paint smears on the white car. If it is the same, then the probability that the blue car is the origin of the blue paint smears has again increased. However, if only three of the four layers of the paint sequence are present in the smears, what now of probability? Ultimately it is the court that will decide the degree of certainty.

Class Characteristics and Individual Characteristics

Probability can be defined as the frequency of occurrence of an event. For many analytical processes this is difficult to define. Consider a homicide at which a complete left shoeprint pattern in blood is observed on a wooden floor. This shoeprint pattern does not match any of the shoes owned by the deceased or the elimination shoeprints obtained from the investigators who attended the scene. A Nike "swoosh" logo is visible in the shoeprint and a quick online review of the Nike shoeprint patterns available indicates that the shoe that made the print is a Nike Air Jordan, model XI Retro. Measurements show it is a men's shoe size 10–10½.

A suspect is arrested wearing a pair of the same size and model shoes whose left shoeprint pattern design elements of chevrons, loops, and small hexagons are also present in the bloody shoeprint. The suspect's shoeprint is said to share the same class characteristics as the bloody shoeprint. Class characteristics are an intentional or unavoidable characteristic that repeats during the manufacturing process. However, in the example above these same class characteristics are shared by all Nike Air Jordan, model XI Retro men's shoe size 10–10½, left shoes. There are likely thousands of such shoes. A class match is the lowest type of match and is of low evidential value by itself. However, when several class characteristics are combined, like in the O.J. Simpson trial where the shoes were determined to be an expensive, rare Italian brand, the evidential value can be quite high.

The other class used to describe characteristics is individual characteristics. Individual characteristics result when something is randomly added to or taken away from an object that either causes or contributes to making that object unique. Examples of random characteristics typically found on the outsole of a shoe include a scratch, a cut or tear, an air bubble, or an inclusion such as a piece of glass or a stone. In the case above, test shoeprints would be made from the suspect's left shoe and these would be carefully compared to the bloody shoeprint from the scene for individual characteristics. How many points of similarity constitute an identification is a point that will be considered in detail in the later discussion of latent fingerprints.

Another topic to be discussed later that impacts the significance of physical evidence is that of forensic databases. Examples of these are the Integrated Automated Fingerprint Identification System (IAFIS) for fingerprints, the Combined DNA Index System (CODIS) for DNA, the National Integrated Ballistics Information Network (NIBIN) for cartridge cases, the Integrated Forensic Automotive Paint Data Query (PDQ) for paint, and the Shoeprint Image Capture and Retrieval database (SICAR) for shoeprints. All of these databases are computerized and searchable and enable investigators to link crimes to each other and to convicted offenders.

Takeaways — Physical Evidence

1. Physical evidence is examined by forensic scientists to either identify a material or to compare one material to another.

2. The object of an identification is to determine the physical or chemical identity of a material to the exclusion of all others with as near absolute certainty as existing analytical techniques will permit.

3. A comparative analysis determines whether or not a suspect item and a standard/reference specimen could have a common origin.

4. Class characteristics are an intentional or unavoidable characteristic that repeats during the manufacturing process.

5. Individual characteristics result when something is randomly added to or taken away from an object that either causes or contributes to making that object unique.

Chapter 11

Latent Fingerprints

The glands make each finger like a self-inking rubber stamp, leaving calling cards on every surface it touches.
— Colin Beavan, *Fingerprints: The Origins of Crime Detection and the Murder Case That Launched Forensic Science*

History and Nature of Fingerprints

In our introductory chapter on forensic science we discussed how at the beginning of the 20th century, the analysis of fingerprints supplanted the Bertillon system of anthropometry as the most reliable means to uniquely identify an individual. At that time, the absence of a single searchable classification system, a centralized database of fingerprints, and adequate communication systems severely hampered the ability of law-enforcement agencies to effectively use fingerprint analysis as a crime-fighting tool. Before we discuss how these obstacles were overcome, let us consider exactly what a fingerprint is, and how it is formed.

Skin is composed of two main layers of cells, the outer layer called the epidermis, and the inner layer termed the dermis. Between the two layers is a boundary of cells called the dermal papillae. The shape and form of the dermal papillae determine the patterns that are seen on the surfaces of the skin on the hands and the soles of the feet. These patterns appear as a series of ridges and furrows as seen in the typical crime scene fingerprints in Figure 11-1. Each ridge in a fingerprint has a row of pores that are duct openings for the sweat glands below.

The mechanism by which fingerprints are formed is determined by the production and nature of human skin secretions including sweat. Body secretions are either produced by the apocrine, eccrine or sebaceous glands. Such glands are found all over the body surface and mostly function in order to regulate body temperature. The palms, the forehead and the soles of the feet have a stronger concentration of eccrine glands than the rest of the body. These eccrine sweat secretions are composed of 99% water, with the balance composed of sodium chloride and other salts, as well as various organic oils.

When a fingerprint comes in contact with a surface, some of the moisture and the accompanying salts and oils are transferred from the finger to the surface, leaving an

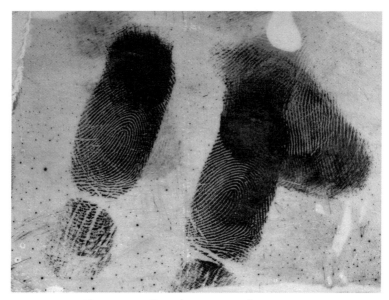

Figure 11-1. Typical crime scene fingerprints.

impression of the friction ridge detail. This is referred to as a latent impression. Latent means not readily visible. Using oblique lighting on most surfaces will often show the impression in more detail. The impression has to be enhanced or developed to be seen fully and collected.

Another type of fingerprint impression, called a patent fingerprint impression, is formed when a foreign material coating the skin of the fingers makes contact with a surface. Patent means obvious. Examples of the foreign material would be substances like blood, paint, or grease. A familiar example of a patent impression would be the ink standards or exemplars collected from individuals. After the ink is applied it becomes the foreign material coating the fingers of the individual. When the fingers are touched onto a card the patent impression is produced. Patent impressions are visible and usually need no enhancement.

A less common type of fingerprint, called a plastic impression, occurs when fingers are pressed into a soft material that will retain the impression of the ridge detail. Examples where a plastic impression would be deposited are into materials such as clay/mud, wet paint, or blood. Plastic or molded impressions are visible and usually need no enhancement.

Fundamental Principles of Fingerprints

There are three fundamental principles of fingerprints that address the uniqueness and stability of fingerprint identification.

- A fingerprint is a unique individual characteristic.
- A fingerprint does not change during an individual's lifetime.
- Fingerprints have general ridge patterns called loops, arches and whorls that permit them to be systematically classified.

The principle that a fingerprint is a unique individual characteristic is supported by the fact that no two individuals of the millions whose fingerprints have been recorded in the last one hundred years, including identical twins, have been found with the same fingerprint ridge characteristics. This does not mean that an individual's single fingerprint print does not have a matching fingerprint somewhere in the world. All that can be concluded from this fact is that, to date, no two people have been found to have matching fingerprints.

Many probability models have been proposed for individuality. The model most quoted is that of Galton in 1892, who gave a probability of finding any given arrangement of ridge details (minutiae) in a fingerprint to be 1.45×10^{-11} (i.e., 1 in 68 billion). Many subsequent models gave an even lower probability number. However, all of these models have obviously not been tested for each of the 7 billion individuals in the world today or even in real-world, large databases. These probabilities may be accurate or they may grossly underestimate or overestimate the truth. It is simply an unknown at this time.[1]

It is obvious that the soles of the feet and the palms of the hands also have friction ridge skin. The friction ridge skin in these areas is also unique, so the term prints is often used as an umbrella term for all impressions caused by contact with friction ridge skin.

We have seen that the shape of the region of dermal papillae cells that lies between the dermis and the epidermis determines the fingerprint ridge details seen on the surface. Dermal papillae are formed in the fetus, and studies show that the future surface patterns are fully formed by the 16th week of pregnancy.[2] The ridge patterns remain unchanged for life except to get larger as the child grows to adulthood. After that they remain unchanged. If the dermal papillae are damaged due to injury, a permanent scar results. This scar adds to the uniqueness of this print. There are no special structures formed by the epidermis or dermis at the site of a wrinkle. Wrinkles are the result of mechanical changes that take place in the skin as it ages. The mechanical properties of the skin cause the skin to be "less stretchable, less resilient, more lax, and prone to wrinkling."[3] The skin becomes loose and simply folds in on itself, creating a wrinkle.

The average fingerprint can contain as many as 175 individual ridge characteristics. However, there are three classes of general fingerprint patterns (loops, whorls, and arches) that form the basis for all ten-finger classification systems. Each of these classes of pattern has several subclasses that assist in classification.

A typical loop pattern is shown in Figure 11-2. A loop has to have one or more ridges entering from one side of the print, then curving back and exiting from the same side. If it opens toward the pinkie finger it is called an ulnar loop, and if it opens toward the thumb it is called a radial loop.

A typical whorl pattern is shown in Figure 11-3. A plain whorl must have one ridge that makes a complete circuit. Other types of whorl include a central pocket loop, a double loop and an accidental loop.

The least common type of general pattern is an arch. Sub-classes include a plain arch or a tented arch. A typical example of a plain arch is shown in Figure 11-4. This is formed by ridges entering on one side of the print and exiting on the other.

Figure 11-2. Typical loop pattern. **Figure 11-3.** Typical whorl pattern. **Figure 11-4.** Typical arch pattern.

Each print that is examined must have sufficient details to determine or exclude the source. The fingerprint found at a crime scene is likely to be a partial print, perhaps representing only a small percentage of a full fingerprint. Lack of clarity in the prints diminishes the examiner's ability to determine or exclude a source of the print. Because the prints have reduced quality of details, the prints must have sufficient quantity of details of these features to determine or exclude a source.

The number of ridge characteristics two fingerprints must share before they can be deemed identical has varied during the last 100 years. Locard indicated that more than 12 clear minutiae establishes certainty.[4] In 1924, Scotland Yard required 16 points.[5] In the United States, in 1973, after a three-year study, the International Association of Identification stated, "No valid basis exists at this time for requiring that a pre-determined minimum number of friction ridge characteristics must be present in two impressions in order to establish positive identification."[6]

Automated Fingerprint Identification Systems

Although the development of classification systems greatly helped the searching of fingerprint databases, the growing sizes of the databases made manual searching increasingly difficult. With the advent of the widespread availability of computers in the 1970s, Automated Fingerprint Identification Systems (AFISs) began to be developed in several countries including the United States, the United Kingdom, France and Japan. In 1999, the FBI launched the Integrated Automated Fingerprint Identification System (IAFIS) that links state AFIS computers with the FBI database. The AFIS scans the fingerprint image and converts it into digital minutiae. Each image is stored in the computer as a geometrical pattern. Using computer algorithms, the computer system searches the database and lists those patterns that are most similar to that of the questioned fingerprint. The list of possible close matches is then compared to the questioned fingerprint by a qualified fingerprint examiner.

Latent Print Development

Latent print development is performed using a myriad of different optical, physical, and chemical processes. These processes are constantly changing requiring dedicated ongoing training for latent print examiners. General procedures have been developed to guide the systematic search for latent fingerprint evidence.[7] An in-depth treatment of the processes is beyond the scope of this book but a discussion of some of the factors that influence the choice of process has value.

An important factor is the nature of the surface upon which the print has been deposited. These surfaces are characterized as either porous, nonporous or semiporous. Porous surfaces are absorbent and include materials like paper, cardboard, and wood. Fingerprints deposited onto porous surfaces absorb into the substrate and are durable to some degree. In contrast nonporous surfaces do not absorb. They include glass, metal, plastics, lacquered or painted wood, and rubber. Latent prints on these substrates are more susceptible to damage because the fingerprint residue resides on the outermost surface. Semiporous surfaces both resist and absorb fingerprint residue. These surfaces include glossy cardboard, glossy magazine covers, some finished wood, and some cellophane.

In addition to the surface, other factors that influence which process to use include:

- Type of latent print residue suspected
- Type of substrate
- Texture of substrate
- Condition of substrate (clean, dirty, tacky, sticky, greasy, etc.)
- Environmental conditions during and following latent print deposition
- Length of time since evidence was touched
- Consequences of destructive processing methods
- Subsequent forensic examinations
- Sequential ordering of reagents
- Seriousness of the crime

Whatever processes are used, the goal is to make the print distinguishable from the substrate and more easily seen. To illustrate this, Figures 11-5 through 11-12 on the following pages show the effects of enhancement processes on two fingerprints on two separate cans.

Accuracy of Decisions Made by Latent Print Examiners

The interpretation of forensic fingerprint evidence relies on the expertise of latent print examiners. Until recently, the accuracy of these decisions was not confirmed in a large-scale study, despite over one hundred years of the forensic use of fingerprints. That changed with the increased scrutiny from reported errors and a series of court

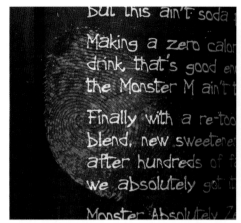

Figure 11-5. Print on can 1 before enhancement.

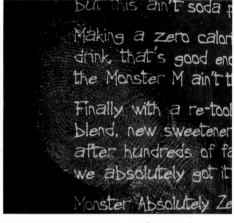

Figure 11-6. Print on can 1 after initial enhancement.

Figure 11-7. Print on can 1 with further enhancement.

Figure 11-8. Print on can 1 with final enhancement.

admissibility challenges to the scientific basis of fingerprint evidence. The National Research Council Report[8] also criticized the ACE-V process. This is where a latent print examiner Analyzes, Compares, and Evaluates fingerprints before having a peer Verify the result if there is an identification.[9]

In response to the misidentification of a latent print in the 2004 Madrid bombing, a FBI Laboratory review committee evaluated the scientific basis of friction ridge examination. This let to an article in the Proceedings of the National Academy of Science[10] reporting the first large-scale study of the accuracy and reliability of latent print examiners' decisions. A group of 169 latent print examiners each compared approximately 100 pairs of latent and exemplar fingerprints from a pool of 744 pairs. The fingerprints were representative of those encountered in forensic casework, comparable to searches of an automated fingerprint identification system containing more than 58 million subjects. This study evaluated examiners on key decision points with pro-

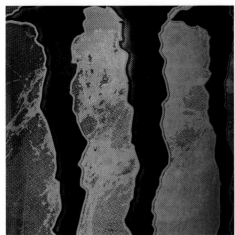

Figure 11-9. Prints on can 2 before enhancement.

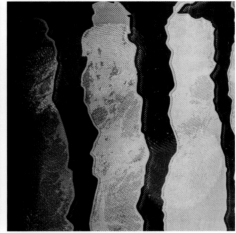

Figure 11-10. Prints on can 2 after initial enhancement.

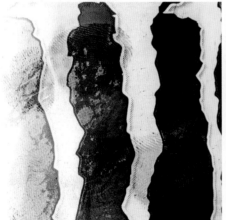

Figure 11-11. Prints on can 2 with further enhancement.

Figure 11-12. Prints on can 2 with final enhancement.

cedures designed to minimize errors. Five examiners made false positive errors for an overall false positive rate of 0.1%. False negative errors (erroneous exclusions) were much more frequent (7.5% of mated comparisons). The majority of examiners (85%) committed at least one false negative error, with individual examiner error rates varying substantially. Though blind verification would have detected the majority of the false negative errors, this is not generally done. Examiners frequently differed on whether fingerprints were suitable for reaching a conclusion. The article concluded that more research is needed.

Fingerprints and the Law

The Federal Rules of Evidence (FRE), FRE 702, Testimony by Experts; and FRE 703, Bases of Opinion Testimony by Experts, are the framework within which scientific evidence is admitted in court. The landmark cases of *Daubert*[11] and *Kumho Tire*[12] refined the rules for admissibility. *Daubert* set forth non-exclusive validity factors for trial courts to use in assessing the reliability of scientific expert testimony:

- Testability: Whether the expert's technique or theory can be or has been tested—that is, whether the expert's theory can be challenged in some objective sense, or whether it is instead simply a subjective approach that cannot reasonably be assessed for reliability.
- Peer Review: Whether the technique or theory has been subject to peer review and publication.
- Error Rate: The known or potential rate of error of the technique or theory when applied.
- Maintenance of Standards: The existence and maintenance of standards and controls.
- General Acceptance: Whether the technique or theory has been generally accepted in the scientific community.

Although the *Daubert* standard is now the law in federal court and over half of the states, the *Frye*[13] standard remains the law in some jurisdictions, incorporated into the *Daubert* general acceptance factor.

Fingerprint identification continues to weather many challenges on each of the *Daubert* factors. The first serious *Daubert* challenge was in *United States v. Mitchell*,[14] in which Judge J. Curtis Joyner denied the defense's motion in limine to bar the government's fingerprint experts from testifying. After a five-day *Daubert* hearing the judge ruled that fingerprint evidence satisfied all *Daubert* factors. The case was appealed and the Third Circuit commented on each of these factors.[15] On the record presented to it, an analysis of the Daubert factors in *Mitchell* showed that most factors either supported, or at least did not disfavor, admitting the government's evidence.

The Third Circuit was concerned that the FBI no longer used a point of comparison system and used an "unspecified, subjective, sliding-scale mix of 'quantity and quality of detail.'" Referring to the AFIS computer check with simulated latent prints (exhibiting only one-fifth of the size of a rolled fingerprint) and that no identification bureau had ever found two matching prints on different digits, the court found this to be the strongest evidence for the government. It concluded that the hypotheses on which fingerprint identifications are based are sufficiently testable, if only to a lesser extent based on experience. The appeals court considered the fingerprint identification community's ACE-V peer review process and stated this may not be peer review in its best form, but on balance, was sufficient to allow admission of friction ridge comparisons and individualizations. Although noting that the error rate was not precisely quantified, the Third Circuit was satisfied that it was low. The maintenance of standards factor was found to be somewhat lacking. The procedural standards of ACE-V were deemed to be insubstantial in comparison to the other scientific and technical disciplines, which did not favor admitting fingerprint evidence. The general acceptance factor received little attention.

There have been several other court challenges to fingerprint evidence since *Mitchell*, all unsuccessful. However, these and all other *Daubert* challenges to forensic evidence have had beneficial effects, causing the forensic community to research its procedures, analysis and peer review. Studies of error rates have removed the complacency that crept in when their views went unchallenged for many years. Forensic scientists have had to re-evaluate how they write their reports and present their findings, helping to make the underlying science and their opinions more reliable.

Takeaways — Latent Fingerprints

1. Skin is composed of two main layers of cells, the outer layer is called the epidermis, and the inner layer is termed the dermis. Between the two layers is a boundary of cells called the dermal papillae whose shape and form determines the patterns that are seen on the surfaces of the skin on the hands and the soles of the feet. These patterns appear as a series of ridges and furrows.

2. A fingerprint is a unique individual characteristic.

3. A fingerprint does not change during an individual's lifetime.

4. Fingerprints have general ridge patterns called loops, arches and whorls that permit them to be systematically classified.

5. The ACE-V process is where a latent print examiner Analyzes, Compares, and Evaluates fingerprints before having a peer Verify the result if there is an identification.

Chapter 12

Firearms and Toolmarks

The vast majority of gun owners don't kill, but people who do kill, tend to kill with guns, and often with illegal guns.

—Alan Dershowitz

The basis for identification in toolmark identification is founded on the principle of uniqueness, wherein all objects are unique and thus can be differentiated from one another. A firearm is considered a specialized tool. The underlying mechanism for the origination of toolmarks is that when a harder object (the tool) comes in contact with a softer object (the work piece), the harder object will impart its marks or features on the softer object. This mechanism for the origination of toolmarks is founded on well-established principles derived from the physical sciences that include physics, metallurgy, metallography and materials science, as well as many mechanical properties presently used in mechanical and industrial engineering.

The working edges of tools, which include components of firearms that contact ammunition, generally consist of some type of hard material, such as steel, to ensure strength and durability of the tool, while work pieces are generally made of softer materials such as lead and brass. These surfaces of a tool that contact a material contain random, microscopic irregularities that are produced during the tool's manufacture, and/or subsequent wear through use and abuse. These irregularities, which

Figure 12-1. Swabbing a weapon to collect DNA.

Figure 12-2. Comparison of breechface marks on cartridge cases.

are formed randomly, are considered unique and can individualize or distinguish one tool from another. Because these irregularities or individual characteristics are typically imparted onto the work piece, the comparative study of the imparted markings allows the tool to be individually associated or identified as having produced the mark. The presence, observation and comparison of these random toolmarks on tools form the hypothetical propositions upon which the discipline of Toolmark Identification is based.

The most widely accepted method used in conducting a toolmark examination is a side-by-side, microscopic comparison of the markings on a questioned material item to known source marks from a tool as in Figure 12-2. The examination process used in Toolmark Identification is similar to that used in the other comparative disciplines in forensic science. This process begins with a study of the most general characteristics (class) of items to be compared, progressing through (subclass) to the analysis and comparison of more detailed characteristics to the most specific characteristics (individual). Any conclusion from this process is based on practical rather than absolute certainty of the underlying (validated) scientific theory.[1]

In the *Journal of the Association of Firearms and Toolmark Examiners* (AFTE) there have been many articles published involving the examination of bullets that have been fired in consecutively produced barrels.[2] They validate the underlying theory that there are identifiable features imparted by a gun on the surfaces of fired bullets that enable a competent firearms examiner to accurately and reliably link them to the barrel that fired them.[3]

In 2005, the FBI designed a validation study to test the accuracy of examinations by trained firearms examiners who use pattern recognition as a method for identification. Eight FBI examiners took the test which consisted of both bullets and cartridge cases. No false positives or false negatives were reported.[4]

Figure 12-3. A bullet under LED lighting on a comparison microscope.

Similarly there have been many publications on firearm and cartridge case identification that test the validity of the basis for toolmark identification.[5] In all of these studies the error rate is either zero or 0.1%.

However, error rates found in studies do not interest a court that is looking at the reliability of actual casework.[6] The proficiencies of individual examiners must be tested for this purpose. Collaborative Testing Service (CTS) currently is the only source of data from which a potential error rate may be inferred. In an assessment of the CTS data for two time periods, the first 1978 through 1997 and 1998–2002, the percentage of false identifications for firearms was 0.9% and 1.0%, respectively. The percentage of false identifications for tool marks was 1.0% and 1.5%. This does not mean that every toolmark identification case report is subject to being right only 98.5% of the time, but rather, that 1.5% of these respondents made an incorrect association. This also assumes that the work was done according to laboratory procedures of quality control, technical peer review and administrative peer review as required by ISO 1725 standards.

Notwithstanding all these validation studies there have been challenges to the admissibility of firearms examination evidence.[7] However, the arguments presented are often unrepresentative of the available literature published by the relevant scientific community (AFTE). A review of that literature indicates that the challenges are found to lack general support. While some legitimate questions are posed with respect to uniqueness of tool marks, the answers provided by the challengers to those questions are not sound.

Takeaways — Firearms and Toolmarks

1. The basis for identification in toolmark identification is founded on the principle of uniqueness, wherein all objects are unique and thus can be differentiated from one another.

2. A firearm is considered a specialized tool. The underlying mechanism for the origination of toolmarks is that when a harder object (the tool) comes in contact with a softer object (the work piece), the harder object will impart its marks or features on the softer object.

3. The examination process used in Toolmark Identification is similar to those used in the other comparative disciplines in forensic science. This process begins with a study of the most general characteristics (class) of items to be compared, progressing through (subclass) to the analysis and comparison of more detailed characteristics to the most specific characteristics (individual).

4. Any individual association or identification conclusion effected through this examination process is based not on absolute certainty but rather on the practical certainty of the underlying (validated) scientific theory.

Chapter 13

DNA Evidence

DNA is like a computer program but far, far more advanced than any software ever created.

—Bill Gates, *The Road Ahead*

What Is DNA?

Deoxyribonucleic acid (DNA) is sometimes called a genetic blueprint because it contains all of the instructions that determine an individual's genetic characteristics. It is well known that the DNA molecule exists as two strands in a double helix conformation. The strands are held together by just four bases: adenine, cytosine, guanine, and thymine. These bases are paired such that adenine is always linked to thymine and cytosine is always linked to guanine.

The type of DNA testing performed is dependent on the nature of the sample. Most laboratories normally use nuclear DNA testing to test biological evidence. Nuclear DNA is found in the nucleus of a cell, packaged in chromosomes. The nucleus of a human cell contains 23 pairs of chromosomes (46 total), half of them inherited from each parent. Regions of the DNA molecule tend to repeat themselves in short, adjacent, or tan-

Figure 13-1. DNA molecule.

dem segments termed Short Tandem Repeats (STR). The areas at which forensic analysts look are always found in the same spots on the same chromosomes. Each specific location is called a locus. The forensic science community typically uses a minimum of 13 genetic loci referred to as the 13 core CODIS (Combined DNA Index System) loci. This enables laboratories to search profiles against other profiles already in the CODIS databank (although some laboratories test more than the 13 core CODIS loci). Each of the 13 loci was chosen because of its high degree of polymorphism, meaning that several different possible genetic types exist for each locus. By examining and identifying these differences, scientists in the laboratory can differentiate between all individuals except for identical twins.

Where Is DNA Found?

The simple answer is everywhere. Usually for humans we associate it with blood, semen, hair, skin and saliva. Sometimes the DNA in the form of visible blood and semen stains is easily seen, but DNA also exists in other less obvious places, such as cigarette butts, the tops of beer bottles and soft drink cans, and envelopes that were licked before they were sealed.

DNA, like all traces, is transferred by contact. When you touch or otherwise make contact with a surface you transfer many skin cells to that surface. So touch DNA can be found on many surfaces, such as a computer keyboard or mouse, a phone or a gun. Sites where the skin rubs against clothing, such as the crotch of a pair of underwear, the collar or underarms of a shirt, the waistband of a pair of shorts, and the headband of a baseball cap, are places where "wearer" DNA can be found. Ski masks, like those discarded by bank robbers, are excellent sources of DNA. With missing persons, where a primary DNA source is not available, a used toothbrush or a hairbrush can be used as a secondary source of DNA to compare with the DNA of unidentified human remains.

DNA in the Lab

When biological evidence is submitted to the lab the forensic scientist begins by examining the items and locating potential biological materials. These biological materials include blood, semen, vaginal secretions, urine, feces, and saliva, that may be encountered in isolation or in combination. The word "materials" is used here because it should be remembered that DNA is molecular level information, while the others convey meaning based on their form.

It is the task of the forensic scientist to differentiate a blood stain from a ketchup stain or from a red wine stain, or to distinguish a semen stain from a mucus stain, or a dairy product stain. To do this we take advantage of the fact that every biological stain has unique properties. We will illustrate this by considering the individual natures of blood and semen.

Blood

Blood is a very complex mixture of a fluid called plasma and cells that float in it. Plasma constitutes 55% of blood fluid. The remaining 45%, in addition to sugar, oxygen, and hormones, contains proteins, blood cells, and platelets. There are red blood cells and white blood cells, each with a specific purpose. The red blood cells, also known as erythrocytes, are shaped like slightly indented, flattened discs. They are by far the most abundant type of cell, and contain hemoglobin. Hemoglobin is a protein which contains iron and it performs the vital function of transporting oxygen from the lungs to body tissues and cells. White blood cells, also known as leukocytes, are the cells of the immune system; they defend the body against infections and foreign materials. Lymphocytes and granulocytes (two type of white blood cells) can move in and out of the bloodstream to reach affected areas of tissue. White blood cells will also fight abnormal cells, such as cancer cells. Platelets (thrombocytes) are involved in the clotting of blood. When a person bleeds, the platelets clump together to help form a clot. If exposed to air the platelets break down and release fibrinogen into the bloodstream. This results in the clotting of blood, for example on a skin wound to ultimately form a scab.

To determine whether or not a stain is blood, a color test is used. The most common such test for blood is known as the Kastle-Meyer or phenolphthalein test.[1] This type of test is termed presumptive, wherein if a positive result is obtained, the material is presumed to be blood, but needs further confirmation. The test works for blood because blood hemoglobin acts like the enzyme peroxidase, which speeds up the oxidation of several types of organic compounds by peroxides. A bloodstain is rubbed with a swab, to which a drop of phenolphthalein reagent is added, followed by a drop of hydrogen peroxide. A vivid pink color results if blood is present. Forensic scientists in training will try the phenolphthalein test on hundreds of different types of stains. Only blood gives a consistent pink color. Some rusts and vegetable juices, most notably horseradish juice, can give a faint positive. Nonetheless, unless a homicide takes place in a horseradish processing plant, then a positive phenolphthalein test is a good indicator that blood is present. However, as it is a presumptive test for blood, further tests are needed to confirm the presence of blood.

Many different tests have been used to confirm that a stain contains blood. The oldest is chemical confirmation of the presence of hemoglobin or its derivatives by the formation of specific crystals.[2] An example is the Takayama or hemochromogen test, in which ferrous iron from hemoglobin reacts with pyridine to produce red feathery crystals of pyridine ferroprotoporphyrin. Another confirmatory test uses the Teichman reagent, consisting of a solution of potassium bromide, potassium chloride and potassium iodide in glacial acetic acid, and is heated to react with hemoglobin. The reaction first converts the hemoglobin to hemin, and then the halides (bromide, chloride and iodide) react with the hemin to form characteristic brownish-yellow rhomboid crystals.

Before we leave the discussion of blood we have to determine whether or not the blood is of human origin. This is most commonly done using what is termed an immunoprecipitin test. Human blood contains proteins called antigens of a type that

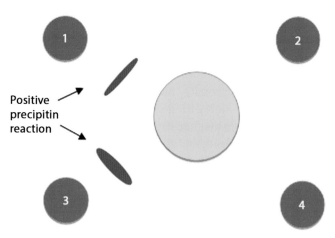

Figure 13-2. Ouchterlony test.

identify the blood as human. The blood or other materials are added to a gel, for what is called the Ouchterlony double diffusion test. In the presence of the anti-human antibodies, the human antigens and a precipitate will form. In the Ouchterlony test this will be seen as a brownish precipitate. The results of a typical test for four blood samples are shown in Figure 13-2. Many YouTube videos also show this process, e.g., http://www.youtube.com/watch?v=h-KptLVJpU0.

In the test shown in Figure 13-2, a brown precipitate has formed in front of samples 1 and 3, but no precipitate has formed in front of samples 2 and 4. So the result of the test is that samples 1 and 3 are human in origin, and samples 2 and 4 are non-human.

Semen

The next major material analyzed is semen, also called seminal fluid, which is fluid emitted from the male reproductive tract that contains sperm cells, which are capable of fertilizing the female eggs. Sperm consists of a head that contains the DNA from the male and a whip-like tail that helps it move. In the human male, sperm cells are produced by the testes; they constitute only about 2 to 5 percent of the total semen volume. The prostate gland contributes about 30 percent of the seminal fluid; the constituents of its secretions are mainly citric acid, acid phosphatase (AP), calcium, sodium, zinc, potassium, protein-splitting enzymes, and fibrolysin (an enzyme that reduces blood and tissue fibers). Tests for the presence of AP are, like the Kastle-Meyer test for blood, considered presumptive. When the Brentamine reagent is applied to the test sample, a purple color forms in the presence of AP. As mentioned above, seminal fluid contains seminal acid phosphatase at elevated levels.

As there are other forms of acid phosphatase in other body fluids, semen stains should give a fast (immediate to within three minutes) purple color reaction depending on the amount of AP present. Slower developing color reaction may be due to a weak semen stain or from AP in other body fluids.

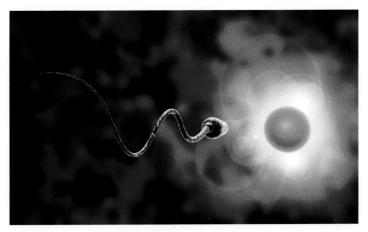

Figure 13-3. Sperm cell.

To confirm the presence of sperm, two dyes that together are called the Kernechtrot-Picroindigocarmine Stain (Christmas Tree Stain) are used to visualize the sperm cells in the presence of other cellular material. The nuclear material of the cell is stained red, while the cellular membranes are stained green. Sperm heads are usually well differentiated with the cap unstained or lightly stained and the posterior (nuclear) portion more darkly stained red. If tails are present they are stained green. This color staining is augmented by phase contrast microscopy in which the staining appears reversed, with the cap appearing darker than the nuclear region.

Some males have low sperm counts or may have no sperm in their semen. For vasectomized males, when the procedure is complete, sperm are still produced by the testicles, but they are broken down and absorbed by the body. To detect semen in samples with no/low levels of spermatozoa observed in a microscopic exam, a p30 or PSA test is usually performed. p30 is a prostate specific antigen that is secreted into semen by the prostate gland. It may be present in other body fluids but is found in semen at elevated levels. To perform the test a proprietary kit such as an ABACard p30 kit is used.

A liquid portion from the test sample is applied after extraction to the sample well on the ABACard p30 kit. Formation of a visible pink line in the test and control regions indicates a positive p30 result. No formation of a visible pink line in the test region, and a visible pink line in the control region indicates a negative p30 result.

Saliva

Similar proprietary cards kits are used to screen for the presence of saliva by detecting human alpha-amylase in forensic samples. Again a liquid portion from the test sample is applied after extraction to the sample well on the card saliva kit. A positive saliva result is when there is the formation of a visible pink line in the test and control regions. No formation of a visible pink line in the test region, and a visible pink line in the control region indicates a negative saliva result.

If the biological material is human the next step is to identify the source. If a sufficient sample is present and is probative, the material is prepared for DNA testing.

DNA Typing

Following the processing of items of evidence to obtain samples for DNA testing, there are five basic steps to follow during DNA typing:

- Extraction of DNA from cellular material.
- Quantification of the amount of human DNA recovered.
- Amplification of the areas of DNA being tested using Polymerase Chain Reaction (PCR) techniques.
- Separation and typing of amplified DNA fragments (typically using capillary electrophoresis, or CE).
- Review, interpretation, comparison and reporting of typing results.[3]

A full treatment of all of these five steps is beyond the scope of this book but we shall briefly discuss PCR, which is what makes DNA analysis such a powerful technique. PCR is a process where potentially billions of copies of the DNA at the locations of interest (typically STRs showing variation between individuals) are made. DNA is mixed with primers for the primer binding sites with fluorescent dyes attached, additional bases, and an enzyme to replicate the DNA. Upon controlled heating the DNA molecule splits into two strands. Each strand will have a long string of bases without their base pairs. Through controlled heating and cooling sequences of DNA at specific temperatures replication of DNA takes place. One sequence will give two copies of the original molecule; two sequences will give four copies. This sequence is repeated 30 times, leading to 2^{30} copies, which is over 1 billion copies. This manufacturing of high numbers of copies of the original DNA permits the analysis of very small amounts of DNA from crime samples. To compare the victim's or suspect's DNA profile to DNA profiles developed from these crime samples, the lab will need to have their known biological samples available for a side-by-side comparison. These known samples are called reference samples. In addition to unknown and reference samples, elimination samples are often collected from consensual sex partners and others, such as first responders, crime scene personnel and analysts working the case so they can be excluded from the investigation.

Y-STR

Y-STRs are Short Tandem Repeats found on the male-specific Y-chromosome. The Y-STRs are polymorphic among unrelated males and are inherited through the paternal line with little change through generations.

In a sexual assault case, evidence such as vaginal swabs will contain both female and male DNA. Differential extraction is often used to attempt to separate the male component (from the sperm cells) from the female component. Often this separation is less than complete. When the "male DNA sample" undergoes the PCR amplification process, any female DNA component also present in the sample is also amplified, masking the male DNA. The more female DNA present the more difficult analysis may be.

This masking is not seen when Y-STRs are examined. Since there is no Y-STR in the female evidence, the contribution of Y-STRs can only come from the assailant(s) in a sexual assault case. In addition only this part of DNA will be amplified.

Mitochondrial DNA

As we stated above nuclear DNA is genetic material present in the nucleus of cells which is inherited half from each biological parent. Mitochondrial DNA (mtDNA) is found in the mitochondria which float in the plasma that surrounds the nucleus. Unlike nuclear DNA, mitochondrial DNA is passed down from the maternal parent only. So mtDNA is not as discriminating as nuclear DNA because siblings and other maternal-line relatives (male or female) will have the same mtDNA.

Mitochondrial DNA does have advantages over nuclear DNA. Each cell only has one nucleus but each cell contains thousands of mitochondria which contain numerous DNA molecules. Nuclear DNA can be very easily degraded or contaminated by environmental conditions whereas mtDNA is much more robust. Therefore it is most often used for hair, teeth, and bones from unidentified human remains.

How Results Are Interpreted

The DNA analysis process provides the analyst with a chart called an electropherogram, which displays the genetic material present at each locus tested (each of the gray bars on the graph below, except for the last one, correspond to a locus; the final gray area is used to indicate the gender of the individual).[4] In a complete profile, each person will exhibit either one or two peaks (alleles) at each locus. The electropherogram shown in Figure 13-4 is an example of a profile from a single individual (i.e., a "single-source" profile).

Loci that display only one allele indicate that the individual inherited the same marker from both parents at this locus. Where two alleles are displayed, the individual inherited different markers. Figure 13-5 shows that the first four loci from the unknown evidence sample collected at the scene match the sample collected from the suspect. (This process would be repeated for all 13 loci.) Note: The height of each peak must exceed a predetermined quantity threshold to be used in the analysis.

In practice, evidence often contains a mixture of DNA from more than one person. These mixtures can be very challenging to analyze and interpret. In Figure 13-6, each marker from the suspect sample is included in the mixture profile collected from the evidence.

To enable profiles to be searched against a large, national database, the FBI created the National DNA Index System (NDIS) in 1998.[5] This national database is part of the Combined DNA Index System (CODIS), allowing law-enforcement agencies throughout the nation to share and compare DNA profiles in investigating cases. As of 2012,

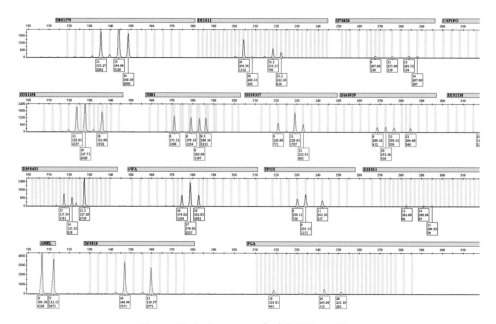

Figure 13-4. A portion of a full DNA profile.

there are more than 10 million DNA profiles in the system and CODIS has produced leads that have assisted in almost 170,000 investigations.

Once a laboratory enters a case into CODIS, a weekly search is conducted of the DNA profiles in NDIS, and resulting matches are automatically returned to the laboratory that originally submitted the DNA profile. CODIS has three levels of operation:

- Local DNA Index System (LDIS)
- State DNA Index System (SDIS)
- National DNA Index System (NDIS)

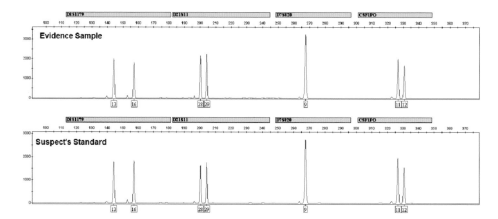

Figure 13-5. Match between two single source profiles.

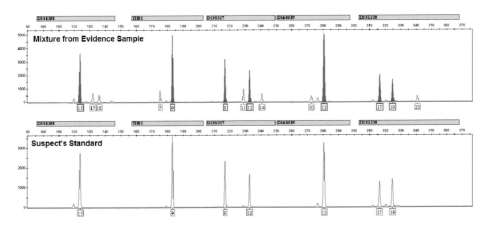

Figure 13-6. Suspect's profile included in mixture.

National Research Council Report and DNA

The National Research Council report recommended changes for many disciplines of forensics but DNA was one major discipline that escaped with little criticism.

> Among existing forensic methods, only nuclear DNA analysis has been rigorously shown to have the capacity to consistently, and with a high degree of certainty, demonstrate a connection between an evidentiary sample and a specific individual or source. Indeed, DNA testing has been used to exonerate persons who were convicted as a result of the misapplication of other forensic science evidence. DNA typing is now universally recognized as the standard against which many other forensic individualization techniques are judged. DNA enjoys this preeminent position because of its reliability and the fact that, absent fraud or an error in labeling or handling, the probabilities of a false positive are quantifiable and often minuscule. However, even a very small (but nonzero) probability of false positive can affect the odds that a suspect is the source of a sample with a matching DNA profile.[6]

The NRC report further stated:

> DNA analysis is scientifically sound for several reasons: there are biological explanations for individual-specific findings; the 13 STR loci used to compare DNA samples were selected so that the chance of two different people matching on all of them would be extremely small; the probabilities of false positives have been explored and quantified in some settings (even if only approximately); the laboratory procedures are well specified and subject to validation and proficiency testing; and there are clear and repeatable standards for analysis, interpretation, and reporting.[7]

Daubert admissibility considerations of the then new technique of DNA led to the "DNA-wars" of the 1980s. For example, the celebrated case of *People v. Castro*[8] held hearings over 12 weeks, featuring a total of 10 expert witnesses on the modified-*Frye* admissibility of DNA evidence. These "DNA-wars" continued on into the 1990s. Today, nuclear DNA evidence is universally admitted as an accepted forensic analysis technique in most courts. However, Judge Donald E. Shelton has sounded a cautionary note that DNA is not infallible:

> Although DNA profiling is clearly scientifically superior to other forensic identification evidence, it is not—contrary to earlier pronouncements—infallible. DNA evidence and its underlying methodology are, of course, subject to human error. False positive DNA results have occurred and will undoubtedly continue to be part of the DNA testing landscape. Proffered evidence may still, as with other forensic science evidence, be the result of mistakes or contamination in its collection, testing, or interpretation. As the technology and methodology of DNA testing has progressed, it is the human errors that may present the biggest evidentiary challenges for trial judges.[9]

Notwithstanding the potential of human error,[10] DNA analysis is so reliable that in a way it has become a victim of its own success. The demand for DNA analysis is steadily increasing and the types of cases it is applied to are also greatly expanding. When you also consider the resources associated with the maintenance of databases of DNA samples from convicted felons, and more recently the addition of legislation in many states to demand DNA samples from arrestees for several categories of offense, it is not surprising that again crime laboratories are demanding more funding and the addition of qualified personnel to tackle the large volume of work that needs to be performed.

Takeaways — DNA Evidence

1. Deoxyribonucleic acid (DNA) is sometimes called a genetic blueprint because it contains all of the instructions that determine an individual's genetic characteristics. It is well known that the DNA molecule exists as two strands in a double helix conformation. The strands are held together by just four bases: adenine, cytosine, guanine, and thymine.

2. Nuclear DNA is found in the nucleus of a cell, packaged in chromosomes. The nucleus of a human cell contains 23 pairs of chromosomes (46 total), half of them inherited from each parent.

3. Regions of the DNA molecule tend to repeat themselves in short, adjacent, or tandem segments termed Short Tandem Repeats (STR). The areas at which forensic analysts look are always found in the same spots on the same chromosomes. Each specific location is called a locus. The forensic science

community typically uses a minimum of 13 genetic loci referred to as the 13 core CODIS (Combined DNA Index System) loci. This enables laboratories to search profiles against other profiles already in the CODIS databank.

4. DNA is found everywhere. Usually for humans we associate it with blood, semen, hair, skin and saliva. Sometimes the DNA in the form of visible blood and semen stains is easily seen, but DNA also exists in other less obvious places, such as cigarette butts, the tops of beer bottles and soft drink cans, and envelopes that were licked before they were sealed.

5. DNA, like all traces, is transferred by contact. When you touch or otherwise make contact with a surface you transfer many skin cells to that surface. So touch DNA can be found on many surfaces, such as a computer keyboard or mouse, a phone or a gun.

6. Following the processing of items of evidence to obtain samples for DNA testing, there are five basic steps to follow during DNA typing:
   • Extraction of DNA from cellular material.
   • Quantification of the amount of human DNA recovered.
   • Amplification of the areas of DNA being tested using Polymerase Chain Reaction (PCR) techniques.
   • Separation and typing of amplified DNA fragments (typically using capillary electrophoresis, or CE).
   • Review, interpretation, comparison and reporting of typing results.

7. The DNA analysis process provides the analyst with a chart called an electropherogram, which displays the genetic material present at each locus tested. In a complete profile, each person will exhibit either one or two peaks (alleles) at each locus.

8. CODIS has three levels of operation: Local DNA Index System (LDIS), State DNA Index System (SDIS), and National DNA Index System (NDIS).

9. Once a laboratory enters a case into CODIS, a weekly search is conducted of the DNA profiles in NDIS, and resulting matches are automatically returned to the laboratory that originally submitted the DNA profile.

10. According to the NRC, "Among existing forensic methods, only nuclear DNA analysis has been rigorously shown to have the capacity to consistently, and with a high degree of certainty, demonstrate a connection between an evidentiary sample and a specific individual or source."

Chapter 14

Trace Evidence

The search for truth takes you where the evidence leads you, even if, at first, you don't want to go there.
—Bart D. Ehrman, *Forged: Writing in the Name of God*

Trace evidence analysis is the nearest you will get today to the classic Sherlock Holmes crime solving method. DNA had not been discovered and drugs were rarely mentioned, with the exception of the "7% cocaine solution." Befitting early 20th-century English society, Dr. Watson's retained British Army service revolver was the only mention of firearms. It was trace evidence and human behavior to which Holmes applied his "methods."

Using Locard's phrase that "every contact leaves a trace," trace evidence is the widest area of forensic analysis. If DNA, drug analysis, firearms/toolmarks, and latent fingerprints are the core forensic disciplines, then trace evidence is the majority of what is left. It encompasses the study of hairs, fibers, paint, polymers, glass, soil, botanicals, explosives, fire debris, and the catchall, miscellaneous.

In recent years, along with latent fingerprints and firearms analysis, trace evidence analysis has come under fire as a soft science, with little or no theoretical or statistical basis for the conclusions reached. While an oversimplification, trace evidence analysis does suffer in comparison to its DNA counterpart. DNA statistical data permits probability statements such as "1 in 64 quadrillion." At best, trace evidence only can provide statements such as "the questioned red nylon fibers could have come from the known carpet or a carpet with similar physical and chemical properties." These limitations have led to a continuing decline in the number of trace evidence cases submitted to crime laboratories. Why would a detective or a prosecutor want to submit trace evidence to hope to establish a link between a victim and a suspect when the best possible result is that "there could be a connection"? Better to submit only DNA evidence that could potentially remove all doubt. The number of trace evidence analysts in crime labs today is dwindling, with available resources concentrated on DNA, latent fingerprint, and firearms analysts. This approach leads to a shortage of ideas on what to do next when the core forms of forensic evidence are not useful. What can be done when there is no DNA evidence?

A quadruple homicide in Des Moines, Washington, in 2003 shows the enduring value of trace evidence. Two victims were beaten and stabbed; two others were shot to death. A suspect eventually was developed through witness interviews, though little

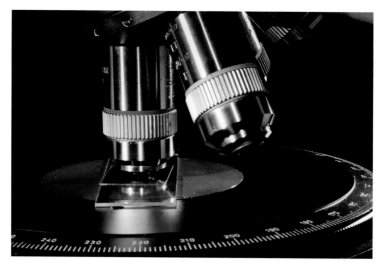

Figure 14-1. Examination of material on a glass slide using a compound microscope.

physical evidence connected him to the crime. A search warrant of the suspect's house turned up a pair of black pants. The Washington State Patrol Crime Laboratory maintains a robust trace evidence analysis section. When the suspect's pants were microscopically examined, the trace analyst noticed several red nylon fibers. He was able to link the distinct vivid red fiber to a sole manufacturer. Crime scene analysts were able to confirm that all three floors of the residence were covered with the same red carpet. Drawing on his native Chicago heritage, the trace analyst recognized that while such red carpet was rare in the Pacific Northwest, it was common among Polish immigrants in Chicago. The manufacturer was able to identify that only a small amount of this carpeting had been sold in Washington state, enough to cover the floors in two houses. This greatly increased the evidentiary value of the carpet fiber analysis in the case.

Expert opinions surrounding trace evidence have suffered from excessive reliability claims. FBI research and training initiatives in the field of hair analysis led to convictions up through the late 1980s. Under prior practices, forensic scientists would state that the hair found on a victim "matched" the hair of a suspect. However, DNA analysis of hair trace evidence has changed this practice, and is able to show that hairs with similar microscopic characteristics do not necessarily come from the same person.

With all these limitations, what value does trace evidence analysis have? This question will be answered by the discussion that follows.

Hairs

There is a widely held belief that it is normal to shed 100 hairs per day. This is based on the assumption that the average scalp contains 100,000 hairs, 10 percent of which are in the telogen (resting) phase. Although this idea is prevalent, it has not been scientifically validated and does not indicate whether shedding remains constant with age or if it is similar between men and women.[1] A casual glance at your personal hairbrush or shower drain certainly will demonstrate that we humans shed hairs every day during normal activities. During the violent activity associated with crime, this increases. Similarly, during sexual intercourse, pubic hairs are transferred and deposited.

Even though microscopic hair analysis cannot lead to human identification, it does have scientific merit and can answer many questions.

Hairs are everywhere in the environment. As most pet owners know, hairs from their pets turn up everywhere in the house. If a dog or cat rubs up against their owner's legs, hairs will be left behind. If the clothing is made of synthetic material, static electricity will make the hairs difficult to remove. This illustrates how animal hairs often are mixed with human hairs at crime scenes. Microscopically, human hairs and animal hairs are easily distinguished. This results in a simple, low cost screening tool in homicides and sexual assaults.

Not all hairs on the human body are similar in appearance. Distinguishing from what area of the body hair evidence originates is easily accomplished by a simple microscopic examination. Head hairs usually are longer and straighter, pubic hair coarser and curlier. The tips of pubic hairs are often abraded from prolonged contact with underwear. In sexual assault cases, they may show surface deposits of blood and semen. Pubic hair in males has some similarity to stomach and chest hairs. Facial hair is initially coarse but becomes softer and wavier as it grows. Underarm hair, leg hair, and arm hair are usually much finer and shorter than other body hairs.

Humans have color-treated their hair for thousands of years. This involves either the removal of natural melanin in the body of the hair by adding bleaching products or adding dye to color coat the surface. As color-treated hair grows, it will show the natural color at the root. As hair grows, the differentiation between the natural, dyed color or bleached color becomes more evident. Successive color treatments will appear as a series of colored bands beginning at the root. Disease and damage due to heat and to the physical and chemical processes that either straighten or curl the hair can be observed microscopically.

Age or gender cannot be determined from the examination of hair. The fact that hair is gray does not necessarily mean the person is old. The only hair that can be differentiated by age is lanugo, the very fine hair found on newborns. Since the late 1960s, length of hair is not a basis for gender differentiation.

In the past, much emphasis was placed on the ability to distinguish racial origin from a microscopic analysis of the different hair diameters, cross-sectional shapes, thickness of cuticle, and distribution of pigments. This only works if the person has fairly pure racial ancestry. As society has become more integrated and more interracial unions take place, the conclusions that can be drawn from an observation of these characteristics have become less definitive.[2]

Despite the versatility of microscopic hair analysis and the conclusions that can be drawn from it, the superior identification of DNA analysis has relegated this form of trace evidence to lesser status.

Fibers

The example at the beginning of this chapter of the vivid red fibers illustrates the potential fiber analysis has in proving an association between suspects, victims, and scenes of crime. Fibers associated with a crime come in the form of natural fibers such as cotton, wool, and rope fibers like hemp and sisal; man-made fibers from natural sources such as viscose rayon; and synthetic fibers such as nylon and polyester. They can be examined microscopically in the same way as hairs, with the same limitations. However, fibers have the advantage in that they can also be analyzed using data gathered instrumentally. Despite this greater scientific footing, fiber analysis is not suitable for individualizing fibers, i.e., associating a fiber from a crime scene with one, and only one, source. Fiber evidence can be used only to associate a given fiber with a class of fibers.

Fiber analyses are reproducible across laboratories because there are standardized procedures. Proficiency tests are routinely provided and taken annually, and the reports are available from Collaborative Testing Services[3] and other proficiency test providers.

Paint

Hundreds of compounds are used in the manufacture of paint. The major components of paint are a polymeric binder and one or more pigments. Binder, solvents and additives in paint are collectively called the vehicle or film former. Paint is applied by brushing, spraying, dipping, or other means, and forms a protective and/or decorative coating. Automotive paints are most commonly encountered in forensic work but structural paints from houses or structures are often seen when dealing with burglaries and tools used for breaking and entering. Artistic paints, which are long lasting and made from naturally occurring oils and pigments, are rarely seen in the crime lab.

Visual and microscopic examinations are typically the first step in a forensic examination of paints and coatings. As is the case with fiber evidence, this is based on a solid foundation of physical and instrumental examination to enable class identification. There also is a possibility of fitting a sample back to a known source, based on irregular borders, brush stroke striations, polish mark striations, or surface abrasion markings. If these samples are paint fragments, the fragments can be identified as having come from that specific source.

Most cars have at least four coats of paint finish: two rustproofing coats, a primer to minimize corrosion, and a topcoat that gives the color of car. A thick clearcoat acrylic polymer protective layer then is added. An examination of the layer sequence of sections of a car provides a characteristic paint history of the vehicle. When two cars collide, a transfer of paint will occur. The transferred paint can be compared to other samples in an attempt to determine the origin. If the vehicle has been repainted over time and the same layering pattern is seen in the transfer sample, the likelihood of a common origin is greatly increased.

Glass

Glass can occur as evidence when it is broken during the commission of a crime. Broken glass fragments can range in size from large pieces to tiny shards. They may be transferred to and retained by nearby persons or objects. The mere presence of fragments of glass on the clothing of an alleged burglar in a case involving entry through a broken window may be significant evidence. The value of this will be enhanced if the fragments are determined to be indistinguishable in all measured properties from the broken window. On the other hand, if the recovered fragments differ, then that window can be eliminated as a possible source of the glass on the subject's clothing.[4]

It is often thought that when a perpetrator breaks into a house or building by smashing a pane of glass in a window from the outside, the glass all falls inward and so will not be found on or near the person who broke the glass. The process of backward fragmentation explains how glass fragments from a broken window get onto a person's clothing. As a general rule glass is strong in compression, but weak in tension. When a force pushes on a pane of glass, the elasticity of the glass causes it to bend in the direction of the applied force, but as the elastic limit is exceeded the glass begins to crack. Initially radial cracks form on the side opposite the applied force, then tension on the side of the applied force causes concentric cracks. That leads to tiny fragments of glass being projected backwards onto the clothing of the person who broke the window and others in the vicinity.

According to Nelson and Revell, although glass fragments were ejected in the direction of the breaking force, glass fragments were also ejected in a backward direction as far as three meters.[5] To ascertain the likelihood of finding glass at random on the clothing of the general public, several studies were undertaken. Notable amongst these was by Petterd et al., who found one glass fragment each on only 6 of 2,008 upper garments examined.[6] This and all of the other studies indicated that it was unlikely that glass fragments would be found on a person who has not been present when a glass object is broken or who has not come into contact with broken glass. The majority of forensic glass examinations that take place are based on the likelihood that the potential suspect has been contaminated by tiny particles of glass resulting from the initial break.[7]

When comparing the properties of recovered glass from a person's clothing with that of the broken window, refractive index is the most commonly measured property in the forensic analysis. This is a function of the composition and thermal history of the glass, measured by automated instrumental methods to a precision of 5 decimal places (e.g., a typical window pane float glass could have a refractive index of 1.51823). In the last 40 years many journal articles have been published on forensic glass examination. A large body of statistical data is available to support the conclusions that can be made when comparing the refractive indices of reference samples from a broken window to glass fragments found on clothing. Though this area of forensic analysis can be a powerful technique for proving either association or dissociation between a suspect and a broken window, it is losing ground to the field of DNA analysis, becoming rarer in crime laboratories today.

Soil

Materials get transferred between the suspect, the victim and the crime scene. Soil on a suspect's shoes may get transferred to a vehicle's carpet. Soil from the wheel well of a vehicle or from a dead victim's clothing may be similar to the soil from the crime scene.

As with many types of trace evidence, forensic analysis of soil involves comparison with known reference samples. Analysis begins with color. There are many distinguishable soil colors. Everyone is aware that soil changes color when wet. The unknown sample and the reference sample first must be thoroughly dried. Next comes low powered microscopy, which can distinguish soils based on the presence of plant, animal, and man-made debris. High power microscopy can assist with the identification of rocks and materials. This task is best performed by a trained forensic geologist.[8] Rocks and minerals are also present in manufactured materials such as brick, concrete, plaster, and safe insulation.

Soils vary horizontally, with landscape and variations often detectable over very short distances. Driving along the highway in many of the western United States affords the view of many multilayered rock formations. The composition of the rock obviously also varies with depth. These factors are of great importance at a crime scene when deciding what reference samples to collect. It is recommended that reference soils should be collected at various intervals within a 100-foot radius of the crime scene as well as at the site of the crime scene. Usually a teaspoon is removed from the surface at each sampling point and packaged in a sealed airtight labeled container. If the crime involves a gravesite then samples at precise depths from the surface must also be collected.

Arson and Explosives Investigation

The difficultly of arson investigations is due to a combination of factors. If the crime of arson is successful, all the physical evidence has been destroyed at its origin. This has been likened to a homicide where the body has been reduced to dust. Arson is the one crime that destroys evidence rather than creates it as it progresses.

A scene must be carefully investigated before it can be determined that a crime took place. Every fire must be treated as a potential arson scene (regarding security, and the preservation and collection of evidence) until clear proof indicates otherwise.

There is a split of training, expertise and jurisdiction between police and fire departments in an arson investigation. The police traditionally are good at warrants, interviews and criminal investigation field work. Fire departments are skilled in interpreting fire behavior and point of origin diagnostic signs.

Fire is defined as an exothermic oxidation that generates detectable heat and light. Exothermic means that the heat is emitted. Oxidation means that the atoms in the fuel combine with oxygen in the air. For a fire to occur several conditions must exist:

- Combustible fuel must be present.
- An oxidizer (e.g., oxygen) must be available in sufficient quantity.
- Energy as some means of ignition (e.g., heat) must be applied.

- For the fire to be continuous, the fuel and the oxidizer must interact in a self-sustaining chain reaction.

If any of these four conditions are removed, the fire extinguishes.[9]

There are many indicators that the investigator can use in reconstructing the path of the fire. None of them is precise, and should be relied on to the exclusion of others.[10] One of the most crucial things in determining the type of fire is the point of origin. It often is the most intense location of burning. Usually at a low point in the building, it may be buried under tons of rubble.

Smoke or damage often shows a V-shaped or conical pattern. This is a consequence of the fact that fires travel upward and outward. These patterns when seen on walls or furnishings can help to indicate the direction of travel of the fire. Samples of debris are collected from potential points of origin of the fire and transported in airtight metal cans to the crime lab where they are analyzed for the presence of volatile accelerants such as gasoline.

We have seen that oxidation is the combination of materials with an oxidizer. The speed of this oxidation can range from the very slow combination of iron and oxygen to produce rust, to the instantaneous detonation of high explosives. For explosive combustion, the various rates of oxidation have been described as:

- Combustion: A rapid oxidation that generates heat and light but does not generate sufficient gases to produce a pressure wave.
- Deflagration: A very rapid oxidation producing heat, light, and a pressure wave that can have a disruptive effect on surroundings.
- Detonation: An extremely rapid reaction that generates very high temperatures and an intense pressure/shock wave that produces violently disruptive effects.

This leads to two categories of explosives, Low Explosives and High Explosives.

Low Explosives burn/deflagrate rather than detonate. They do so at less than 3,000 feet per second and are primarily used in pyrotechnics (fireworks) and as propellants. They can be initiated by heat, shock, friction and/or chemical means and do not require a blasting cap to initiate. Examples are black powder, and single-base smokeless powder that contains nitrocellulose. Nitrocellulose propellants ignite at 190°C; with modest confinement, the increased pressure leads to deflagration.

High Explosives detonate rather than burn and do so at more than 3,000 feet per second. They are relatively insensitive and generally require another explosive to start the detonation reaction. Examples of high explosives that are used as primary or initiating explosives are lead azide, mercury fulminate, and picric acid. Examples of high explosives that are used as main charge explosives are Trinitrotoluene (TNT) and Pentaerythritol tetranitrate (PETN).

Although materials such as TNT explode with violent intensity, traces of the unexploded material can often be detected on portions of the explosive device or nearby surfaces. At the crime lab these traces are released from the host material and the resultant volatile explosives are analyzed by similar methods that are used to analyze fire debris samples. These methods involve the use of instruments such as gas chromatography mass spectrometry (GCMS), capillary electrophoresis (CE), and high pressure liquid chromatography (HPLC).

In the summary assessment of the discussion on the analysis of explosives evidence and fire debris in the NRC report, the following appears:

> The scientific foundations exist to support the analysis of explosions, because such analysis is based primarily on well-established chemistry. As part of the laboratory work, an analyst often will try to reconstruct the bomb, which introduces procedural complications, but not scientific ones. By contrast, much more research is needed on the natural variability of burn patterns and damage characteristics and how they are affected by the presence of various accelerants.[11]

Takeaways — Trace Evidence

1. Based on the mechanism by which evidence is created, wherein according to Locard "every contact leaves a trace," all evidence can be termed trace evidence.

2. Trace evidence encompasses the study of hairs, fibers, paint, polymers, glass, soil, botanicals, explosives, fire debris, and the catchall, miscellaneous.

3. Microscopic hair analysis cannot lead to human identification. However microscopic hair analysis does have scientific merit and can answer many questions.

4. Fiber analysis has the potential to prove an association between suspects, victims, and scenes of crime.

5. The analysis of paints and coatings is based on a solid foundation of physical and instrumental examination to enable class identification.

6. Although in the case of someone smashing a window most glass fragments are ejected in the direction of the breaking force, glass fragments are also ejected in a backward direction as far as three meters, and will be discoverable on the suspect's clothing.

7. Soils show variation both horizontally and vertically.

8. If the crime of arson is successful, all the physical evidence has been destroyed at its origin. This has been likened to a homicide where the body has been reduced to dust. Arson is the one crime that destroys evidence rather than creates it as it progresses.

9. Although materials such as TNT explode with violent intensity, traces of the unexploded material can often be detected on portions of the explosive device or nearby surfaces. At the crime lab these traces are released from the host material and the resultant volatile explosives are analyzed by similar methods that are used to analyze fire debris samples.

Chapter 15

Drugs

Cocaine is God's way of telling you that you are making too much money.
—Robin Williams

Prior to the late 1960s, illicit drugs were controlled under various different federal laws. The Controlled Substances Act of 1970[1] brought together a number of laws regulating the manufacture and distribution of narcotics, stimulants, depressants, hallucinogens, anabolic steroids, and chemicals used in the illicit production of controlled substances. All substances were placed in one of five schedules, I–V, based on medicinal value, harmfulness, and potential for abuse or addiction.

Schedule I drugs, substances, or chemicals are defined as drugs with no currently accepted medical use and a high potential for abuse. Schedule I drugs are the most dangerous drugs of all the drug schedules with potentially severe psychological or physical dependence. Some examples of Schedule I drugs are: heroin; lysergic acid diethylamide (LSD); marijuana (cannabis); 3,4-methylenedioxymethamphetamine (ecstasy); methaqualone; and peyote.

Figure 15-1. Robotic sampling of drug cases.

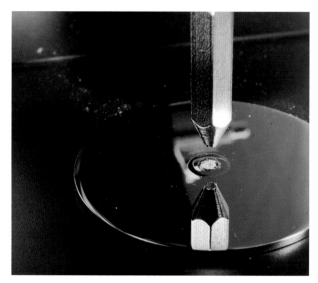

Figure 15-2. Direct sampling of a white powder.

Schedule II drugs, substances, or chemicals are defined as drugs with a high potential for abuse, less abuse potential than Schedule I drugs, with use potentially leading to severe psychological or physical dependence. These drugs are also considered dangerous. Some examples of Schedule II drugs are: cocaine, methamphetamine, methadone, hydromorphone (Dilaudid), meperidine (Demerol), oxycodone (OxyContin), fentanyl, Dexedrine, Adderall, and Ritalin.

Schedule III drugs, substances, or chemicals are defined as drugs with a moderate to low potential for physical and psychological dependence. Schedule III drugs have less potential for abuse than Schedule I and Schedule II drugs but more than Schedule IV. Some examples of Schedule III drugs are: Combination products with less than 15 milligrams of hydrocodone per dosage unit (Vicodin), products containing less than 90 milligrams of codeine per dosage unit (Tylenol with codeine), ketamine, anabolic steroids, and testosterone.

Schedule IV drugs, substances, or chemicals are defined as drugs with a low potential for abuse and low risk of dependence. Some examples of Schedule IV drugs are: Xanax, Soma, Darvon, Darvocet, Valium, Ativan, Talwin, and Ambien.

Schedule V drugs, substances, or chemicals are defined as drugs with lower potential for abuse than Schedule IV and consist of preparations containing limited quantities of certain narcotics. Schedule V drugs are generally used for antidiarrheal, antitussive, and analgesic purposes. Some examples of Schedule V drugs are: cough preparations with less than 200 milligrams of codeine or per 100 milliliters (Robitussin AC), Lomotil, Motofen, Lyrica, and Parepectolin.

Society's attitude toward drugs is changing. On October 14, 1982, President Ronald Reagan declared illicit drugs to be a threat to U.S. national security. (One of the authors was hired under a federal grant as a result of what was called "Ronald Reagan's War on

Drugs.") On May 13, 2009, R. Gil Kerlikowske, the director of the Office of National Drug Control Policy, signaled that though the Obama administration did not plan to significantly alter drug enforcement policies, it would not use the term "war on drugs," saying it was "counterproductive." After recreational marijuana initiatives passed in Washington and Colorado in November 2012, President Barack Obama said the federal government had "bigger fish to fry" and would not make going after marijuana users a priority. In August 2013, it was reported in the *Huffington Post*:

> The United States government took a historic step back from its long-running drug war, when Attorney General Eric Holder informed the governors of Washington and Colorado that the Department of Justice would allow the states to create a regime that would regulate and implement the ballot initiatives that legalized the use of marijuana for adults.

Notwithstanding all the changes in government attitudes in the last 30 years, drugs form the largest percentage of items submitted to crime laboratories for forensic analysis. As can be seen above in Schedules I–V above the type of drug submitted can vary tremendously. It may also be in the form of liquid, rock-like chunks, many different colors of powder solids, leafy material, tablets, capsules, cigarettes, pipes, syringes, and an array of drug paraphernalia. With such a variety of drugs and the different forms in which they can appear, there are diverse types of testing that must be employed.

Testing usually begins with a screening test that typically results in a characteristic color change when small amounts of reagents are added to the suspected controlled substances. These screening tests are typically named after the chemists who devised them. Examples are the Duquenois-Levine test that gives a purple color in the presence of marijuana, or the Marquis test that turns purple in the presence of opiates or brown when methamphetamine is present. These tests are for screening only, and to identify drugs to the exclusion of all other known substances a confirmatory test must be used. Such confirmation tests are usually done using instrumental methods such as infrared spectroscopy, gas chromatography, liquid chromatography, and mass spectrometry. These and other methods of analysis were discussed in depth in 2011 in the Scientific Working Group for the Analysis of Seized Drugs.[2] In addition to the methods of analysis, this report also included a recommended code of professional practice for drug analysts, education and training, and quality assurance.

The NRC report stated: "The analysis of controlled substances is a mature forensic science discipline and one of the areas with a strong scientific underpinning. The analytical methods used have been adopted from classical analytical chemistry, and there is broad agreement nationwide about best practices."[3] The report went on to say, "The chemical foundations for the analysis of controlled substances are sound, and there exists an adequate understanding of the uncertainties and potential errors. SWG-DRUG has established a fairly complete set of recommended practices."[4] This level of confidence in the techniques and practices surrounding drug analysis is in marked contrast to the criticisms leveled at other forensic disciplines. Not surprisingly, there now are relatively few challenges made to the chemical analysis of seized drugs in criminal cases.

Takeaways—Drugs

1. All controlled substances are placed in one of five schedules, I–V, based on medicinal value, harmfulness, and potential for abuse or addiction.

2. Society's attitude toward drugs is changing.

3. Drugs may be in the form of liquid, rock-like chunks, many different colors of powders, solids, leafy material, tablets, capsules, cigarettes, pipes, syringes, and an array of drug paraphernalia. With such a variety of drugs and the different forms in which they can appear, there are diverse types of testing that must be employed.

4. The NRC report found that the analysis of controlled substances is a mature forensic science discipline with a strong scientific underpinning.

Chapter 16

The Gatekeeper's Perspective

Common sense is that which judges the things given to it by other senses.
—Leonardo da Vinci

Everyday life is complicated, increasingly dependent on science and technology to provide the answers to the questions it presents. This is reflected in how disputes are resolved in our legal system. Advocates bring in any science that will help win a case. The emphasis on results, rather than information quality, compromises how the legal system resolves scientific issues. Judges are acutely aware of this.

The clash of scientific ideas in the courtroom adds complexity to a judge's life, requiring an understanding of a broad spectrum of knowledge far beyond purely legal analysis. The relative importance of experts is highly dependent on the individual case. The credibility of the trial stories of each party has a controlling effect on how much weight is given to the testifying experts.

The Limited Guidance of Cases on Expert Testimony

Beyond a very general level, the case law on sorting out expert testimony isn't particularly helpful to judges in their gatekeeper functions. *Daubert* was a very important step for the federal courts to take, with the basic principle that non-science should not be tolerated as science. Who could argue with that? The Supreme Court went on to give reasonable guidelines for what science is.

Daubert has served as a focusing tool, making judges more aware of their role in sorting out expert testimony. *Daubert* provides the framework for a totality type analysis, combining peer-review publications, credentials and acceptance within the scientific community. A judge must analyze what the criticisms are of a challenged expert's opinion and the credibility of the sources upon which the opinion is based.

What Qualifies Judges to Rule on Scientific Issues?

As a group, judges are reasonably well equipped to process peer review scientific literature when challenges to expert opinions are made in a case. Many state and federal

judges either have prior background in science or math, or have had specialized training in deciding these issues since their appointment to the bench. Judge Andrea Darvas is representative of this group:

> I am able to comprehend most forms of expert testimony. My undergraduate
> background was in life sciences, with a bachelor's degree in zoology. At one
> point I was premed. I also attended a program at the Advanced Science and
> Technology Adjudication Resource Center (ASTAR), an organization created
> to educate judges on science and technology issues through a boot camp type
> approach. This course aims to give judges a grounding in the evaluation of
> scientific evidence. It starts with Science 101, "This is what science is and is
> not." These classes are cutting edge, taught by top people in their fields, relat-
> ing them to issues that trial judges have to decide. The idea was that those of
> us who got certified in this program would become resources to other col-
> leagues on the bench, correcting the deficits of a traditional liberal arts back-
> ground, where everything is a matter of opinion.[1]

Judge Robert Robert Lasnik's prior background in social science has adapted well to
understanding scientific and technical evidence in the cases that come before him in federal court:

> I have a master's degree in counseling. I had to take courses involving statis-
> tics in graduate school. My undergraduate degree was in psychology and so-
> ciology. Though I don't have hard science background, the social science
> courses I took in college have been helpful to me as a judge in understanding
> statistical significance.[2]

How Do Judges Evaluate the Reliability of Experts?

There are a number of ways for a judge to assess the reliability of experts in making
command decisions about who testifies and on what subjects. Has the expert been allowed to testify before in federal or state court? Have they published articles in peer-re-
viewed journals? Do others in the field espouse a similar perspective? Has there been
any controversy or debunking of the theory? Has there been any credential padding? It
is surprising how often the latter happens.

Judges recognize that true experts are scientists, not advocates. A scientist focuses on
issues without preconceptions, intrigued by possibilities, open to alternative hypotheses. An advocate will reflexively agree with the position of the attorney who hired them
and disagree with the opposing attorney. Juries pick up on this right away. Experts who
are advocates enjoy far less respect and trust.

> **Example:** A veteran county medical examiner was a scientist first and fore-
> most. Jurors really picked up on this expert's objective, scientific "call it as I see
> it" frame of mind, resulting in tremendous credibility. In homicide cases, while
> he typically would offer opinions for the prosecution on issues like the angle
> of entry of a bullet wound, he readily would concede reasonable points on
> cross-examination by the defense. "If the victim was standing in this position

with his arms held out in this manner, the bullet could have entered in a different manner than what you just described, correct?" "Yes." "The victim could have been in an aggressive posture rather than a defensive one at the time the bullet pierced his arm and entered his chest." "Absolutely, that's entirely consistent with the facts."

Prosecutors worried that these candid responses would create reasonable doubt. What this really did was to show the jury how credible this medical examiner was. His opinions always were based on the evidence. He was not going to reach conclusions just because the prosecutor needed them.[3]

Even for those judges who have little science in their formal educations, they quickly learn the indicia of reliable science on the job. The basic common-sense capacity to evaluate fairly the information presented for decision is a central aptitude of good judges:

> I am often called upon to make judgment calls in an area where I have no personal experience. I have to start with what I know to be reasonable and then apply that information to what is presented to me by the experts in a case.[4]

Deciding between the persuasiveness of scientific articles is very similar to comparing legal precedents. Just as cases can be distinguished on the facts, so can scientific articles. Judges look for the scientific literature that is most analogous to the situation before them, getting a feel for what is going to be the most helpful and makes the most sense. It all comes down to what seems reasonable under the circumstances:

> **Example:** In divorce cases, typically there is a battle between the appraisers on each side on the value of the family home, plugging comparable sales into a formula. All of this is somewhat subjective and forces the judge to rely on his/her own general knowledge as a homeowner in the community.[5]

All judges know that some journals are more highly ranked than others, such as the *New England Journal of Medicine*. If an article appears there, it is likely to have large acceptance within the scientific community.

Federal judges are faced with hard science questions more frequently than their state court counterparts, having to preside over class actions and intellectual property cases. Resources are provided to them in the federal system to close any knowledge gap which may exist: "It is not uncommon for me to get tutorials on technical or scientific issues from court appointed experts. I am not a bit shy about using them."[6]

How Judges See Their Gatekeeper Role

Federal and state trial judges see their role as determining whether expert testimony meets the minimum standards of reliability and integrity, filtering out a level of manipulative junk science:

> I have a certain reliability threshold for an expert. You must convince me that your expert has the right credentials and relies on legitimate science in reaching their opinions before I will let an expert testify. Once this minimum is met,

my philosophy is, "Let both sides put their experts on and try their case. May the better side win." My style is to let the information come in and have the jury sort it out, unless I am convinced that it has no substance. It is not my job to decide who has a better expert or case theory. I will not attempt to influence the outcome of a case through expert testimony.[7]

Judges have a practical and philosophical inclination to let jurors hear the testimony of each side and then decide the case on that basis. The judge's position usually is, "In the adversarial system, each side gets to put on their case and then we let the jury decide." It is rare for state court judges to throw out expert testimony unless it is on the fringe:

I never have gotten any portion of an opposing expert witnesses' testimony excluded. Judges seem reluctant to get too aggressive in their gatekeeping functions. It seems that lawyers have to do it for them through cross-examination. "So when it comes down to it in this case, this is just your opinion, isn't it?" "Do you have any data on this I can look at, beyond your own anecdotal experience?" "Where is it?" "How can I evaluate your experience?"[8]

Judicial Concerns over How Attorneys Present Experts

Jurors are very receptive to scientific proof. Like the rest of us, they love to impress others with how smart they are. Judges often are in the best position to see how well the presentation of an expert is going over with the jury:

The credibility of an expert is heavily dependent on common sense. Having a lot of initials behind your name doesn't get an expert anywhere if their ideas don't make sense. No matter how learned or experienced, the effectiveness of expert witnesses is closely tied to communication skills. Expert opinions and the foundation for them must be explained to both the court and the jury.[9]

Presenting expert credentials often is overdone, appealing more to the vanity of the expert and the lawyer than in meeting the needs of the jury.

Judges know that juries better understand and retain what they absorb through visual aids, particularly with scientific evidence:

If you are introducing evidence on gas chromatography or mass spectroscopy, let the jury see what the equipment and the lab it sits in look like. If the jury can picture what your scientist was doing when he formed his opinions, they have a better basis for accepting them.[10]

The way in which an expert's information is communicated to a jury is of great concern to a judge:

It baffles me why some lawyers will fawn all over a jury during voir dire or closing, but never once look at them during the presentation of evidence. If they did, it often would tell them that it is time to wrap things up. A furrowed brow also can tell you that the juror is trying to grasp it all but is troubled by something the witness just said. This tells you to back up and straighten it out.[11]

Too often, judges see attorneys making their own expert testimony far too complicated:

> Juries know that the evidence comes from the witness stand and are anxious to receive the benefit of an expert's special knowledge. Don't squander it with an unnecessary, overladen two-minute question containing your final argument. Think of Bob Edwards' interviews on National Public Radio. "Why?" "What's that?" "Is that good or bad?" This type of question keeps your attention where it belongs, on the interviewee.[12]

Judges and the *CSI* Effect

Veteran trial judges express little concern over the impact of the so-called "*CSI*" effect. Skilled lawyers always set the expectations of jurors at the beginning of a trial, preparing them that real life is different from television. Jurors quickly find that real criminal trials are far different from those in the entertainment world. The pace and timing is much slower. While television criminal trials may last 20 minutes, real ones typically last the better part of a week. Television trials never show the frequent recesses, which always drive jurors crazy.

Judges give lawyers the opportunity to confront television shaped expectations of prospective jurors during voir dire. In cases that don't have much scientific evidence, prosecutors will ask: "Do you expect to see DNA evidence in every case?" "Do you realize that many cases don't have it?" This reduces the expectations and influence of those who watch television crime shows. By the end of jury selection, it is understood that *CSI*-type evidence does not happen in every case, or that it is even necessary to prove guilt.

How Much Expert Testimony Do Judges Exclude?

The loose criteria of the *Rules of Evidence* do not require experts to be real scientists. If a witness has a science degree in an area arguably related to the subject matter of the case, they usually are considered an expert. Family practitioners in many states are qualified to testify about all medical issues, including things as complicated as brain surgery.

In criminal cases, the scientific evidence is almost always admitted. Prosecutors don't really need to go out on a limb to get it in:

> It is rare for me to exclude scientific evidence from a case, as the rules of admissibility in our state are very open to it, trusting the jury to figure it out. In all my years as a criminal department judge, I've never had a full-blown *Frye* hearing, though I certainly have ruled on *Frye* type issues with frequency. We just don't get that much novel scientific evidence. Though the defense often will try to claim that prosecution evidence is novel, usually it isn't.[13]

For example, studying decomposition of the human body at the University of Tennessee was enough to allow a prosecution expert to testify about what the smell in the trunk of Casey Anthony's car was in her murder trial.[14]

Judges have the same liberal threshold for defense experts, even oddball ones, all in the name of giving the defendant a fair trial:

> **Example:** Handwriting analysis was an issue in a criminal case. The defendant called a graphologist as an expert. This person was not a scientist, but a psychic type who attempts to tell people's personalities by looking at the characteristics of their handwriting. The judge came close to excluding this on motion of the prosecutor, but a layperson is permitted to compare handwriting. Though the judge had serious reservations about the validity of this testimony, he couldn't think of a reason to keep it out and wanted to give the defendant a fair trial. The graphologist got to give her opinion to the jury.[15]

The empirical data suggests that while helpful in setting basic guidelines, *Daubert* has not much changed the actual process of qualifying experts. Judges still tend to exercise a fairly lax regulation over experts, with most following the philosophy of letting lawyers try their cases. Relatively little is done to regulate the manner in which expert testimony is presented:

> I can imagine a circumstance where an expert is so off the wall that I might raise a question about it on my own. However, if the lawyers involved in a case are competent, this is an unlikely scenario.[16]

What Lines Do Judges Not Want to See Crossed?

Though judges typically apply a liberal standard toward allowing expert testimony, this is not to suggest that anything goes. The power of judges to exclude experts has a cautionary effect on the trial bar:

> The claimed science behind an expert opinion must be looked at in a very detached and sober way. As a judge, I want to find a way to infuse a body of science that is accepted as legitimate into the resolution of disputes. I don't want it to come down to who has the best looking or smoothest talking expert.[17]

There are two lines that judges do not want to see crossed in the presentation of testimony. The first is whether the opinions offered are within the accepted boundaries of an expert's field. If an expert attempts to present opinions beyond his/her field, the judge will restrict the scope of what the expert can testify about. The other area of judicial concern is when the expert intends to testify about something that is essentially a credibility determination. The judge is going to be very protective of the province of the jury. Even here, though, certain allowances are made if scientific research can assist the jury in determining credibility questions:

> **Example:** Psychologists testify regularly for the defense on the unreliability of eyewitness identification. Prosecutors always move to exclude them, but the

judges almost never do, citing the weaknesses in eyewitness identification revealed by scientific studies.[18]

Hired Guns

In some generic forms of litigation, with similar issues in cases across multiple jurisdictions, a small group of experts often appears over and over, not unlike the actors in a theater repertory company. At the state court level, medical expert panels testify repeatedly for insurance companies. Experts who advocate in this manner typically are very well spoken, making it tough for opposing counsel to prove to a jury that they are not to be believed.

Offering scientific opinions in court for the money is more an ethical problem than a scientific one. Though they should know better, some experts become wedded to a script for financial gain, advocating for one side. Similar manipulation often is seen in the legislative process, with experts testifying in hearings on behalf of one side or another. In turn, this shapes public opinion over time, through this information being reported in the news media.

Integrity concerns about the trustworthiness of experts who testify frequently adds to the judge's gatekeeper burden, as noted by the National Academy of Sciences in its 2009 report. For enough money, a lawyer can find an expert to say nearly anything. These kinds of hired guns tend to take extreme positions, becoming a self-sustaining industry. There is a certain cynicism that has been built up around their use:

> Some experts can be trusted and others cannot. There are corrupting influences of advocacy at work here. Medical experts used to testify for the tobacco industry that cigarette smoking was not linked to lung cancer, even after the Surgeon General's report in 1964. Cumulatively, the expert industry makes millions of dollars per year testifying for a particular side in litigation. Some favor plaintiffs, others defendants.[19]

The Role of Motion Practice in Triggering Gatekeeper Rulings

Though it is not common to keep out expert testimony, judges certainly are asked to do so often enough. The judicial gatekeeper function most often is triggered by motion practice:

> If an expert is either not qualified generally or specifically to offer a particular opinion, I expect opposing counsel to make a motion and explain why. What's wrong with the expert's testimony under the rules of evidence? Then it is up to the party calling the expert to meet those objections, giving me a context in which to make a decision.[20]

A motion to strike an expert or limit his/her opinions usually sets the stage for a ruling on these kinds of issues: "Judge, I'm concerned about this witness expressing an opinion on this subject, as it is beyond his expertise. I also am concerned about opinions that involve credibility and invade the province of the jury."

Pretrial hearings can be used to determine whether or not an expert's testimony is generally accepted in the scientific community, though many judges do see this as adding another layer of complication to the resolution of cases: "If we bring the experts in and try and resolve this issue before the case begins, this will require significant resources and not result in a record that decides the issue."[21]

An alternative to pre-trial hearings with live witnesses is motion practice relying on sworn declarations from each side's expert as to what they believe the scientific community accepts in an area. Judges tend to prefer this more compact format, as it is sparing of their time and resources. Each side can supplement the declaration of their experts with scientific treatises or articles from the literature. Prior testimony by the expert on the same issue also can be helpful:

> I will consider whatever is submitted by both sides on whether the testimony is generally accepted within the scientific community. This is much more helpful to me than going through an offer of proof with direct and cross-examination of an expert in the courtroom prior to trial. It is a more orderly and economical way to handle this issue.[22]

Lawyers Have Become the Real Gatekeepers

As a practical matter, it is the lawyers who have become the real gatekeepers in the post-*Daubert* era. The lawyer for each side has to exercise due diligence and make sure that all the experts in the case are qualified to offer opinions. To some extent, this is self-regulating. There are a host of economic and practical reasons for this. No lawyer is going to invest huge resources in the case that relies upon speculative, shaky expert testimony. If a case is not likely to be viable, an experienced lawyer will have a good sense of this and not take it on. There is a strong disincentive for a lawyer to put significant resources into it. Hence, it is uncommon to see lawyers pushing the envelope with experts presenting off-the-wall, oddball scientific theories. After a rigorous pre-screening by counsel and the challenges to experts in pre-trial depositions, the court is likely to allow those experts endorsed by each counsel to testify at trial.

Takeaways — The Gatekeeper's Perspective

1. The greater role science and technology plays in legal cases reflects what is happening in our modern world.

2. The clash of forensic ideas adds another layer of difficulty to a judge's life, going far beyond purely legal analysis.

3. Advocates focus on any science that will help them win a case, discrediting that relied upon by the opposing party. This emphasis on results, rather than information quality, compromises how the legal system resolves scientific issues.

4. Beyond a very general level, the case law on sorting out expert testimony isn't particularly helpful to judges in their gatekeeper functions.

5. *Daubert* has served as a focusing tool, making judges more aware of their role in sorting out expert testimony. It provides the framework for a totality type analysis, combining peer review publications, credentials and acceptance within the scientific community.

6. As a group, judges are reasonably well equipped to process peer-review scientific literature when challenges to expert opinions are made in a case. Many state and federal judges either have prior background in science or math, or have had specialized training in deciding these issues since their appointment to the bench.

7. There are a number of ways for a judge to assess the reliability of experts in making command decisions about who testifies and on what subjects; the case law for sorting out expert testimony isn't particularly helpful beyond a very general level.

8. Even for those judges who have little science in their formal educations, they quickly learn the indicia of reliable science on the job. The basic common-sense capacity to evaluate fairly the information presented for decision is a central aptitude of good judges.

9. Judges recognize that true experts are scientists, not advocates. A scientist focuses on issues without preconceptions, intrigued by possibilities, open to alternative hypotheses.

10. Deciding between the persuasiveness of scientific articles is very similar to comparing legal precedents. Just as cases can be distinguished on the facts, so can scientific articles.

11. Federal and state trial judges see their role as determining whether expert testimony meets the minimum standards of reliability and integrity, filtering out a level of manipulative junk science.

12. Judges have a practical and philosophical inclination to let jurors hear the testimony of each side and then decide the case on that basis.

13. Judges are often in the best position to see how the mix of communications skills among testifying experts impacts the jury.

14. The way in which an expert's information is communicated to a jury is of great concern to a judge.

15. Counsel often don't pay enough attention to on how expert information is being received by a jury.

16. A common fault judges see in the presentation of expert testimony is the tendency toward unnecessary complexity.

17. Veteran trial judges express little concern that the so-called "*CSI*" effect is having a major impact on trials. Skilled lawyers always set the expectations of jurors at the beginning of a trial, preparing them that real life is different from television.

18. The loose criteria of the Rules of Evidence do not require experts to be real scientists. If a witness has a science degree in an area arguably related to the subject matter of the case, they usually are considered an expert.

19. The empirical data suggests that while helpful in setting basic guidelines, *Daubert* has not much changed the actual process of qualifying experts. Judges still tend to exercise a fairly lax regulation over experts, with most following the philosophy of letting lawyers try their cases.

20. If an expert attempts to present opinions beyond his/her field, the judge will restrict the scope of what the expert can testify about.

21. When an expert intends to testify about something that is essentially a credibility determination, a judge will be very protective of the province of the jury.

22. Integrity concerns about the trustworthiness of hired gun experts who testify frequently add to the judge's gatekeeper burden, presenting ethical issues at times.

23. Though it is not common to keep out expert testimony, judges certainly are asked to do so often enough. The judicial gatekeeper function most often is triggered by motion practice.

24. Pretrial hearings can be used to determine whether or not an expert's testimony in a case is generally accepted within the scientific community, but this extra step poses a strain on limited judicial resources.

25. An alternative to pre-trial hearings with live witnesses is motion practice relying on sworn declarations from each side's expert.

26. As a practical matter, it is the lawyers who have become the real gatekeepers in the post-*Daubert* era.

27. There are a host of economic and practical reasons why lawyers do not want to get out on a limb with experts who rely on marginal, oddball theories.

Chapter 17

Casting Director

Casting is everything. If you get the right people, they make you look good.
—Todd Solondz

Thinking about the experts to use in a case is just like being a casting director for a play or movie. You start with ideas in the back of your head about who might fill the parts and then you start scouting the possibilities. It is important to keep a critical eye on the scientific and technical issues throughout.

It is hard to find well-qualified experts to review a case who will do a good job of testifying. It is often just a matter of cold calling, combined with personal networking, Google and resume research. There is a good bit of serendipity involved, with necessity being the mother of invention. Ideas pop into your head, such as: "I've got a friend who used to work in this department at the university. I'll call her for names."

The question largely is answered if you are representing a big company. Industry has favorite scientists they call on when these things come up. Drug companies in particular have in-house scientists, who are both smart and well-paid.

Figure 17-1. Lawyers cast for expert roles.

145

Aversion to Expert Witness Work

Many experts don't want to do legal consulting work. It requires too much effort and exposure to confrontation. If full disclosure was required at the outset, you would have to say something like this to a new prospective expert:

> "We'd like you to review volumes of material, write a report and then be grilled at a deposition for about 3 or 4 hours by opposing counsel. Later on, we'd like you to spend days getting ready to come into court and testify. After you've done the fun part of teaching the jury about the issues in the case, you'll get ripped apart by opposing counsel for at least 2 hours."

Top people in their field vastly prefer to do research, writing and teaching. It takes a certain kind of expert personality willing to take on both a deposition and then a cross-examination at trial.

Why Would Any Good Expert Agree to Serve?

Given all the negatives, why would top people in their fields ever agree to be an expert witness in a legal case? One core reason is the understanding that they have something of value to offer the legal system, providing expertise on a difficult and important issue. Lawyers often appeal to new potential experts from this angle, saying, "We need someone well qualified like you to teach the jury so that they will make the right decision here."

Beyond this, forensic work provides a great learning opportunity for experts. Reviewing cases can provide a wealth of information about their field, professional pitfalls and the legal system. For example, doctor witnesses in malpractice cases learn from the difficult experiences of colleagues, bringing this forward into their own teaching, writing and patient care. This is far preferable to learning the hard way as the target of a malpractice complaint.

Finding the Right Expert: Networking, Hard Work and Luck

Networking to get the right experts really is a process of trial and error. You usually won't know the top experts to call immediately. You first identify a list of possibilities, then narrow it down, searching for those who will meet your needs. You will have to educate the candidates about what you need and that they must be definitive in their opinions. When you present the legal "more probable than not" standard to doctors and scientists previously unfamiliar with it, they are puzzled, often saying, "I don't understand this. It isn't relevant to me or my work." They have trouble grasping or agreeing with the legal standard of proof.

Some lawyers regularly make efforts to get on a plane and meet potential new experts, even if they don't have a specific case for them at the moment. There is a constant pressure to refresh your expert pool with new faces. Who else can you get interested in doing forensic work? Some experts in certain medical fields get asked all the time, particularly in obstetric cases. Given all the effort required to recruit qualified experts, many consider their names to be work product:

> I am reluctant to share my experts with other lawyers, as this is proprietary. In the real world, lawyers have to give thought on how to promote their own practice. Frankly, the experts I am able to use in the case are part of the value that I offer to clients. I will discreetly share information about experts with other lawyers who would do the same for me, but not beyond this select group.[1]

Searching the Literature

The first thing to do in identifying a good potential expert is to go to the literature and see who has written peer-review articles on the topics at issue in a case. It gives you a leg up if you get a person who is recognized as knowledgeable in his/her field. All things being equal, an expert whose work has appeared in peer-review journals is superior to one who merely knows what is going on in the field, but has not published.

You must perform meticulous scrutiny of anything a potential expert ever has written or relied upon that could conceivably apply to your case. Make sure that they haven't said something in print that is different from what they are telling you in your case. If they have, you don't dare use them. Always read a whole chapter in detail if your expert relies on it, just to make sure that there is nothing directly contrary a few pages later.

Personal Experience with the Issue

If an expert has personal experience with an issue in the case, that always gives their testimony more of a ring of authenticity. "I saw the same thing happen" is always more powerful than just referring to an article in the literature. A jury is more likely to believe evidence-based medicine than the all-purpose claim, "I trained at a great institution and this is what I was taught."

The testimony of treating health-care providers carries great weight. This is particularly true if it is the first time they have testified in a courtroom. The jury will find a treating medical expert highly persuasive if they believe that this doctor really wants what is best for the patient and wants to help them get better. This human level is always the most important one for the jurors.

How Will Your Expert's Personality Fit in the Courtroom?

You always have to think about the personality of an expert and how it will translate into the courtroom setting. A pleasant manner, knowledge and good communication skills are a winning combination. The credibility of experts also revolves around their perceived expertise by the jury. Does the expert carry himself with authority and knowl-

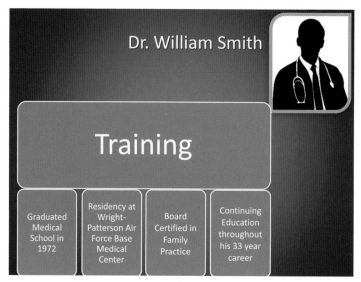

Figure 17-2. Jurors favor treating doctors.

edge? We know it when we see it. At a stylistic level, experts with some form of British accent often are well-liked, perceived to be charming and credible, right out of a BBC television show.

Strength of character is a real plus, but this becomes a major negative if it lapses into know-it-all arrogance. Nothing quite turns off the jury like this. You can't afford to have any experts that cross over this line. The common touch in an expert witness is critical to juror acceptance. Experts always have to keep a sense of perspective and humility, understanding that the jury often has no prior experience in the field.

Communication Skills

Juries decide the battle of the experts by weighing all the human factors. No matter how learned or experienced, the effectiveness of experts is closely tied to communication skills and the ability to explain science in a way that will be understood and believed. While experts know things that people outside their field do not, they must make sense and track with common experience. It is important to determine the comfort zone for each expert in relaying information and then figuring out how that will translate in the court. The best forensic experts transmit information in an interesting, economical and user-friendly way.

Experts who come from an academic background often are good communicators, as teaching students is similar to teaching jurors. Using simple words that lay people are familiar with is important, explaining the foundation concepts and terminology so that the judge and jury will understand the opinions in the case. This is similar to when relevant scientific principles are used as background for a news story.

If you have a choice between a leading scientist in the field who is not a good communicator and someone who is mediocre, but very well spoken, go for the best communicator every time. The jury will relate to that person better and accept their testimony as true. There is some truth in the scene from the movie *Philadelphia* where Denzel Washington says to an expert, "Explain it to me like I am a third grader." There is a real danger with experts the jury loves, as this can cause loss of focus on the validity of the underlying scientific theory. Unless the other side has an effective cross-examination, the communicator carries the day. Some experts have difficulty in reducing their opinions to everyday language. The use of too many technical terms will cause them to lose the jury. The genius who may understand the science better, but is unable to communicate it to the average person, will be all but useless in the courtroom.

Advocates Lack Credibility

Objectivity is by far the most important quality in an expert. A true scientist focuses on all the possibilities, open to alternative hypotheses. Experts who make reasonable concessions while building the other side's case do not come across as advocates, with greater overall credibility. However, some forensic experts are biased, with opinions that don't track with basic sense. They seem to know what they are going to say, looking at the records only enough to be familiar with them. This tends to get them into trouble on their assumptions.

Jurors can be impacted negatively when they learn that an expert only works for one side or the other. These experts can be painted into a dogmatic corner rather easily on cross-examination: "Doctor, have you ever rendered an opinion that a doctor in a medical malpractice claim did anything wrong?" "No, I haven't." "So you always show up as an expert for the defense in these cases. You don't think that any doctor ever does anything below the standard of care, do you?"

As it is, jurors are skeptical about lawyers coming into a case. While they ordinarily look at doctors and scientists in a much less critical light, the law can have a corrupting influence on this too. The usual juror good will toward these experts vanishes if any cross over the line and become an advocate:

> Experts who are advocates end up with far less respect and trust. An advocate
> will reflexively agree with the position of the attorney who hired them and disagree with the opposing attorney on cross-examination. The jury picks up on
> this right away.[2]

The credibility of an expert also will suffer if they place too much reliance on the information provided by the attorney. Experts who react emotionally when challenged on cross-examination, losing their cool, also are viewed as advocates, unprofessional in their demeanor. No matter how smart the expert, this will tend to discredit them, as jurors expect scientists to be dispassionate.

Some experts who testify frequently are cagey, avoiding being seen as advocates by making a concerted effort to consult for both sides. This seeming evenhandedness enhances the expert's credibility in the eyes of the jury: "This person must really know because he/she is asked by both sides to sort these things out."

Bonding with Your Experts

You have to bond with your experts and get them to believe in the importance and correctness of your position of the case. Once they do and have signed on as a part of your army, it will be very hard for your opponent to shake them from that opinion. If anything, they will get even stronger thereafter.

Though many details will be sketchy in the early going, potential experts ultimately must get all the information they need to render a valid opinion in the case. Nothing is worse then having your expert asked a key piece of data that either you didn't give or they didn't read, and you assumed they had. It makes them look incompetent.

The Two Things All Lawyers Want from Their Experts

No matter what side we represent, all lawyers are looking for two basic things from experts. The first is that they have to be teachers whose testimony will help move our case forward. It is critical for the expert to help explain to the jury why our client should prevail. The second is that they do no harm by making damaging admissions to opposing counsel. This requires a well-ingrained street sense and appreciation of the perils of the adversary system. The same rules apply for both experts and lay witnesses.

If an expert you call says something that hurts your case, it causes irreparable harm, as it will be taken as true by the jury. Experts who have not done a great deal of testifying always are a bit of a calculated risk here. Sensitive to the prospect of being seen as an advocate for one side, they may give away too much on cross-examination. If your expert concedes on cross that something "could be possible" this shouldn't really matter as the legal standard of proof is "more likely than not." But it does. Jurors look on this as a sign of weakness when experts concede that, "This could have happened." While lawyers educate new experts not to agree with opposing counsel's hypotheticals, the object lesson doesn't always take.

The Need to Be Crisp and Definitive

Jurors are very conscientious, looking for concreteness and accuracy in making their decision. The different approaches of science and law can make it hard for experts to be definitive in the way the law requires. That's one of the elements that a lawyer has to evaluate in assessing the juror appeal of an expert. Doctors in particular tend to hedge their bets, "It could be this, it could be that, clinical correlation is advised." You want an expert who can deliver a crisp, unequivocal opinion: "This is what it is, and why." Successful lawyers apply the casting director criteria to all potential experts, eliminating those who cannot do this:

> After meeting with some doctors, I have concluded that I could not possibly use them. They won't stand up for their opinions and waffle around too much. Often, they struggle to communicate in a group setting and won't even look you in the eye in a one-on-one encounter. This can only reflect badly on my case. I don't tell these doctors to their face, but leave their offices knowing I will not call them.[3]

Special Considerations for Doctor Experts

Though this is covered in greater detail in Chapter 23, it bears repeating that the antagonism in medicine toward the legal system will make your job difficult in recruiting medical experts, particularly if you represent a plaintiff suing a doctor, nurse or hospital. It is very hard to get doctors to testify on the plaintiff side against other doctors in medical malpractice cases. The scientific challenge and importance of the case to good medical practice are critical selling points in these circumstances.

Testifying in a case raises the unwelcome prospect of time away from a doctor's practice. Most do not want to be involved in any legal case, even providing testimony about the treatment and prognosis of their own patients. It often is frustrating for plaintiffs to get treating physicians to render a competent medical-legal opinion. Doctors live in a world were they have to routinely tell their patients that they will do well, seeing the glass as half full rather than half empty. Plaintiff's lawyers can encounter a reluctance to say that a patient will do badly over time, even if this is a distinct possibility. Doctors tend to believe that a poor prognosis can become a self-fulfilling prophecy.

Developing a trust relationship is critical to overcoming the distaste physicians have to testifying in medical-legal cases. Treating physicians are more receptive when they know that their input is important to the case. Some variation of the following statement is helpful in motivating them: "The jury wants to hear from you. They're going to believe a treating physician much more than any expert either side brings in. You weren't picked by anybody for litigation purposes. You are the person the patient picked to help get them better."

Face Time and Cross-Pollination

Face time with experts is critical. You have to work on multiple experts simultaneously, trying to synchronize their opinions. You need to understand their experts' fields as best you can before spending time with them. Pick up from each everything you can about the case. Be alert for any mention of, "Here's a problem, I worry about this." Cross-pollination occurs when you go back and forth between the experts, raising the difficult questions. Add all this up into a unified picture and then go back to each expert individually, getting him/her to ratify it.

"The Usual Suspects"

The selection of experts in legal cases is a bit incestuous, with a tendency to see the same ones over and over again in certain types of cases, much like a theater repertory company. For example, this happens in motor vehicle tort cases in state court, where certain medical experts testify repeatedly for one side or the other. This can put these experts in tenuous circumstances:

> Doctors who end up doing only litigation work are an interesting group. It's a slippery slope, particularly if you're retired, not doing medicine anymore. You need income and attorneys start calling you. The more compliant you are, the more attorneys will call you. After a while, this tends to put pressure on a doctor's professional objectivity and credibility.[4]

Perhaps feeling a bit stung by the insinuations made by opposing counsel, scientists who do testify regularly point out the benefit they confer to the legal system:

> Why do I serve as an expert witness? An honest part of the answer includes financial gain. I certainly earn money testifying in court. But there are other more altruistic reasons as well. The administration of justice in cases with scientific issues requires expert input. I really do know the answers to some of these questions, based on the research that has been done in my laboratory. These are the kinds of things I do every day.[5]

Many veteran trial lawyers agree that it often is not just about the money:

> I can't believe that most forensic experts just do it for the money, though there are some that make a lot of money from testifying. Most don't make enough for this to be the total explanation. Some feel a calling to help sort these issues out. Part of it may be ego, "They need me to figure this out."[6]

How does an expert become one of those who testifies frequently? A big part of the answer is that they are easy to contact and will do it. You don't have to stretch to go find them:

> Often enough, I go to experts that I have worked with before and trust. I know they will look at a case and give me a fair shake. This is a matter of expedience, convenience and reliability. I also will think about using experts who were effective as witnesses for the other side in prior cases.[7]

There also is a tendency to overuse those experts who are skilled in explaining things in lay language. Jurors like them because they can understand what they are saying.

Many lawyers go the path of least resistance, selecting experts that they know are available and reliable. It is a hassle to find experts that are fresh and new who will agree to testify. Experts who have busy careers, such as doctors, have their time spoken for. It is inconvenient and disruptive to get involved in a case.

Judicial Response to Frequent Experts

Judges hear the same kind of opinions from experts who testify frequently. In a bench trial, the judge will tend to discount these experts, relying instead on informed gut instincts. It is hard not to if the testimony merely repeats what has been said on many other occasions. For example, in family law cases with allegations of domestic violence, a husband often will be sent to one of a small group of treatment providers for anger management, concluding that he needs treatment. The defense then calls an opposing expert who concludes, "Oh no, this was just situational, he does not need treatment. The husband is not a domestic violence perpetrator." But judges recognize that it is an entirely different matter for a jury who hasn't heard an expert before. To jurors, the testimony is fresh and new.

Experts Who Don't Make the Cut

Even when you have done everything right with expert selection and preparation, a certain number of your casting director decisions will not make the final cut. Be prepared not to use some experts who have written a great report with helpful opinions. For reasons that were not apparent earlier in the case, concerns develop over how they might be perceived by the jury. For this reason, you always list more experts than you intend to use and see how well they hold up. You must evaluate the credibility of each expert and how well they will come across in trial. You pick the ones you like and know will hold up, tossing the rest.

Takeaways — Casting Director

1. Thinking about the experts to use in a case is just like being a casting director for a play or movie.

2. It is hard to find experts who are willing to review a case and do a good job of testifying.

3. Many experts don't want to do legal consulting work. It requires too much effort and exposure to confrontation.

4. Quality experts need to feel that they have something to offer to the jury and the legal system, providing expertise on a difficult issue.

5. Forensic work provides a great learning opportunity for experts.

6. Networking to get the right experts is a process of effort, luck, and trial and error.

7. The first thing to do in identifying a good potential expert is to go to the literature and see who has written peer-review articles on the precise topic at issue in the case.

8. You must perform meticulous scrutiny of anything a potential expert ever has written or relied upon that could conceivably apply to your case.

9. If an expert has any personal experience with an issue in the case, that always gives their testimony more of a ring of authenticity.

10. You always have to think about the personality of an expert and how it will translate into the courtroom setting.

11. Arrogance by an expert in front of a jury is a deadly sin.

12. Experts must be good teachers who help to move your case forward.

13. Any concessions by an expert are dangerous, as these will be taken as absolutely true by a jury.

14. The different approaches of science and law can make it hard for experts to be definitive in the way the law requires.

15. The underlying antagonism between law and medicine makes it difficult to recruit medical experts, particularly for plaintiffs.

16. Developing a trust relationship is critical to overcoming the distaste physicians have to testifying in medical-legal cases.

17. Face time with experts is critical.

18. Cross-pollination occurs when you go back and forth between the experts, raising the difficult questions in a case.

19. The selection of experts in legal cases is a bit incestuous, with a tendency to see the same ones over and over again in certain types of cases.

20. There is a tendency to overuse those experts who are skilled in explaining things in lay language.

21. In a bench trial, the judge tends to view the canned opinions of shopworn experts skeptically, but it is different for a jury, who has not heard these experts before.

22. Even when you have done everything right with expert selection and preparation, a certain number will not make the final cut.

23. Always list more experts than you intend to use, so you aren't caught short if you are forced to drop one.

Chapter 18

Experts and Attorney Work Product

Make a habit of two things: to help, or at least to do no harm.
—Hippocrates

An opinion by your own expert that is contrary to your case theory can have devastating consequences. Juries understand that the adversary system requires careful script control by attorneys. They anticipate that experts always will give opinions favorable to the party calling them. More often than not, this is exactly what happens. Typically, attorneys get what they are looking for from the experts they contact. But this is not always true.

Any human system has the potential for mistakes and unforeseen outcomes. Experts can and do disappoint the attorneys who hire them, delivering negative opinions. The very thought of this makes attorneys nervous, as self-inflicted wounds always hurt the most. While jurors may discount an expert's favorable opinions as advocacy driven and lacking credibility, admissions against interest are judged quite differently, seen as absolute truth. "It must really be true if the party's own expert says something negative about the case."

Experts who go off the expected script and give negative opinions during the consultation process are summarily dropped. Sometimes the issue is not the expert's actual opinions in a case, but rather, qualifications, bias or ethics matters. This can come at any point in the process, from the initial consultation to informal opinions to reports to depositions. When these problems surface later in the pre-trial process, after the expert's report has been given to opposing counsel, or in a deposition, asserting work product can be more difficult. In this chapter, we will examine how much an expert gone wrong can be used to embarrass or weaken the case of the party who hired them.

When experts have opinions harmful to the party calling them, the doctrines of open discovery and attorney confidentiality come into conflict. While discovery was created as an orderly way to exchange information and resolve disputes efficiently, it did not abolish the confidentiality protecting the attorney-client relationship. Just as communications between lawyers and clients are privileged, so are many of the steps a lawyer takes in building a case. Judges attempt to draw a sensible line between discovery and confidentiality.

There is a general recognition that one party should not expect to be able to prove its case with the work product of the opponent. But potential advantage from the other

Figure 18-1. Conflicting goals of discovery and attorney work product.

side's wayward expert often is too much to resist. An opponent may attempt to resurrect the expert in some manner, asserting waiver. This is high-stakes battle, as expert "friendly fire" can inflict enormous potential damage.

Range of Discovery Obligations for Experts

FRCP 26(a)(2)(B) and 26(b)(4)(A) make clear that any underlying facts or assumptions, opinions and final reports are discoverable when an expert is expected to testify. At the other extreme, FRCP 26(a)(2)(D) explains that when an expert is employed by counsel merely for advice in preparation for litigation, any documents or opinions generated in that capacity are undiscoverable absent "exceptional circumstances." But if counsel changes an expert's designation from "testifying" to "non-testifying" prior to trial, what then? How long can trial counsel protect these opinions and documents as work product by changing the expert's designation?

A Split of Authority

There is a clean split of authority in the cases on expert disclosure. One long-favored approach dictates that a testifying expert may be redesignated as "non-testifying," insulating her from discovery. This shift can occur at any time until the testimony is used in summary judgment or trial.

Another evolving approach is less forgiving. It insists that work product protections for consulting experts are permanently waived after formal identification in discovery or disclosure of a report. At this point, the expert is a "testifying" one for discovery purposes, regardless of any designation to the contrary. This has significant implications for a lawyer's discretion to redesignate an expert or claim discovery protections. The relationship between attorney work product and expert testimony has received little attention in the case law, especially where redesignation is concerned. One court described this issue as a "vexing and surprisingly little explored question."[1]

The Protections of FRCP 26(b)(4)

The core of the work product doctrine for expert testimony is found in FRCP 26(b)(4). The December 1, 2010, amendments significantly expanded work product protections for experts. Prior courts read FRCP 26(a)'s disclosure provisions to extend to draft expert reports, as well as all communications between counsel and a testifying expert.[2] To remedy this, FRCP(b)(4)(B) was amended to allow work product protection for all expert draft reports "regardless of the form." FRCP(b)(4)(C) extends this to all attorney-expert communication, except on compensation and any facts, data, or assumptions the expert relied upon.

These amendments were intended to strengthen expert work product protections. The Committee was concerned that "routine discovery into attorney-expert communications and draft reports has had undesirable effects.... Attorneys may employ two sets of experts—one for purposes of consultation and another to testify at trial—because disclosure of their collaborative interactions with expert consultants would reveal their most sensitive and confidential case analyses."[3] They recommended protections for communications and draft reports, reducing expert preparation anxieties and litigation costs, promoting more open communication between attorneys and their hired experts.[4]

Testifying vs. Consulting Experts

The 2010 amendments retained the same work product distinction between testifying and non-testifying (or "consulting") experts first codified decades ago. Under FRCP 26(b)(4)(A), any expert presented at trial is subject to discovery, required to do a written report under FRCP 26(a)(2)(B). Consulting experts who are not expected to testify are protected from disclosure under FRCP 26(b)(4)(D).

The party who retains an expert chooses whether he or she will testify. Even an expert who initially is identified as offering testimony can be stricken. However, there is debate over whether the designation change from "testifying" to "consulting" will restore work product protection.

The Impact of Redesignation on Discovery

Changing pre-trial designations of experts has different consequences, depending on which line of authority is applied.[5] The first, described by some courts as the majority position,[6] holds that changing an expert's designation from "testifying" to "non-testifying" can shield unwanted expert opinions, even after they have been disclosed. A party who no longer intends to call an expert witness for testimony does not have to respond to depositions, interrogatories, or other requests absent a showing of "exceptional circumstances."

The Illinois case of *Ross v. Burlington Northern R. Co.*[7] is frequently cited for the restoration of work product protection.[8] In *Ross*, the plaintiff redesignated an expert as a consulting one after endorsing the witness for trial and revealing his opinions. The court denied the defendant's attempt to force the plaintiff to produce the expert for deposition, restoring "consulting expert" protection under FRCP 26(b)(4)(D) (then FRCP 26(b)(4)(B)).[9] Plaintiff was given "the prerogative of changing his mind" until actual testimony was given,[10] based on background support in *Durflinger v. Artiles*.[11]

Though the expert in *Ross* had not yet made full disclosure of his opinions,[12] many other cases have reached the same result, even after an expert has surfaced and provided opinions. In *Lehan v. Ambassador Programs, Inc.*, the defendant's medical examiner under FRCP 35 was listed as a trial witness and his report disclosed.[13] When defendant later withdrew this expert, the plaintiff moved to call him. The court refused to allow this access absent "exceptional circumstances."[14] Similarly, in *Estate of Manship v. U.S.*, the court held that the mere endorsement of an expert as a testifying witness did not waive work product protection.[15] This designation is revocable, "even if a testifying expert witness' designation is withdrawn after his/her opinions have been disclosed."[16]

Many other opinions have blocked discovery of an expert after redesignation, even following disclosure of an opinion or report.[17] As one court explained:

> This approach is grounded in the policies underlying the distinction between the manner in which Rule 26(b)(4) treats testifying experts versus consulting experts.... Rule 26(b)(4)(A) is designed to allow the opposing party an opportunity to adequately prepare for cross-examination at trial, a concern that does not exist when the expert will not be called at trial. Thus, fairness requires that [what is now Rule 26(b)(4)(D)]'s protections apply to a consulting expert who will not be called to testify at trial, regardless of whether the party who retained the expert at one time had intended to call the expert to testify.[18]

Redesignation to Insulate Experts

A smaller number of courts have taken the "cat is out of the bag approach,"[19] finding that the designation as a testifying expert or disclosure of opinions removes the "exceptional circumstances" protection against discovery requests. These courts either have replaced the "exceptional circumstances" requirement with a Rule 403-style balancing test, or simply permit discovery as though the expert were still a testifying one.

Many opinions credit *House v. Combined Ins. Co. of Am.*[20] as the origin of this position. *House* held that, once counsel designates an expert as "testifying," they have waived the "consulting expert" privilege and are subject to discovery. The work product protections of the "exceptional circumstances" standard no longer apply.[21] Discovery access to a redesignated expert is based on the discretion of the trial judge, balancing the probative value of this evidence against any potential prejudice.[22] While several decisions subsequently followed a similar approach to *House*,[23] it has often been described as the minority position.[24]

However, since 2009 the *House* approach has gained some favor, particularly in the Seventh Circuit. Building on a dictum in *S.E.C. v. Koenig*,[25] several courts have departed from the majority view in *Ross, et al.* In *Koenig*, the defendant had argued that if he had known the plaintiff had intended to call the defendant's own expert at trial, this expert would have been withdrawn to prevent it. The court reasoned that doing so would not have helped, because "[a] witness identified as a testimonial expert is available to either side; such a person can't be transformed after the report has been disclosed.... *Disclosure of the report ends the opportunity to invoke confidentiality*" (emphasis added).[26] Other district court opinions in the Seventh Circuit have followed this dictum. Together, they stand for the proposition that providing an expert's report ends the power of redesignation to quarantine the expert.[27]

What Is the Bottom Line?

The split of authority on the ability of a lawyer to bury retained experts creates a troubling uncertainty. It puts a premium on thorough vetting *before* identifying experts as trial witnesses. A fight over discovery and work product should be anticipated if an expert is redesignated as non-testifying after the expert veers from expectation. That fight may be more difficult to win after the expert's report has been provided, or his/her testimony offered in a summary judgment motion. By then, it is likely too late. While the weight of authority over the last 20 years still favors insulation of the expert through redesignation, the outcome in any particular case is difficult to predict.

Takeaways — Experts and Attorney Work Product

1. An opinion by your expert that is contrary to your case theory can have devastating consequences.

2. Juries anticipate that experts always will offer opinions favorable to the party calling them.

3. Any human system always has the potential for unforeseen outcomes. Experts can and do surprise the attorneys who hire them, delivering negative opinions.

4. Experts who go off the expected script during the consultation process usually are summarily dropped from the roster. But sometimes this occurs later on, after the expert's report has been given to opposing counsel, such as at a deposition. At this point, dropping the expert becomes more difficult.

5. When experts have opinions harmful to the party calling them, the doctrines of open discovery and attorney work product protection come into conflict.

6. While discovery was created as an orderly way to exchange information and resolve disputes efficiently, it did not abolish the confidentiality protecting the attorney-client relationship.

7. FRCP 26(a)(2)(B) and 26(b)(4)(A) make clear that any underlying facts or assumptions, opinions and final reports are discoverable when an expert is expected to testify.

8. FRCP 26(a)(2)(D) explains that when an expert is employed by counsel merely for advice in preparation for litigation, any documents or opinions generated in that capacity are undiscoverable absent "exceptional circumstances."

9. There is a clean split of authority in the cases on expert disclosure.

10. One long-favored approach dictates that a testifying expert may be redesignated as "non-testifying," insulating the expert from discovery. This shift can occur at any time until the testimony is used in summary judgment or trial.

11. Another evolving approach is less forgiving. It insists that work product protections for consulting experts are permanently waived after formal identification in discovery or disclosure of a report. At this point, the expert is a "testifying" one for discovery purposes, regardless of any designation to the contrary.

12. The split of authority has caused uncertainty over whether the designation change from "testifying" to "consulting" will restore work product protection. It puts a premium on thorough vetting *before* identifying experts as trial witnesses.

13. A fight over discovery and work product should be anticipated if an expert is redesignated as non-testifying after the expert veers from expectation.

14. The fight against shielding an expert may be more difficult to win after the expert's report has been provided, or his/her testimony offered in a summary judgment motion.

Chapter 19

How People Learn

I am always ready to learn although I do not always like being taught.
—Winston Churchill

Lawyers must effectively communicate scientific and technical information so that it is understood, believed and remembered. In this sense, every lawyer must be a teacher. Accomplishing this requires a basic understanding of how people learn, which is the focus of this chapter.

The Story Drives the "Stickiness" of Your Case

Your case story is a central factor in determining whether new information will stick. A good story motivates an audience to pay attention to details and remember them. Human beings are hardwired to think in terms of stories. It goes back to times when we all gathered around campfires. It starts in childhood and carries over into adult life. We all like stories about characters we can identify with that evoke strong feelings. That is how knowledge is passed on. We take sides, based on our values, cheering for some and hissing at others.[1]

Jurors base their decisions on the parties and their respective stories, often developing a leaning early on. This influences how they listen to the testimony. They absorb the things that bolster their perception of the case. The character of your client is a critical part of this process. For corporations, the representatives who testify shape the perception of the entire organization. After the key experts testify, most jurors know which way they are going.

To be an effective teacher, you must have a well-trained ear and keep a continuous sense of the viability of your case story. How will this play? Tools such as focus groups can give insight into how people will respond to it. The facts and the story of a case drive a jury's decision more than the advocacy of the lawyers: "In strategizing on how to present my cases, I focus on the ultimate culture of stories, which are critical to learning."[2]

For example, an important part of the story in a medical malpractice case is the character of the care. The lawyers for both sides put jurors in the scene with photos of the medical settings where critical events occurred. The doctor or hospital is presented by the plaintiffs as missing important steps while the defense shows the defendant as detailed oriented and conscientious, providing good patient care. Which side of the story jurors buy into determines what jurors will believe and remember.

Stories provide jurors the perspective through which all the expert testimony is viewed. For example, in a medical malpractice case involving an unusual complication after neck surgery that caused brain damage, the defense used a story to show the surgeon knew what he was doing. The surgeon had encountered a similar case once before as a resident. He had called his professor and asked, "What should I do?" His professor responded emphatically, "That patient is bleeding from the operation. Get him to the operating room immediately." When this same complication happened to the plaintiff many years later, the defense had the surgeon recall this story for the jury, using it later in closing argument: "The most important person in this case was one we didn't hear from directly. It was the professor that trained our surgeon."[3]

The Multi-Media Impact on Learning and Persuasion

A substantial body of research has proved the effectiveness of multi-media communication: "Learners can better understand an explanation when it is presented in words and pictures than when it is presented in words alone."[4] Human beings need visuals to recognize patterns. Combining words and pictures is not a new idea. For centuries, many people were illiterate, requiring that pictures be used to convey religious or political information. During the Renaissance, Leonardo da Vinci's notebooks combined his drawings with handwritten observations, covering every field of science known at that time.

Though pictures are powerful, a countervailing intellectual snobbery dismisses them as less "serious" than text. Scott McCloud captures this paradox in "*Understanding Comics*":

> As children, our first books had pictures galore and very few words because that was 'easier.' Then, as we grew, we were expected to graduate to books with much more text and only occasional pictures—and finally to arrive at 'real' books—those with no pictures at all…. Words and pictures are as popular as ever, but this widespread feeling that the combination is somehow base or simplistic has become a self-fulfilling prophecy.[5]

Two Processing Systems

The brain receives information through two basic processing systems, one language based, and the other with images.[6] When learning from text and pictures, pictures can always be retrieved from both memory systems. Pictures have the stronger impact of the two.

Working Memory and Retention

Our working memory determines what we hold onto and what we discard. It has an astonishingly limited capacity. Much of what is presented to us quickly disappears: "Novel information must be processed by a structure that … retains [it] for no more

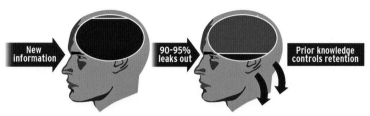

Figure 19-1. The ability to retain new information is limited.

than a few seconds."[7] Our long-term memories control and define our capacity to encode and remember information. The average brain can only hold about seven elements of information at any given time.[8] Without some effort, all the contents of working memory will evaporate in about 20 seconds.[9] It is only when short-term and long-term memory connect that we learn.

The Challenges of Teaching about Science and Technology

Details of science and technology are hard for many lay people to learn. Forensics requires us to develop a strategy which compensates for the fragility of working memory. It is not just a matter of "dumbing down" information. Human beings are not tape recorders. New information is evaluated and absorbed in light of we already know. If it is not connected to our fund of knowledge, it quickly disappears.

Even with all the visual potential of the computer, much information still is presented verbally, whether in the classroom or the courtroom. This ignores the proven

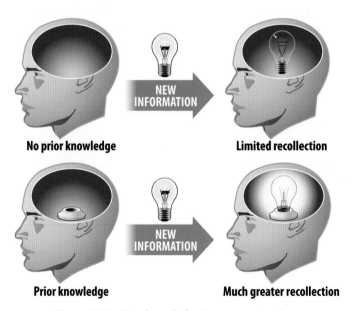

Figure 19-2. Prior knowledge increases retention.

superiority of visual information over auditory. Common sense alone tells us that pictures are stronger and more believable than words. Media sage Marshall McLuhan captures why:

> Most people find it difficult to understand purely verbal concepts. They suspect the ear; they don't trust it. In general we feel more secure when things are visible, when we can "see for ourselves." ... All kinds of "shorthand" [metaphors] have been developed to help us see what we hear.[10]

How Words and Pictures Reinforce One Another

Words and pictures together give audience members a deeper, more connected understanding.

Pictures serve four basic functions in learning:

1. Reinforcement. Overlaps the words, a second opportunity for learning.

2. Simplification. Less detail, more easily absorbed.

3. Interpretation. Illustrates what is difficult to understand from words alone.

4. A Hook. More easily coded and placed in memory.[11]

Some concepts, such as spatial relationships, are far better conveyed by pictures than words.[12]

It is a challenge to make experts interesting and likeable for the jury without being too obvious about it. The technical information experts present is more interesting using visuals. Experts can draw on butcher paper as they testify. Objects can be passed around to the jury to feel and examine. These can be simple things, like a fetal scalp electrode in a birth injury.

Using PowerPoint with Experts

There is no question that PowerPoint is the tool of choice for most lawyers in presenting experts. For that reason, we want to spend some time analyzing its effectiveness.

As incredible as it may seem, there actually was a time when people made effective presentations without PowerPoint. The time-honored teaching method centered around writing on the board. Mathematics teachers once used overhead projectors with a scrolling celluloid roll full of black grease pencil equations.

PowerPoint is just a slightly higher-tech version of traditional show-and-tell group presentation tools. The effectiveness varies, depending on the subject, techniques and skill of the presenter.

How Effective Is PowerPoint?

While there are many opinions on the subject, surprisingly little research exists on the overall effectiveness of PowerPoint. Multi-media expert Edward Tufte, savages it as "evil":

Imagine a widely used and expensive prescription drug that promised to make us beautiful but didn't. Instead the drug had frequent, serious side effects: and induced stupidity, turned everyone into bores, wasted time and degraded the quality and credibility of communication.... The standard PowerPoint presentation elevates format over content.[13]

Naturally, Microsoft has an entirely different view of PowerPoint, presenting it as an essential tool of modern spoken communication. Does PowerPoint "captivate" as Microsoft claims, or is it "evil" as Tufte would have it? Or is the truth somewhere in between?

Research Studies on How Visuals Aid Learning

A few credible studies shed light on the connection between visual presentations and audience retention. The 1981 Wharton Study titled, "A Study Of The Effects Of The Use Of Overhead Transparencies On Business Meetings,"[14] has been much cited. It compared business meetings conducted with visuals to those without, using the most common presentation aid of the time, overhead transparencies. Simulated meetings in the study were closely modeled on the real business world.

The Wharton study concluded that presenters using overhead images were seen as better prepared, more professional, persuasive, credible and interesting. They achieved a much higher degree of consensus in the group.[15] Decisions were reached more quickly when overheads were used, with shorter meeting time.

Research concluded at the University of Minnesota in 1986 (the UM/3M study)[16] evaluated the effects of visuals in sales presentations. The influence of the speaker and audience information retention were far better with visuals:

1. Speakers with visuals were 43% more persuasive.

2. Increased audience attention and comprehension.

3. Speakers with only average skills were seen as much better by the audience.

The UM/3M study also determined that:

- The combination of verbal and visual is much more effective than verbal alone.

- Only a small amount of information delivered verbally is remembered after three days.

- The audience remembers much more information received visually and verbally after three days.

Both the Wharton and University of Minnesota studies support that:

1. Speakers using visuals are more effective.

2. The audience retains more information.

3. Greater persuasion results.

These general principles applying to using PowerPoint to present scientific and technical information in a legal case. As with any tool, it all comes down to the skill of the user.

Things to Avoid When Using PowerPoint

A screen is an eye magnet. If you flash something on it, the audience immediately diverts its attention from you to look at what is on the screen. If there is text on the screen and you are talking at the same time, people will try to read and listen at the same time. They won't succeed in doing either very well. If push comes to shove, they will prefer to do their own reading and ignore you. Anything that makes you invisible to your audience is not good.

There is a temptation for content-driven lawyers to put too much information on a slide, overloading the audience. Bullet points don't necessarily make information more digestible. A dozen slides with five bullet points on each assumes that people are mentally capable of taking in a list of 60 points. Most speakers overestimate how much information people can actually absorb in a single presentation.

Bullet Points

- ## This is a Bullet Point
- ## Boring
  - ### And hierarchical
- ## Very often bullet points are too long
- ## Reading is faster than talking
  - ### That's why you're already here and I'm not

PowerPoint can cramp your style, turning you into a presentation robot, only opening your mouth when a slide is on the screen. There is a tendency to use slides as verbal crutches for yourself rather than visual aids for the audience.

Tufte is highly critical of what he calls the "dreaded slow reveal" of most slides, with similar annoyance as a dripping faucet. The goal of a successful PowerPoint is to match the pace of the information to the audience's ability to absorb it, not too fast or too slow, but just right.

PowerPoint slides should be constructed with these principles in mind:

1. Words and pictures are great together, but the fewer words the better.

2. Keep weeding your material to get a simple message.

3. Relate the image to something the audience already knows.

Figure 19-3(a). Use of a common object to create size perspective.

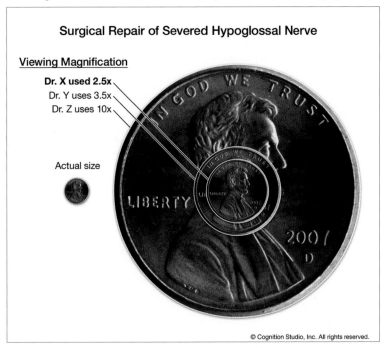

Figure 19-3(b). Surgical magnification is paired with the coin size image.

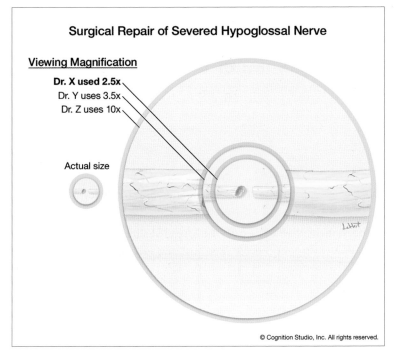

4. Use well-designed pictures that reinforce your message.

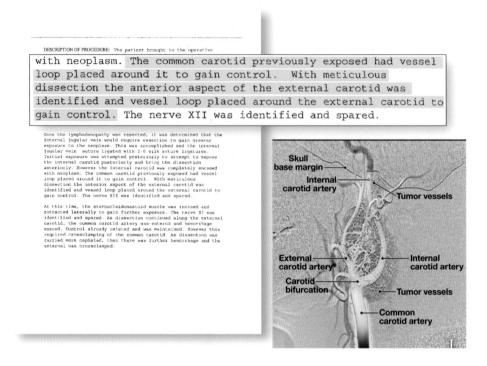

Figure 19-4. Medical drawing illustrating the words of an operative report.

5. Sequence from the simple to the complex.

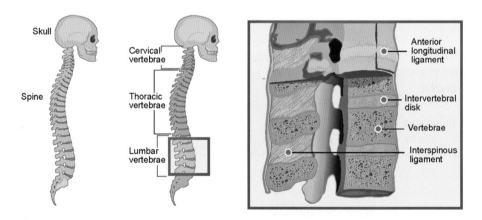

Figure 19-5. An audience will understand better when you go from the simple to the complex.

6. Use graphic devices such as arrows, close-ups and highlights.

Figure 19-6(a). Graphic devices aid retention.

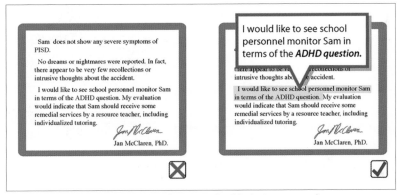

Figure 19-6(b). Use graphic devices to highlight important language.

Figure 19-6(c). Use graphic devices to call out the importance of concessions by opposing experts.

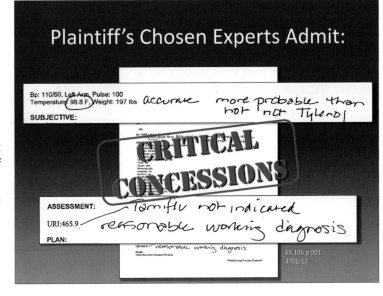

7. Use site maps, timelines or visual tables of contents.

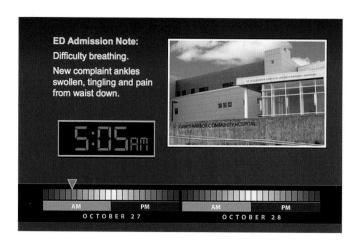

Figure 19-7(a). Timelines help us to understand a sequence of events.

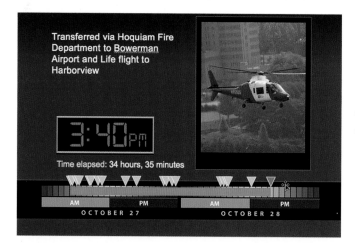

Figure 19-7(b). Timelines can show the impact of choices.

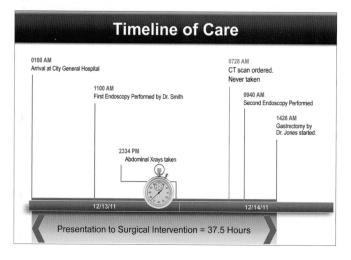

Figure 19-7(c). Timelines can deflect the blame, showing limited involvement by those who came later.

8. Present problems and solutions visually.

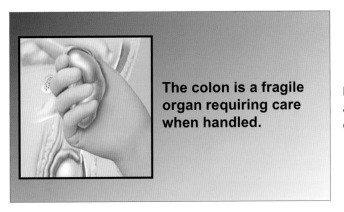

The colon is a fragile organ requiring care when handled.

Figure 19-8(a). Visualizing a basic risk in a hernia operation.

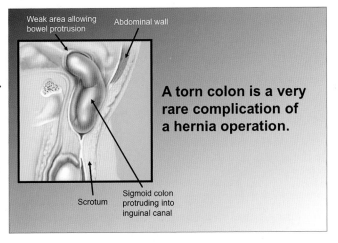

Figure 19-8(b). More specific identification of what happened in the procedure.

A torn colon is a very rare complication of a hernia operation.

Figure 19-8(c). Showing the solution that would have prevented the problem.

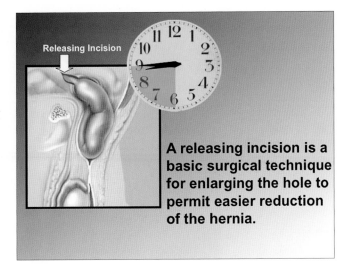

A releasing incision is a basic surgical technique for enlarging the hole to permit easier reduction of the hernia.

Dr. Smith Properly Obtained Informed Consent for His Working Diagnosis
Reasonable Working Diagnosis of URI
Treatment Options
• Antibiotics not for virus
• No anti-viral med for URI
• OTC cold remedies limited for pregnant patients
• Fluids, rest
• Tamiflu not an option for URI
Plan:
• To OB for protein and re-check
• To ED if worsen
• Contact clinic as needed
ASSESSMENT:
URI:465.9
PLAN:
Tamiflu not indicated
reasonable working diagnosis
EX 106 p 001

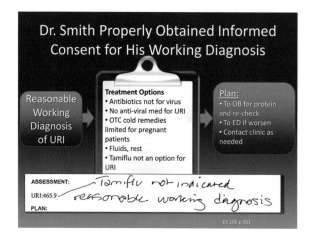

Figure 19-8(d). Visualizing proper procedure, working diagnosis and treatment.

9. Coordinate your actions as a speaker with screen images, but don't be enslaved by them.

Helping the Trier of Fact to Retain Science and Technology

There are a number of techniques you should use in presenting scientific or technical information with experts, making it easier for the judge or jury to retain.

1. Make clear what each expert will address. The points must be limited, not attempting too much.
2. Regulate the pace at which the new information is presented, so that it can be absorbed.
3. Use a conversational, less formal style.
4. Use words and pictures in a way that will allow people to construct a mental model of the information in their own minds.

Jane Smith's Pre-Op Symptoms
Headaches
Decreased range of motion
Pain radiating to both shoulders
Low back pain
Neck pain, stiffness
Pain, numbness in both biceps
Pain, numbness in both hands
Dr. Jones saw Ms. Smith for six months prior to surgery
No sustained improvement after more than 12 months of conservative management
17

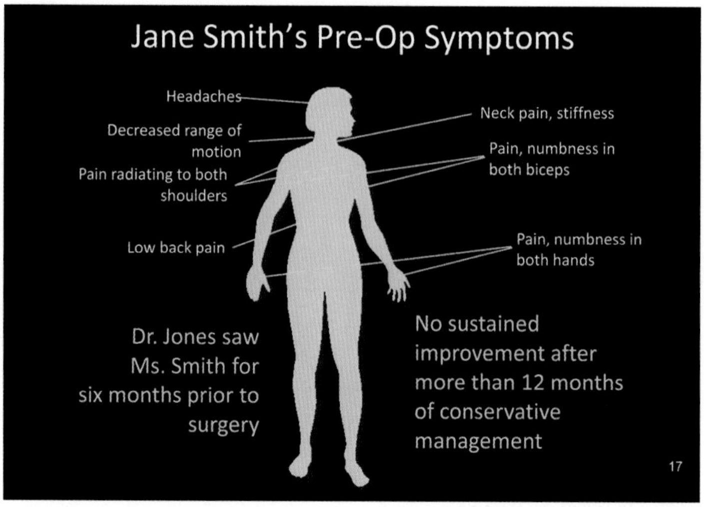

Figure 19-9(a). Mental model of all patient's problems prior to surgery.

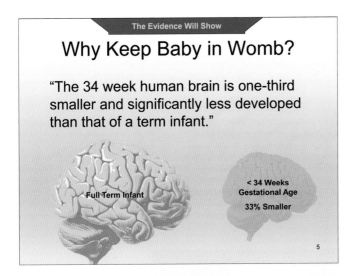

Figure 19-9(b). Showing why delayed delivery promotes brain growth.

Figure 19-9(c). Connecting mechanics of injury to tendon rupture.

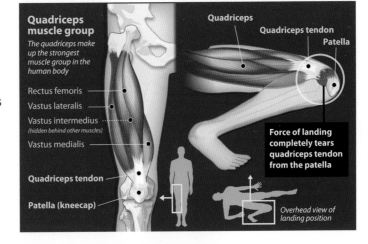

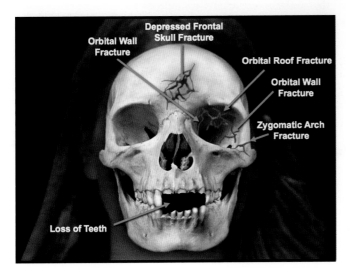

Figure 19-9(d). Showing locations of fractures listed in medical record.

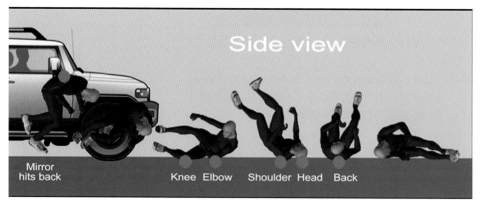

Figure 19-9(e). Relating mechanics of trauma to medical record.

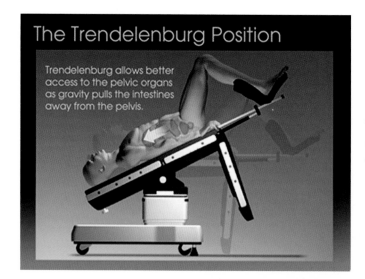

Figure 19-9(f). Visualizing medical procedure with explanation.

Figure 19-9(g). Explaining the structural difference between cold and flu viruses.

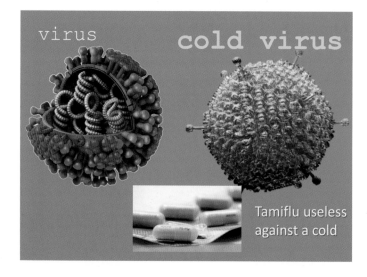

5. Use visuals to describe both problems and solutions.

6. Immediately engage the interest of your audience, sustaining it throughout an expert's testimony.

7. Vest the audience in what you are doing. If they get something helpful or useful from an expert, they will continue to pay attention to the testimony.

Different Learning Styles

In addition to the limitations of working memory, another major challenge to the retention of forensic evidence is the variability of learning styles. There are individual differences in how people perceive and process information. Audience members can look at the same presentation and interpret it differently. The capacity to remember and understand is personal to each individual. Information is not received in exactly the same form from one mind to another.[17] Some are visual learners who more readily absorb information from a diagram or a model. Others get lost with these and need verbal explanations. Yet another group learns through tactile manipulation, holding objects that they can engage with. These variations require you to develop a mixed-media strategy for your case, something for everyone, accounting for these individual differences in learning styles.

Figure 19-10. Use of different media in expert testimony.

Graphics: A Critical Instructional Tool

The design and use of instructional graphics is one of the most versatile means of addressing the principles of effective learning. We have a particularly strong graphic tradition in our culture, which a lawyer can draw upon in presenting information. Graphics help us to "get it" quickly:

> It seems that when problems are translated into more concrete graphic forms, it is often easier to solve them ... making the solution to a problem "transparent" by representing it in another form. Simply presenting problems as diagrams often lets us quickly "see" the solution.[18]

Graphics perform the critical task of simplifying the complex, so the working memory is not overwhelmed. Research has shown that realistic pictures can have too much information in them, which in turn overloads the audience with irrelevant detail.[19] Graphic forms such as a map have far less realistic detail than photographs. By reducing the number of features in a graphic, the location of the remaining features becomes easier to see. Idea mapping with graphic techniques improves the comprehension of concepts as well. The use of symbols can indicate that one idea is related to another, improving comprehension.

The Bottom Line: Multi-Media Learning Works

Though the research on multi-media learning still is in its infancy, irrefutable evidence of its basic effectiveness now exists: "Multi-media works ... It is better to present ... both words and pictures than using words alone."[20]

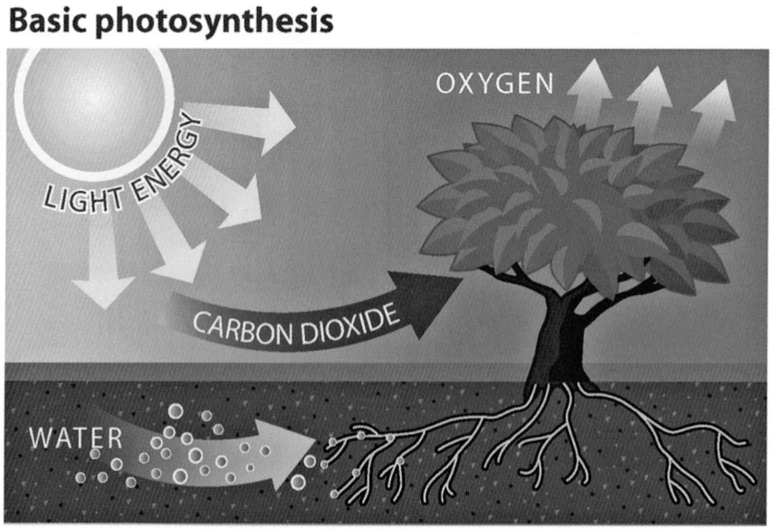

Basic photosynthesis

Figure 19-11. Use graphics to simplify complex scientific information.

Professor Richard Mayer of the University of California at Santa Barbara divides his results into two basic areas—retention of information and transfer. While the retention of information is a self-evident concept, transfer is even of greater interest to lawyers. Transfer goes beyond rote memorization to measure the ability to apply basic concepts to new situations. The deeper the learning, the greater the transfer. Multi-media learning has an even more dramatic effect on transfer than it does on memorization of detail.[21]

Unanswered Questions

Much research remains to be done on which particular combinations of words and pictures are the most effective in persuading an audience. Communication is both art and science:

> Pictures interact with text to produce levels of comprehension and memory that can exceed what is produced from text alone…. The good news is that we now know that pictures can indeed facilitate students processing of text information…. The bad news is that we do not know very much about why and how….[22]

Despite all the advancements in technology, multi-media communication has not reached its real potential as an educational tool. In order for this to happen, we must change the ways we look at an audience. Cognitive scientist Donald A. Norman reminds us of the critical importance of keeping a human focus: "Today we serve technology. We need to reverse the machine-centered point of view and turn it into a person-centered point of view: Technology should serve us."[23]

The Bottom Line: Visuals Work

While the debate over the effectiveness of PowerPoint likely will continue, there is no question that using visuals dramatically increases learning. This is of great importance in the presentation of forensic evidence, as this scientific and technical information may be unfamiliar to both the judge and the jury.

Takeaways—How People Learn

1. Effective communication is critical in the presentation of science and technology information for a judge or jury to understand, believe and remember it.

2. Every lawyer and his/her expert must be a teacher.

3. This requires a basic understanding of how people learn.

4. Your case story is a central factor in whether or not information sticks with the audience.

5. Jurors figure out which direction they are going in based on who the parties are and the story of the case.

6. The halo effect that comes from a good story is an audience that is motivated to pay attention to the details of the expert testimony.

7. We all like stories about characters we can identify with that evoke strong feelings. We take sides, based on our values, cheering for some and hissing at others.

8. You must have a well-trained ear and keep a continuous sense of the viability of the story. How will this play?

9. Stories provide jurors the perspective through which all the expert testimony is viewed.

10. Human beings need visuals to recognize patterns. Combining words and pictures is the most powerful form of communication.

11. The brain receives information through two basic processing systems, one language based, and the other with images.

12. When learning from text and pictures, pictures can always be retrieved from both memory systems. Pictures have the stronger impact of the two.

13. Our working memory determines what new information we hold onto and what we discard. It has very limited capacity.

14. Much of what is presented to us quickly disappears.

15. Our long-term memories control and define our capacity to encode and remember information.

16. Information about science and technology is hard for many lay people to learn. Forensics requires us to develop a strategy which compensates for the limitations of working memory.

17. Visuals have proven superiority over auditory in teaching. Common sense alone tells us that pictures are stronger and more believable than words.

18. PowerPoint is the tool of choice for most lawyers in presenting experts. It is a slightly higher-tech version of traditional show-and-tell group presentation tools.

19. A screen is an eye magnet. If you flash something on it, the audience immediately diverts its attention from you to look at what is on the screen.

20. If there is text on the screen and you are talking too, people will try to read and listen at the same time. They won't succeed in doing either very well.

21. There is a temptation for content-driven lawyers to put too much information on a slide, overloading the audience.

22. Bullet points don't necessarily make information more digestible.

23. PowerPoint can cramp your style, turning you into a presentation robot.

24. There are individual differences in how people perceive and process information. Audience members can look at the same presentation and interpret it differently.

25. Some are visual learners who more readily absorb information from a diagram or a model. Others get lost with these and need verbal explanations. Yet another group learns through tactile manipulation, holding objects that they can engage with.

26. These variations require you to develop a mixed-media strategy for your case, something for everyone.

27. Graphics perform the critical task of simplifying the complex, so the working memory is not overwhelmed.

28. Idea mapping with graphic techniques improves the comprehension of concepts as well.

29. While the retention of information is a self-evident concept, transfer is even of greater interest to lawyers. Transfer goes beyond rote memorization to measure the ability to apply basic concepts to new situations. The deeper the learning, the greater the transfer. Multi-media learning has an even more dramatic effect on transfer than it does on memorization of detail.

30. Despite all the advancements in technology, multi-media communication has not reached its real potential as an educational tool. In order for this to happen, we must change the ways we look at an audience.

31. Adding visuals can improve your presentation of scientific and technical information, with more effective communication, greater audience retention and enhanced perception of you as a presenter.

Chapter 20

Teaching Judges and Juries about Science and Technology

Science and technology revolutionize our lives, but memory, tradition and myth frame our response.

—Arthur M. Schlesinger

How do you take apart a scientific problem and figure out how to present it so that non-scientists will understand it? Too many citizens now come to jury duty with the idea that science does most of the work:

> Many jurors may think that DNA will provide the answers for any crime that occurs. The police just collect the DNA from the scene and tell us who did it. If only it were that simple.[1]

Though scientific and technical information provides only part of what is necessary to represent a client's interests in a legal case, it is a very important part, requiring you to effectively teach the trier of fact about it.

The Steep Learning Curve

The learning curve for most lay people on scientific matters is steep. This includes you in the early stages of a case as you try to familiarize yourself with the forensic aspects. Veteran prosecutor Mark Larson's initial struggles with DNA are typical of what every litigator and trial lawyer goes through:

> DNA evidence has no real intuitive quality. I remember thinking to myself in the early days, "How do we explain this stuff?" Even after laying all of it out, an element remained mysterious to me.[2]

In addition to the associated burden of learning new information, there is a corresponding excitement from the intellectual challenge. Science- and technology-heavy cases require you to go beyond comfortable legal theories and stretch yourself. It is not an easy process. Just starting out, it is very hard and stressful to know how to ask all the right questions about the background science involved. It is not just a matter of reading up and doing the homework.

Use Your Experts as Teachers

Experts are a great resource. Your constant request to them should be, "Teach me." This approach will end up giving you everything you need to provide a well-rounded picture of the background science. Experts also give jurors that are on your side the tools and incentive to advocate for the result you want back in the jury room. The teaching they get from experts is an important part of all this:

> Representing plaintiffs in medical malpractice cases, I want the jury to conclude "Just like the experts said, Dr. Smith never should have missed this. They told us why too. Remember that thing they showed us? Remember that diagram one of the experts drew? It showed right there that this condition was visible, they should've seen it and taken action. They shouldn't have missed it."[3]

Spending time with your experts is necessary to a thorough understanding of what is going on. You need to check your fear, start reading the literature and reaching out to experts in the field:

> When I first started doing DNA cases as prosecutor, the crime lab put together a board for us with photos and explanations. Here is an item taken from the crime scene. This is how we take DNA samples from it. Here is what we do in the lab to test the samples.
>
> However, the board itself was much too complicated, full of graphs and grids at this end. It only really made sense to someone who had spent a few years working on DNA cases. And yet, this board became part of our office culture. Young prosecutors will ask me "Where is this board I've been hearing about?" Whenever this comes up, my reply is: "We have it, but you can't use it. You need to learn the science behind it."[4]

Learn the Science

In the first instance, recognize that the science is not beside the point. Don't just think, "I know the law, I can figure this out on my own." View the preparation of your case as an interdisciplinary problem. Any lawyer with a science and math background is going to have a leg up in this process. If you can't do it yourself, bring in those who have the necessary scientific and technical expertise. Colleges and universities are great resources in this effort.

Prepare a simple checklist of the scientific issues in the case, a baseline to use in building your proof. How do you engage in the same kind of critical analysis of science that we are taught to do in cases? Always ask yourself, "What are the underlying assumptions here?" This part of the analysis can get you part of the way there, particularly if any elements do not make sense or match up.

Evidence-Based Medicine

Evidence-based medicine has made a big difference in how experts are used in legal cases. Risk factors determine when a drug should be given or a medical procedure performed. Research informs best practices, which are turned into guidelines by professional groups. Experts educate the jury how these standards were developed and look at the surrounding clinical considerations, identifying the right approach to a problem: "If my doctor has followed these, I am likely to win, even with a bad patient outcome."[5]

Latent Injuries and Toxic Torts

Latent injuries and toxic torts are more difficult, as the critical issue of causation is expressed in terms of relative risks, with multiple elements totally or partially contributing to the outcome (e.g., worker gets lung cancer who was exposed to airborne asbestos fibers in the workplace and smoked cigarettes). With latent injuries, so much doubt can be created with alternate theories of causation. What can we expect science to prove? What is the threshold for declaring something a significant contributing factor? Do we need different causation standards to accommodate the difficulties of proof? Do we let all the relevant science come in and then let the judge or jury decide?

Keep It Simple

The effective presentation of expert testimony requires an understanding of how people learn best, the ability to simplify difficult concepts and an appreciation of the dynamics of a courtroom setting. The battle over the actual scientific and technological details is not what matters most.

Figure 20-1. Simple drawings can be very effective.

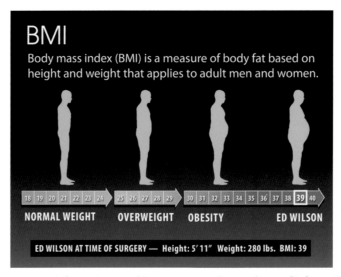

Figure 20-2. Information graphics can summarize a volume of information.

In the courtroom, the ability to explain science in a way that can be understood is at a premium. You always have to keep in mind that while the trier of fact is highly motivated to pay attention and reach the right outcome, he or she will not be able to understand the scientific or technical aspects like an expert.

Keeping it simple is the most persuasive form of advocacy. It is a mark of superior achievement for a lawyer to present complex matters of science and technology in a simple, understandable way. Too many lawyers cannot seem to reduce complexity to more understandable components: "There are three words in the front of the trial notebooks of every member of our firm, 'simplify, simplify, simplify.'" [6]

We now are in a place where most jurors understand the basic idea behind science that appears in trials in the news and popular culture. While foundation still is important, it should be done sparingly. It is far better to approach forensic evidence in a more summary fashion: "Here are the tests we ran and why. These are the kinds of things you can expect when you run these kinds of tests. These are the results we got. They were peer reviewed. Here is what they mean in terms of some kind of probability."

While science is complex, it can be communicated in a simple but persuasive way. Chief Criminal Deputy Mark Larson of the King County, Washington Prosecutor's Office explains their "stick to the basics" philosophy in presenting scientific evidence:

> In the beginning, many prosecutors felt the need to describe all the steps of DNA testing in detail. No longer. While we want our lawyers to know this stuff, we don't want to go overboard on the foundation, boring the jury so they lose the significance of the evidence. The peak for us comes with the basic question: "What is the probability of having the same genetic profile in the general population?" It's that last number that everyone is waiting for. We rarely even show visuals matching up the DNA bars anymore.[7]

Most prosecutors now treat DNA experts in the same way as fingerprint experts. Fingerprint testimony is fast, going from the basics to the specific findings. The same thing happens now with DNA testimony. "What is it?" "Where do you find it?" "What sort of testing is done on it?" All of that can be done in short order in the usual case, as most jurors are familiar with this through the mass media and popular culture. Even so, a reflexive attachment to detail remains among our peers. This is particularly true when it comes to using certain favorable scientific articles too often: "I have been told by jurors, 'I got tired of seeing that same article over and over again. You kept putting it up there. Enough is enough.'"[8]

The technicalities of any subject likely will bore most jurors. If you go on long enough, you will lose them entirely. Don't use big words or a technical term when everyday language will do. If it's a heart attack, don't say "myocardial infarction." If it's a vascular problem in the case, talk about plumbing. If it's a neurological problem, talk about electricity. Everyone can relate to this, having had a plumbing or electrical problem at one point or another.

Show and Tell

When an expert is using a chunk of an article or a textbook, it is helpful to the judge and the jury to put the portion being read up on the screen. The whole page is too much information and the jury's attention will wander. The expert must explain what this means in the context of the case. Why is this important? How long has this been known?

Start out with a board containing definitions of the technical terms important to the case. Stop your experts when these terms are used. Refer back to the board and have them interpret and explain so the jury is tracking with the testimony. "Okay, then this means ... ?" It also is important to repeat what you say in different ways, reinforcing the new information.

Active Listening: Stay Engaged and Ask Follow-Up Questions

Active listening is one of the most important things in presenting expert testimony. Pay close attention to what the expert is saying. Don't be looking down at your notepad for the next question. Resist the temptation to show off your superior knowledge of the expert's field. You need to be constantly translating and explaining the import of the testimony as the need arises. Otherwise, there is a real risk that some or all of what the expert is saying will go over the heads of the jury.

Every single time that expert uses language that is not within the everyday experience of the jurors, you must step in and get the expert to explain it. "Timeout. You just used a word that I am not sure I know the meaning of. Could you stop for a moment and explain it to us?" This must be done in a humble and self-effacing manner, rather than making a negative comment about the capacity of the jury to understand.

The Need to Track with Common Experience

In order to be seen as credible, the specialized knowledge of an expert has to track with common experience. It can't be too far out there, laden with jargon or esoteric terms. It has to make some basic sense. A counterintuitive forensic opinion will take a lot of explaining to sell, if at all. Effective experts understand this and shape their testimony accordingly:

> I realize that most jurors do not have any direct background in my field of expertise. I attempt to present my opinions in a way they can follow just on the basis of common sense. This also makes it difficult for the lawyers opposing me to attack.[9]

Using concrete examples is critical for translating scientific terms, stepping through them very simply, using experiences from everyday life that people can relate to. It's almost as if you're trying to explain the science to your child. You start at the beginning and don't make any logical leaps. "Everybody has fingerprints. Each is unique in certain ways and not in others."

> **Example:** A medical malpractice case involved an oral surgeon cutting a nerve rather than a blood vessel. Veins and nerves look different. The plaintiff's standard of care expert presented this simply. He reduced it to a simple equation, veins are blue and nerves are white. Before you cut, examine and identify as

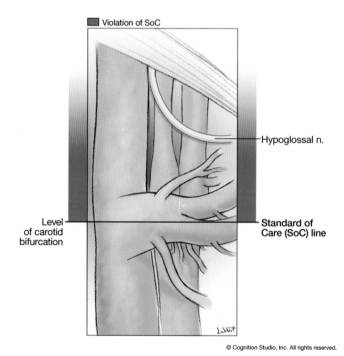

© Cognition Studio, Inc. All rights reserved.

Figure 20-3. Explaining the surgical standard of care.

to type, making sure which is which. The rule for oral surgeons is similar to the measure twice cut once rule for carpenters.

The defense tried hard to convey to the jury that it was not necessarily as easy as all that, "When you're inside a person's body, there's a lot of muck. Everything is coated with blood. It is hard to tell one from the other. You think you've identified it before you cut, but in fact you might be mistaken. These things happen."

But the plaintiff's interpretation prevailed, laid out simply and convincingly by a persuasive medical expert who did not appear to be an advocate. It also was well documented through the simultaneous use of visual aids.[10]

It is very helpful to use examples from the everyday experiences of the jurors. In a highway design case, expert information should track with juror experience as drivers. Even if some or all of the jurors do not have an understanding of the science involved from their everyday lives, simple examples can give them a practical grasp of what happened. Opinions have to be delivered in concrete terms too. This is not only for the nonmathematical members of the jury, but also to keep the expert on target.

For example, biomechanics quantifies the forces involved in motor vehicle collisions, using principles of momentum transfer from physics. This can be explained by an analogy to billiards, where a moving ball collides with a stationary one, transferring energy. In automobile collisions, cars of different weights do the same basic thing on the roadway. The same analogies to everyday life can be used to explain the G forces that act on the human body in a collision, such as comparing it to hitting the ground after jumping up.

The Side with the Best Teachers Often Wins

In part, experts help you win by being teachers, explaining why the jury should go in a particular direction. It's not about the opinion so much as it is the teaching. It's about giving the jury the tools to go back and say, "This side should win because of these reasons."

Judges and juries can react to experts differently. The best teacher wins with a judge. Sometimes for the jury, it's the best communicator. These are separate issues. The teacher has to be able to get through in a certain intellectual, educational and emotional level. But a communicator has the capacity to manipulate the audience like a salesman.

What makes a good teacher? First of all, they really have to know their stuff and explain it in a way that others can understand. There is certain air of confidence that infuses a good teacher's overall manner, inspiring confidence in the quality of the information they give us. Even though they know more than we do, they can't be arrogant. And if it's a medical expert, it has to be the kind of doctor that the jury members themselves would like to go to. "Dr. R. is so caring and competent. She really knows what she is doing."

Many experts teach in a university setting in their field. This background readily transfers to testifying in court, giving a keen appreciation of how to put the material

Figure 20-4. The teaching function of experts is critical to success.

across to an audience: "Having taught students for many years allows me to tell if jurors are tracking what I am saying from the witness stand. You can tell when they are nodding off, or looking quizzically, 'What the heck is he trying to tell me?'"[11]

You need to put up illustrations with the testimony so that it makes sense to the jurors. The best teachers show their students as they tell them: "As a teacher in the courtroom, drawing simple illustrations of the scientific principles I am testifying about makes my testimony more understandable."[12]

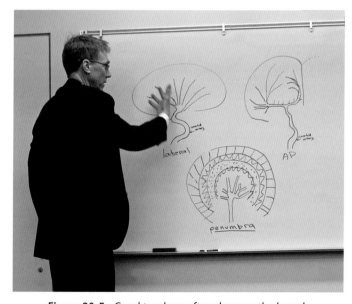

Figure 20-5. Good teachers often draw on the board.

Use of Visuals in Teaching

It is quite important to identify the visuals that will best help the expert educate the jury.

Ask your experts to visualize the jury as a class. When do we want to use a screen and what do we want to put on it? What are the best ways to explain the science involved in the case? Do we want to use a model here? Do we want to pass a physical object around to the jury during the testimony? If so, what, and where do we get it? Who will bring it to court?

Animations and flowcharts make medical processes more understandable to jurors. Animations once were incredibly expensive, but now you can often find them for free on YouTube.

Animations are increasingly used with medical expert testimony, making it more compact and vivid:

> **Example:** For fetal inflammatory response in birth injury cases, we have developed a very effective short animation explaining how this leads to brain damage. Very simple terms are used. This bypasses the need for an expert to get deep into the terminology, putting the jurors to sleep.[13]

Patient education videos are quite effective at explaining medical issues and can be adapted for use in the courtroom with expert testimony. Anatomic drawings are helpful too, but should not be too graphic or scary.

The use of PowerPoint was covered in Chapter 19. Slides usually aren't very dynamic. You can't edit them on the fly very easily. If time pressures develop, there is a tendency to start skipping slides, leading to a disjointed information flow. However, PowerPoint has distinct advantages in certain situations. For example, imaging studies often are hard for juries to follow. Graphics can make this much easier.

CT scans just show horizontal slices of a patient's anatomy from head to toe and are even harder to make sense of. It is not like an MRI, where the jury can readily

Figure 20-6. Good teachers make use of PowerPoint images.

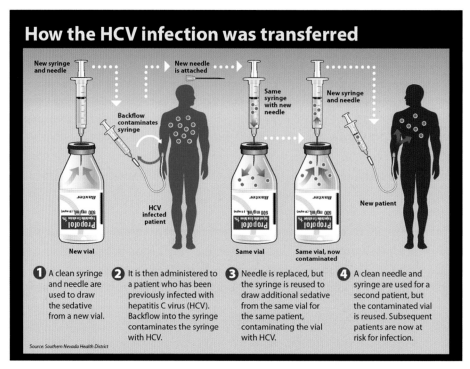

Figure 20-7. Information graphics summarize and show detailed science so that lay people can understand it.

identify what they are seeing: "Wow, that's the brain." But, unlike an MRI, a CT scan can visualize the points of bleeding inside the brain. The disadvantage is that no one slice is going to show all the bleeds because there are different levels, meaning it is three-dimensional. Consequently, the jury needs to be oriented where the images on the screen are located in the patient's body. "This is where the face would be, this is the back of the head." Graphics help judges and juries to understand what they are seeing.

> **Example:** A brain injury case involved a CT scan showing six different areas of bleeding in multiple levels. These could not be shown on any one image. Without a cumulative visual reference, the expert neuroradiologist's testimony would be confusing.
>
> To get around this problem, a short PowerPoint correlated individual images of the patient's brain with locations on a model of the head. The neuroradiology expert explained why the trauma led to this diffuse injury of the brain, showing multiple areas of bleeding on the CT. This showed the jury that the expert had objective evidence to back up his testimony.
>
> The actual CT image slice appeared on the screen and the expert used a model of the brain to help the jury locate and interpret what they were seeing. Then the CT images were colorized in red with arrows to better identify the areas of bleeding.[14]

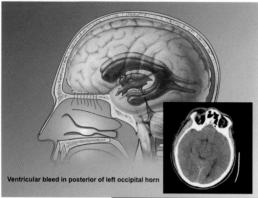

Ventricular bleed in posterior of left occipital horn

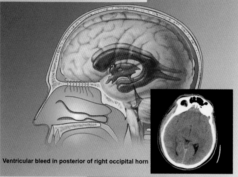

Ventricular bleed in posterior of right occipital horn

Figures 20-8(a)–(c). Graphics can help locate what part of the body is displayed in a series of CT scans and where abnormalities are.

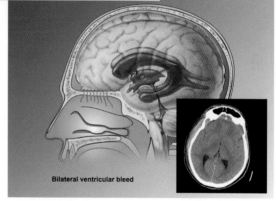

Bilateral ventricular bleed

Perceived Expertise

All the research shows the impact of perceived expertise. Does the expert carry herself with authority and knowledge? We know it when we see it. You always have to think about the personality of an expert and how they will translate into the courtroom setting. Strength of character is a huge thing.

One of the best medical experts I have ever had is an orthopedic surgeon and professor at our regional trauma center. If your pelvis is ever crushed, it is self-evident that this is the guy you want to put you back together. He's literally an artist too, able to do beautiful medical drawings.

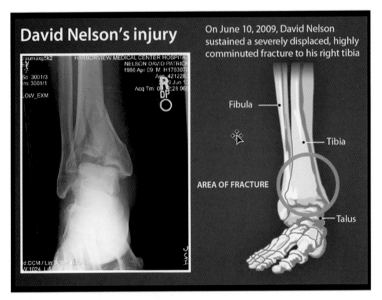

Figure 20-8(d). Graphics make imaging studies easier to understand.

As a trauma surgeon, it's just natural for him to take charge. He is a force of nature, a medical wizard with supreme mastery of his field. I had to figure out how his great self-confidence would play at trial. Was it going to help me or hurt me? Fortunately, he is not arrogant, despite all his accomplishments. This made all the difference.

He showed up in the courtroom to testify in my case just after finishing his rounds, still in his scrubs. He got up on the witness stand and became the center of attention in a very positive way. "Do you have the X-rays?" "Can someone dim the lights?"

I didn't have to do anything, other than sprinkle in some token questions, "Doctor, what are we seeing here?" This surgeon was simply magnificent and the jury loved him: "This wonderful doctor takes such good care of his patients. He really knows what he is doing." His opinions in the case were unassailable. It was beyond question that he knew what he was doing and the jury hung on his every word.[15]

Effective experts cover a wide range of styles. Some have bigger personalities than others. As the director of your case, it is important that you think carefully about the role that each expert will play:

Example: An expert I use regularly in medical malpractice cases has a bit of a "why you?" quality. He is a great communicator with a very solid resume, but it is his membership on a national standards committee in his medical specialty that makes him important to me. He audits hospitals for errors and bad outcomes, which gives him a national authority claim. When juries hear that he regularly reviews the adequacy of practices in hospitals, it clicks: "Now I get why you called this guy."[16]

Movement and Choreography

Just as in the classroom, movement can energize an expert's testimony and make it more compelling:

> I always evaluate the teaching ability of my experts. I try to get them off the witness stand, out of the chair, interacting with a model, chart or illustration. This relaxes the experts and makes them more dynamic, taking the testimony beyond a lecture, involving the jury in the learning process.[17]

Choreography is one of many roles a lawyer plays with expert witnesses. You need to know if your expert is a walker, a talker, a sitter or some combination. Questions must be asked about the expert's preferred presentation style. "Are you more comfortable sitting around the table?" "Do you like getting up and moving around?" "Or perhaps some combination of the two?" "What do you want to use as exhibits?" "How about some basic anatomical drawings?" "We had some illustrations made for this case, what do you think of these?" "Anything wrong with them?" "Would you change them in any way?" "How and why?" "What's wrong with them?" "Can this help you explain your opinions here?" "What else do you need?" Accomplished trial lawyers have the same sense of their experts that film directors do of actors, figuring out how to show their talents off to best advantage:

> **Example:** One expert surgeon I work with is highly effective, but does not want to get out of the witness chair. I've got to make sure that he has a laser pointer and foam core boards with anatomical diagrams. The laser allows him to interact with the board without getting up and pointing at it with his finger. He can teach just as effectively from his seat with a laser pointer.[18]

Sometimes this can include physical movement, which adds energy and engagement to testimony:

> One of the techniques I use as a teacher is to get physical, both in the classroom and in the courtroom. I literally will jump up and down in explaining things. "When I just landed, I generated 3 G's of force." Moving around definitely helps keep the audience awake.[19]

Figures 20-9(a) and (b). Movement makes experts more interesting. Figure out what choreography you will use with your expert.

Live Demonstrations in the Courtroom

While there is some risk of an unintended result, a live demonstration of a scientific principle in front of a jury can have a powerful impact. If well-conceived, this can cause all the jurors to reach the same conclusion as the expert:

> **Example:** Even though the bumper was not damaged, plaintiff argued that the steel frame of her car was bent in a collision. Defendant's expert went to the dealership and bought an identical piece of foam in the bumper. He brought

Figures 20-10(a)–(d). Live demonstrations from the witness stand can make your expert more interesting: a demonstration of simple black powder fingerprint technique is shown here.

it into the courtroom and whacked it on a steel beam, showing how applied force would damage it.[20]

Even though experts are, by definition, people of superior accomplishment, any display of arrogance is likely to be fatal to acceptance by the jury. Humility and a genuine desire to be helpful go a long way toward establishing credibility.

> I strongly dislike pontificating from the witness chair, saying to the jury, "I am the expert, you have to listen to me." I prefer a more relaxed teaching style, "Here's what the data looks like and the conclusions supported by it."[21]

Takeaways — Teaching Judges and Juries about Science and Technology

1. The learning curve for most lay people on scientific matters is steep.

2. Science- and technology-heavy cases require you to go beyond comfortable legal theories and stretch yourself.

3. Your constant request to experts should be, "Teach me."

4. Prepare a simple checklist of the scientific issues in the case, a baseline to use in building your proof.

5. Evidence-based medicine has made a big difference in how experts are used in legal cases.

6. The effective presentation of expert testimony requires an understanding of how people learn best, the ability to simplify difficult concepts and an appreciation of the dynamics of a courtroom setting.

7. In the courtroom, the ability to explain science in a way that can be understood is at a premium.

8. Keeping it simple is the most persuasive form of advocacy.

9. We now are in a place where most jurors understand the basic idea behind science that appears in popular culture, such as DNA in crime shows.

10. While science is complex, it can be communicated in a simple but persuasive way.

11. When an expert is using a chunk of an article or a textbook, it is helpful to the jury to put the portion being read up on the screen.

12. The technicalities of any subject likely will bore most jurors.

13. Don't use big words or a technical term when everyday language will do.

14. Start out by defining the terms that are important to an understanding of your case and refer back to these throughout the testimony.

15. Listen actively to what your experts are saying and stop them whenever they lapse into technical jargon, asking to explain the concept in lay terms.

16. Using concrete examples is critical to understanding scientific terms.

17. Experts help you win by being teachers, explaining to the jury why they should go in a particular direction.

18. The best teacher wins with a judge.

19. Sometimes for the jury, it's not necessarily the best teacher, but the best communicator.

20. Good teachers really know their stuff, are confident and explain things in a way that we can understand, both showing and telling us.

21. It is quite important to identify the visuals that will best help your experts educate the jury.

22. Animations, videos and flowcharts make medical processes more understandable to jurors.

23. PowerPoint can be effective, but the use of it needs to be limited and thought through carefully.

24. All the research shows the impact of perceived expertise. Does the expert carry herself with authority and knowledge?

25. As the director of your case, it is important that you think carefully about the role that each expert will play.

26. Choreography is one of many roles a lawyer plays with expert witnesses. You need to know if your expert is a walker, a talker, a sitter or some combination.

27. A live demonstration of a scientific principle in front of a jury can have a powerful impact.

28. Arrogance is usually fatal to any expert's acceptance by a jury.

Chapter 21

Deposing Experts

*I was bold in the pursuit of knowledge, never fearing to follow truth and reason
to whatever results they led, and bearding every authority that stood in their way.*
— Thomas Jefferson

A deposition is an important opportunity to find out information from opposing experts, testing assumptions and obtaining admissions. It is preserved as sworn testimony, admissible at trial.

Deposition Planning

The utility of a deposition greatly depends on advance preparation. Knowledge is power. The more you figure out in advance, the better your deposition will be. The time spent planning a deposition should be equal to or greater than that required for the cross-examination of a critical witness at trial. This invariably involves brainstorming with trusted colleagues on the best use of:

1. Legal theories.
2. Potential themes.
3. Key facts.
4. Case-related documents.
5. Written discovery responses.

One of the main goals of experts' depositions is to find out what they will vouch for as reliable. Under the Civil Rules, opposing counsel is required to provide a copy of their reports and anything they relied upon in reaching their opinions. Thereafter, serious research into all this foundation follows. Do any of these sources contradict the expert? They often do. If so, this should be explored at the deposition.

Strategy

It is a big part of expert deposition strategy to ask about the journals they read regularly and the books on their shelves. Often enough, there is contrary information in these sources. This sets you up nicely for asking questions at trial like, "Isn't it true that you told me at your deposition that this is a reliable journal that you read regularly?" "Absolutely." "Well, let me direct your attention to an article in this journal that is directly opposite to what you are saying in this case."

There is great potential for gathering useful information from opposing experts in a deposition. Most lawyers will take advantage of it, particularly if facing an expert for the first time. If you are going to cross-examine this person at trial, you need to size them up and get a feel for them. A deposition is the place to do that. Who is he/she? A usual suspect, bought and paid for by the other side? An advocate? Or a fundamentally reasonable person? The more mainstream the expert, the more likely you are to get some concessions in the deposition that support your case.

A deposition gives you the opportunity to demand everything the expert has and look it over carefully. Not infrequently, expert files will have damaging documents. Email exchanges with counsel can be unguarded and informal too, with impeachment potential. Sometimes you will find a gem that your whole cross-examination can be organized around.

> **Example:** In a traffic fatality case, an accident reconstruction expert had a pre-liminary calculation sheet in his file that was directly opposite to his testimony. He had to change his figures, throwing out the first set of calculations in order to get to the conclusion he wanted. The expert's own document basically proved the other side's case. This ended up having devastating consequences for the expert's credibility in the later trial.[1]

The Downside of Expert Depositions

There is a countervailing school of thought for only taking expert depositions sparingly, based on an analogy to the measurement effect. This is a scientific rule that says, in essence, you can't measure something without changing it. In conducting experts' depositions, you cannot gather information without simultaneously educating them, at least somewhat, on where you are going in the case. While it is taken to help you prepare for trial, a deposition also may help an opposing expert better prepare for and withstand your cross-examination at trial. For this reason, some lawyers prefer not to take expert's depositions, instead gathering information from other sources, such as lawyers who have encountered the same witness in another case, along with transcripts, reports and other potentially impeaching material. Opposing counsel often may not be aware of the full extent of what is out there regarding an expert.

You have to make a decision on how hard to go after an expert in a deposition. Do you hold your most devastating questions back for trial? This often is the smartest move, as otherwise your opponent will figure a way to repair the damage before trial. If you pull out all your big guns and hit an expert hard, causing them to crumble, the other side simply won't call this expert at trial, substituting another better prepared one in the lineup.

Example: In a breach of contract suit brought by a city against a professional sports team after the new owners sought to move the team out of town, the city called an economist to establish the monetary losses this would cause. Unknown to the lawyers for the city, this economist had issued a virtually identical report in another case, changing only the names and the figures. Opposing counsel knew this prior to taking the deposition of this economist, but elected not to reveal that he had the report prior to trial, preferring the element of surprise. This proved to be a brilliant strategy, as the heavy media coverage made much of the debacle, with the city's economist in ruins after the cross-examination. If this identical report had been inquired into at the deposition, the city likely would not have called the witness at trial.[2]

Why Take an Expert's Deposition?

- An opportunity to gather everything the expert relied upon in rendering opinions in the case.
- If you have not encountered the expert before, allows you to size them up as a person, getting a feel for their style and habits, assessing their jury appeal.
- Lock in details and pin them down, identifying the most promising areas for cross-examination at trial.
- Get admissions on the positive in your case that the expert will agree with.
- Test factual assumptions and legal theories.
- Cut through opposing counsel's filter.
- Foundation for motion practice.
- Create a video record which can potentially be devastating for the expert at trial if there are fundamental inconsistencies.

What to Do in a Deposition

- Ask lots of questions, using an open format until you get a hook, then close in, forcing specifics.
- Get a copy of everything the expert reviewed, as well as all emails exchanged with opposing counsel. These can contain potentially damaging information.
- Find out all articles, books and journals the expert regards as authoritative. Following the deposition, you will need to go through these looking for inconsistencies.
- Force witnesses to talk about things they don't want to.
- Focus on answers that fit your theory of the case.
- Listen very carefully to the answers as witnesses will often give you spontaneous gifts. Follow up on these vigorously.
- Test different approaches with a witness to see what works best.
- Have visuals that argue your theory of the case and put the witness on the spot.

The Value of Videotape Depositions

Videotape every expert deposition, taking the time prior to trial to carve out potential impeachment clips, using the transcript as a reference. You must review each clip to make sure it is as effective as the transcript makes it seem. Conversely, some questions and answers are more effective than they appear on the transcript because of body language or lengthy delays before the witness answers the question.

It is critically important to have these ready to show at trial. Index every deposition of opposing experts according to topic. Every cross-examination question you ask an expert in court should be correlated to a page and line reference from the deposition, allowing you always to lock the witness into what you want them to say. If they don't go there, you can show the deposition clip, allowing the jury to see the inconsistency for themselves.

Forgetting for a moment the content of what an expert has to say in a deposition, the visual appearance of the expert on a video also can be a huge factor. Often times, depositions are taken under informal circumstances. The best trial lawyers are excellent at cleaning up the appearance of their experts before bringing them into court. In some cases, it is almost a total makeover. If there is a noticeable contrast between the appearance at deposition and trial, that can cause the jury to doubt the credibility of both the expert and the lawyer who called them.

> **Example:** An opposing engineering expert was somewhat disheveled at his deposition, with an unkempt, bushy beard. The court reporter's conference room table also was too high, making him look a bit like a kid sitting at the adult's table. Though the expert was cleaned up for trial, his different appearance in the deposition video clips impeached his credibility when shown to the jury.[3]

Takeaways — Deposing Experts

1. A deposition is an important opportunity to find out information from opposing experts, testing assumptions and obtaining admissions, preserved as sworn testimony admissible at trial.

2. The utility of a deposition greatly depends on advance preparation.

3. The time spent planning a deposition should be equal to or greater than that required for the cross-examination of a critical witness at trial.

4. One of the main goals of a deposition of an expert is to find out what they will vouch for as reliable.

5. A deposition gives you the opportunity to demand everything the expert has considered and look it over carefully.

6. Not infrequently, experts will have damaging documents in their file, or in email exchanges with counsel. They may not even realize this.

7. There is a countervailing school of thought for only taking expert depositions sparingly, based on an analogy to the measurement effect. This is a scientific rule of thumb that you can't measure something without changing it.

8. Some lawyers prefer not to take expert's depositions, instead gathering information from other sources, such as lawyers who have encountered the same witness in other cases.

9. You have to make a decision on how hard to go after an expert in a deposition. Do you hold your most devastating questions back for trial? This often is the smartest move.

10. Videotape every expert deposition, taking the time prior to trial to carve out potential impeachment clips, using the transcript as a reference.

11. It is critically important to have these clips ready to show at trial.

12. Changes in the appearance of the expert between the deposition and trial can impeach credibility, particularly when it looks as if this is being used to manipulate the jury.

Chapter 22

Using the Literature

Science never solves a problem without creating ten more.
—George Bernard Shaw

In cases with scientific or technical issues, spending considerable time, energy and resources on the relevant peer-review literature is inevitable. Any time an expert identifies a textbook or certain articles as being authoritative, you have to read, absorb and figure out how best to use this information. While this often is stimulating, it also can be overwhelming.

Print Alone Does Not Make It True

Just because something makes it into print doesn't make it true. A prime example of this is the shocking 2012 revelation that, when carefully scrutinized, only 6 of 53 landmark cancer studies in the literature (11%) had reproducible data.[1] Subsequent researchers merely assumed the truth of the basic findings in these studies. The authors concluded:

> The scientific community assumes that.... the main message of [a] paper can be relied on and the data will, for the most part, stand the test of time. Un-

Figure 22-1. Cases often involve a large amount of scientific information.

fortunately this is not always the case.... This [lack of reproducibility] was a shocking result.[2]

Publishing generally is a profitable enterprise and scientific and technical journals seek to capitalize on this opportunity. As a result, almost anything can see print, whether it truly is good or not. The results of a particular study may not be replicated and it may just sit there, inert, not attracting much attention. However, the fact that it exists in the literature means that it can be cited as authoritative in a legal case.

Where research gets published is very important. What is the reputation of the journal? How many other people have published on this subject? Have these results been replicated? The peer-review system is particularly good at scrutinizing research that gets published in top journals, such as *Science* or *Nature*. Anything that appears in these is likely to be quite good. In terms of science, if something appears in a textbook, that means it has been known for at least a decade before the book was published. Textbooks are the last places that new information shows up.

Indicia of Reliability

Analyzing the relative positioning of the scientific literature used in a case is a rational way for a judge to assess the strength of each side's arguments. What journal is this in? Has the data been verified by others in the field? Are these results cited often? Is it backed up by research? The alternative would be to do a crude quantitative analysis, doing a headcount of the articles for one position or the other. Has an expert written peer-review articles on the precise topic at issue in the case? This can give you a leg up to get an expert who is recognized as knowledgeable in his/her field. All other things being equal, an expert whose work has appeared in peer-review journals is superior to one who merely knows what is going on in the field, but has not published.

A careful study of the articles written by any particular expert may reveal a certain amount of resume padding. Are these review articles or independent research? Review articles basically collate other studies, take their data and add it all together. This is more like a book review then writing the book itself. It is like taking a group of books and summarizing the common conclusions, "This is what all these guys are saying. Here is what we can learn from combining all the data."

The Pluses and Minuses of Using Scientific Literature

While textbook sections and journal articles generally can be helpful, inevitably these lead to unproductive battles between counsel on which authorities are better. Often all this does is just show the judge or jury that there are two sides to this coin. This is not good if your side has the burden of proof. The only way this makes sense then is if the great weight of authority is on your side, like the burning of fossil fuel as a cause of global warming.

Medical literature should only be used when it is crisp and clean. There is a big danger that it will confuse the jury. How much information is enough? You don't want to overdo it. If you have a study that is right on point, spend some time on it. But research typically is not black and white, written in an academic style that is not particularly crisp. Most academic books are sufficiently esoteric that your points will tend to get lost in the nebulous language. Academics want to give with one hand and take away with the other. There are two sides to everything. It can be very difficult to find sufficiently clear statements without a nearby point going the other way. That isn't going to work if you are looking for impeachment material. You've got to read the book enough yourself to find clear sound bites that help your case, making sure that there isn't another one going the other way.

There are many peer review journals and textbooks to choose from on almost any subject that comes up. You also have to make sure that you have sufficient authoritative sources so that you can't be accused of picking and choosing. You must avoid the one school of thought versus another. Make sure you know which school of thought you are dealing with. There is a tendency to use the articles you like too much in the examination and cross-examination. Jurors get tired of seeing the same articles over and over again. Enough is enough.

Overall, the use of learned treatises in the courtroom is a mixed bag, with considerable downside potential. Trial judges often advise restraint in this area: "There is some risk in putting learned treatises before jurors. They may not process some or all of it due to the technical nature. Secondarily, they may be bored to death by it."[3]

In measured doses, learned treatises can be effective against opposing experts, providing ammunition for a substantive attack. If you have a treatise written by somebody at Harvard, then it is not you crossing the witness, but this author at Harvard, as well as the editors at the *New England Journal of Medicine* who published it.

The Challenges of Using Literature Effectively in Cross

Blowing up a page from a treatise with callouts of the language you like can have a real impact on the jury, particularly a sentence going to the core of the dispute in the case. However, pulling this off requires both economy and precision. "You are familiar with the *New England Journal of Medicine*? Are you aware of this article which appeared in it? I would like to read you this sentence." If an article is in language which the jury can understand and directly contrary to what the expert said on direct, it is powerful impeachment. If the witness has to scramble to explain away the inconsistencies and looks evasive, the cross-examiner really scores points in the exchange.

Lawyers who try to use literature that is not crisp and clean in cross-examination quickly get into trouble, particularly if the expert knows it well. This often is the expert's cue to give lengthy speeches of interpretation, which you have to stand and listen to, doing the slow burn. You also have to be careful not to fall into the accusation that you have taken things out of context. An expert will not passively read the section you want and ignore the rest of the document. The whole article will be brought into this discussion, with lengthy speeches and loss of control over the expert.

EXCERPT FROM *ACCIDENT RECONSTRUCTION PRINCIPLES*
by Louis R. Charles

Page 75: Perception-response time begins when an object or condition for concern enters the driver's visual field, and concludes when the driver develops a conscious awareness that something is present.

This is an area where experts frequently move to the extreme corners of the range to prove their point and support their opinion.

point and support their opinion. The reaction times under normal conditions in accident avoidance braking maneuvers range from 1 second to 1.5 seconds.

Given a reasonably clear stimulus and a straightforward situation, there are good data indicating that most drivers, i.e., 85–95 percent, will respond by about 1.5 seconds after first appearance of the object or condition of concern.

The evidence also indicates that the minimum perception-response time for this straightforward situation is about .75 seconds. Thus, the probable range of perception-response times for reasonably straightforward situations should be .75 to about 1.5 seconds. Please note these values are not chiseled in stone on tablets along with other commandments.

Figure 22-2(a). Simple visuals emphasizing critical information are effective.

Figure 22-2(b). Combine learned treatises and critical case facts.

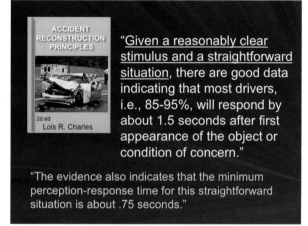

Even if you avoid the speeches, using literature with an expert runs the risk of winning the battle and losing the war. A series of quotes from the literature gets into too many details, losing the jurors. This also slows down the pace of cross, diluting the drama. You must come up with an advance strategy to speed up the process, having what you need right at your fingertips, easy to refer back to. The helpful quotes need to be extracted from the book and preserved, ready to use in a way that allows the jury to follow along.

Takeaways — Using the Literature

1. In cases based on scientific or technical information, it is almost impossible to avoid going to the peer-review literature to help prove your case.

2. There is a large volume of scientific journals and the quality of the articles in the literature can be variable.

3. The peer-review system is particularly good at scrutinizing research that gets published in top journals. Anything that appears in these is likely to be quite good.

4. Look for experts who have written on the precise topic at issue in the case.

5. All things being equal, an expert whose work has been published in peer-review journals is superior to one who merely knows what is going on in the field, but has not published.

6. While textbook sections and journal articles generally can be helpful, inevitably these lead to unproductive battles between counsel on which authorities are better.

7. The only way that using the literature makes sense is if the great weight of authority is on your side.

8. Medical literature should only be used when it is crisp and clean. There is a big danger that it will confuse the jury.

9. Most academic books are esoteric and points tend to get lost in the nebulous language. Academics want to give with one hand and take away with the other. There are two sides to everything.

10. In measured doses, learned treatises can be an effective tool in the battle against opposing experts, providing a basis for substantive attack.

11. Blowing up a page from a treatise with call outs of the language you like can have a real impact on the jury, but this must be done with precision and economy.

12. Lawyers who try to use literature in cross-examination that is not crisp and clean quickly get into trouble, particularly if the expert knows it well.

Chapter 23

Law and Medicine

Medicine is a science of uncertainty and an art of probability.
—Sir William Osler

Doctors and attorneys are alike in many ways. Members of both professions are highly educated, intelligent and articulate, seeing themselves as strong individual advocates. Doctors are trained to focus on what is best for their patients, which has a powerful and lasting effect. Lawyers do much the same thing for their clients, though with a different kind of advocacy.

Unlike law, however, medicine is not a collection of rules. Medical textbooks do not contain lists of rules, as the focus is on the complexities. Medicine is an art and a science, both subjective and objective. Rarely black and white, simple rules often do not provide a complete explanation for what happens in medicine. Doctors must pay careful attention to the larger clinical picture unfolding in front of them, as some cases don't fit narrow rules.

It often is difficult for medical experts to be definitive in the manner demanded by the legal system due to the difference of approach between the two disciplines. Issues are much more shades of gray in the real world of medicine, as opposed to the more black and white legal context. The standard of practice can vary from one area of medicine to another, further complicating matters.

Culture Conflict between Law and Medicine

The culture conflict and dynamic tension between medicine and law goes far beyond the differences that exist between science and law. In medicine, doctors presume innocence and truth. If a patient tells a physician something, it is presumed true until the medical evidence shows otherwise. In law, it often is the reverse. Lawyers are trained to be skeptics, challenging the truth of what others say.

A big difference between doctors and lawyers is that doctors never get challenged. Most doctors spend their days in patient care, doing examinations, reviewing or conducting test results, examining imaging studies. They discuss patients with colleagues and give orders to nursing and technical staff, all of which are accepted and followed without question.

When a staff member is instructed by a doctor to do something, they don't ask why, they just do it. Doctors speak confidentially with patients, nursing staff and other doctors, document events on the patient's chart, based solely on how they perceive them. None of this has to be cleared through anybody else. The courtroom environment is the exact opposite, where nearly everything a doctor says is cross-examined and challenged.[1]

Disagreements do occur between doctors in the same area of practice on the right approach to patient care. It also is not uncommon to have different opinions between practitioners in one specialty and another. These discussions certainly can be adversarial, but more in an educational, scientific sort of way: "Why do you think about that? What is the evidence for that?" There is a certain matching of wits, but overall, it has a much more altruistic focus on what is the best for the patient:

Nobody has any ulterior motive, there is nothing to win or lose, nobody is trying to win any money. Doctors in the medical setting are interested in learning the truth in a very pure way. How can we help this patient with a serious medical problem?[2]

The daily life of lawyers is directly opposite to physicians on the adversarial dimension. Lawyers get challenged all the time by clients, opposing counsel, partners, judges, and juries. While lawyers accept this kind of pushback as part of the job, doctors don't. Medical professionals ordinarily are highly esteemed for their pivotal role in preserving life and health. When lawyers second-guess medical opinions in legal cases, challenging anything that is subjective, doctors bristle with resentment:

A big part of the career satisfaction of being a doctor is the respect medicine gets from all members of our society. However, this is largely absent in the courtroom environment.[3]

In the back of the doctors' minds, lawyers are the one profession that can trump the respect they otherwise get, including the ultimate disrespect of bringing a malpractice

Figure 23-1. There is a culture conflict between law and medicine.

lawsuit against them. No other profession has this much potential power over doctors. This helps to explain the bad feeling in medicine toward attorneys:

> Everybody makes mistakes and the fear of being sued among doctors is huge. It's pretty much a given that, at some point, this will happen.[4]

Being sued is an extraordinarily traumatic event for the doctors who have been through a malpractice lawsuit. While they may not say bad things about their former patient for bringing a case against them, they most certainly will about the patient's attorney. Just as every family has a story about health care, so does every physician about being sued, the medical equivalent of urban folk legends.

The scrutiny of the legal system tends to shine a light on problems in medical care, which creates a fundamental antagonism between the two professions. It has been shown through multiple studies that health-care providers make mistakes with some frequency. In 1999, the widely publicized Institute of Medicine report, *To Err Is Human,*[5] estimated that mistakes in hospitals resulted in up to 98,000 patient deaths per year. This figure went up dramatically in 2010 when the Office of Inspector General for the Department of Health and Human Services attributed 180,000 deaths of Medicare patients alone to deficient hospital care.[6] In 2013, the Journal of Patient Safety estimated that between 210,000 and 440,000 patients each year suffered harm in a hospital setting that contributed to their death.[7]

Medical Reaction to Lawyer Questions

Doctors called to testify in a legal case often resent the lack of medical context of the attorneys. Lacking experience with patient care, lawyers are seen as a dangerous combination of knowledge and no wisdom:

> Though he's been reading nonstop about a medical issue for months, an attorney doesn't really have a clue. That's what makes them so dangerous. They're smart, aggressive and knowledgeable, but with no real clinical sense.[8]

The verbatim transcript of legal proceedings is unnerving to physicians, with every mistake they might make preserved forever on the record:

> Testifying in a legal case is such a scary, foreign environment for most doctors, particularly since we don't do it often. It's all so exposed and public, very different from the privacy of a medical setting.[9]

It is very uncomfortable for a physician to be on the witness stand with every word scrutinized, open to challenge in a public forum:

> All our training emphasizes being a problem solver. The last thing any doctor wants to do is point an accusing finger at somebody else and say, "Why did this happen, how come this, how come that?" We focus on solving and fixing our patients' medical problems.[10]

The Emotion of Being Cross-Examined

Cross-examination is designed to create doubt, using skepticism. It reflects the passionate, adversarial component of the law. This is very different from medicine, an emotional flashpoint for doctors. The legal process also forces doctors to take sides, which makes most of them very uncomfortable, as do questions about fees, accusations and personal attacks.

While nobody likes to be attacked on cross-examination, doctors take particular offense, given the extreme deference they normally get. Questions from lawyers are very different from when patients ask them, "Why did I get this condition? Why are you doing this procedure?" While patients ask questions reflecting their need for information on matters of great personal importance, this is not generally adversarial. Not so with lawyers' questions, which can sting, insinuate and accuse.

Being cross-examined by lawyers is an emotionally charged experience for doctors. They often see it as a battle in which they are attacked without regard to the truth. In malpractice cases, this becomes even more personal. Medical experts for the defense often are there not only to give their opinions, but also to defend their own. In other matters, such as insurance company examinations in personal injury cases, defense medical experts are more focused on the money. However, even there, antagonism between doctors and lawyers remains a background element.

Doctors who have gone through testifying in court quickly pick up on the rules of engagement:

1. Even though lawyers may act like they don't know much, they really do.
2. Opposing lawyers want to make you look bad, so expect a barrage of difficult questions.
3. Do not take things personally.
4. Be smooth and composed in your manner.
5. Be as clear and careful as you can.
6. Read transcripts, understanding how attorneys ask questions and how your answers will look in transcript form.

Differences in Medical and Legal Standards of Proof

There is a basic difference between the way doctors and lawyers approach causation. Most of what doctors do in making a diagnosis is to try and identify the cause of a patient's illness, followed by appropriate treatment. The legal standard of proof is largely irrelevant to this, as are the questions lawyers typically ask. The "more probable than not" legal causation standard strikes most doctors as a foreign concept that has no role in science:

My own experts will say, "I'm just not certain that this is true." I respond, "Well you need to understand, doctor, that we lawyers live in a different world. We are not scientists and use a vaguer standard."[11]

Lawyers always want physicians to reduce things to probabilities, breaking down the fault for what happened into pieces, 70% here and 25% there. Doctors usually don't deal with these kind of numbers in patient care. On the defense side of civil cases, trial counsel subtly hold up the medical standard of proof as more solid than the legal one of more probable than not:

> The legal standard of more probable than not is not worth anything scientifically and has no relevance in medicine. As defense counsel, I point up to the jury how the plaintiffs are relying upon the laxness of the more probable than not standard, saying "if we get to 51%, we win. It is more probable than not."[12]

Changing Attitudes toward Information Sharing

The greater openness and sharing of information with the patient has caused increased tension between law and medicine. Traditionally, physicians were reluctant to tell patients anything beyond basic diagnosis and treatment. "Here is your diagnosis, this is what you should do," end of discussion. Often times, patients would not even know what their symptoms meant. Professional separateness and superiority of medicine was reinforced by the use of Latin when giving instructions to a pharmacist or to another colleague.

The whole patient model now has changed to a partnership concept, building good relationships with patients through open communication. Under the old system, if the doctors made a mistake, the patient had no idea what had gone wrong or why. Under current practice standards, mistakes are to be disclosed to the patient. Younger doctors generally are able to accept this. Older colleagues are aghast, "Are you kidding? Do what?"

This new ethic of full disclosure feeds right into the fear of being sued and the whole idea of defensive medicine. The latter is a term doctors use for the idea of doing more than they should in order to avoid being sued. Defensive medicine is the straw man that often is brought up as a reference point for the gut fear of lawyers and the legal process.

Difficulty of Testifying against Colleagues

Doctors who testify for plaintiffs in medical malpractice cases open themselves to the accusation of being "traitors to their class." Criticizing a colleague in a public way is much more uncomfortable than being an expert for the defense:

> Defense medical expert work actually is relatively easy, saying good things about colleagues. It's tougher to say bad things about them on the plaintiff's side. I realize that the defendant physician is somebody like me. I've made mistakes too. Going after somebody's professional judgment and career in open court is tough. We usually do it in the privacy of the peer review process.[13]

Evidence-Based Medicine

The change to evidence-based medicine is important. Traditional medicine was very dependent on where doctors trained. By a process of consensus, the senior clinicians got together and came up with what they thought were the best practices. Medicine relied heavily on individual clinical judgment, which may or may not have had a valid scientific basis:

> When I trained, the head of a department would literally write down, "Here is what I expect you to do in specific cases. This is what the best practice is." That was top down management, using top down guidelines. Anybody that deviated from the department chair's guidelines would be in big trouble.[14]

While there may have been a very strong belief among doctors that something works, the evidence may show otherwise. Common medical procedures, done with the best of intentions, turned out either not to help or actually harm patients. The top down consensus method steadily has been replaced by evidence-based medicine. The body of scientific research now shapes the standards of evidence in a very structured manner.

One of the questions always asked now is, "Does the evidence actually provide a foundation for this or is it all based on expert opinion?" Expert judgment alone has proved to be shaky ground. Many specialty groups now issue guidelines for the best clinical practices in their respective areas. Part of the challenge is to retain some flexibility in how these guidelines are applied. For example, what may work for a 35-year-old may be very different for an 80-year-old.

Some things are absolute medical fact. Others have been shown by new evidence to be completely unfounded. One example of the latter is the past practice of prescribing estrogens to post-menopausal women. There was a time when this was universally believed to be a good practice. But the medical evidence of adverse patient outcomes proved otherwise and this practice now has been completely reversed. More recently, after following a group of 90,000 women for 25 years, researchers in Canada discovered that women who received yearly mammograms did not have improved survival statistics for breast cancer. One of the recurrent problems from what has been accepted as good medical screening practices is overdiagnosis and overtreatment.[15]

There are better medical standards now, backed up by more evidence. In most of the high-profile areas of medicine, like management of chest pain and screening for certain kinds of cancer, there are good standards for physicians to refer to. In some sense, a testifying physician has become an interpreter of these evidence-based standards, which provide a comfortable foundation and greater definition.

Changes in Expert Testimony with Evidence-Based Medicine

Evidence-based medicine has made a big difference in how lawyers use experts in cases. For example, if the use of antibiotics is at issue in a case, lawyers have to look at the clinical considerations surrounding this. Risk factors determine when a drug should be given or a medical procedure performed. Research informs best practices, which are turned into guidelines by professional groups. Experts must inform the jury of the right approach to a problem, based on how these standards were developed.

Lawyers defending malpractice cases adopt the medical model in presenting expert opinions, as the scientific standard of proof is more stringent than the legal one. The defense tells the doctor's story from a very basic perspective:

> Why did you want to be a doctor? How hard was it to get into medical school? How do you learn your specialty after graduation? How did you get into your residency? How competitive was it? Describe your on-the-job training.[16]

The medical chart is critical in any medical malpractice case. What was known at the time becomes the basis of any liability argument or defense. The jury sees and hears from the doctor, who addresses questions like: "What clinical factors did you consider? Was this an emergency? Should something have been done immediately?" An important part of the defense story is to describe the character of the care, presenting the doctor as detail-oriented and conscientious, ordering tests and making reasonable judgments.

Takeaways — Law and Medicine

1. Unlike law, medicine is not a collection of rules.

2. Medicine is an art and a science, both subjective and objective. Simple rules often do not provide a complete explanation for what happens.

3. Medical malpractice cases are an emotionally charged topic among doctors, significantly coloring their view of the legal system.

4. Medical professionals ordinarily are highly esteemed for their pivotal role in preserving life and health, given great deference. Lawyers are the one group that can trump this, with the power to aggressively confront doctors.

5. Lawyers get challenged frequently in their work, while doctors do not. This difference plays an important role in the animosity that exists between the two professions.

6. In medicine, doctors presume innocence and truth. If a patient tells a physician something, it is presumed true until the medical evidence shows otherwise. In law, it often is the reverse.

7. Disagreements do occur between doctors on the right approach to patient care.

8. Being cross-examined by lawyers generates much background emotion, as doctors see it as a battle in which they are attacked without regard to the truth or the proper clinical context.

9. The standard of proof in law often is irrelevant in medicine. There is a basic difference between the way doctors and lawyers approach causation.

10. Doctors take the more precise and data-driven approach of science.

11. Lawyers always want physicians to reduce things to probabilities, breaking down the fault for what happened into pieces, 70% here, 20% there and 5% there. Doctors never have to deal with those kind of numbers or causation analyses in most patient-care scenarios.

12. Under the traditional approach, physicians were reluctant to tell patients anything beyond the diagnosis and prescribed treatment.

13. Under the old system, if the doctors made a mistake, the patient had no idea what had gone wrong or why.

14. Under current practice standards, mistakes are to be disclosed to the patient.

15. This new ethic of full disclosure feeds right into the fear of being sued and the whole idea of defensive medicine.

16. Doctors who testify for plaintiffs in medical malpractice cases open themselves to the accusation of being "traitors to their class."

17. Traditional medicine was very dependent on where doctors trained. By a process of consensus, the oldest doctors got together and came up with what they thought were the best clinical practices. Medicine relied heavily on individual clinical judgment, which may or may not have had a valid scientific basis.

18. While there may have been a very strong belief among doctors that something works, often the evidence will show that it doesn't.

19. One of the questions always asked now is, "Does the evidence actually provide a foundation for this or is it all based on expert opinion?" Expert judgment alone has proved to be shaky ground.

20. There are more and better medical standards now than before, backed up by more evidence.

21. A testifying physician has become an interpreter of these evidence-based standards.

22. Evidence-based medicine has made a big difference in how lawyers use experts in cases.

23. Lawyers defending malpractice cases adopt the medical model in presenting expert opinions, as the scientific standard of proof is more stringent than the legal one.

Chapter 24

Using Data, Statistics and Probability

There are three kinds of lies: lies, damned lies, and statistics.
—Benjamin Disraeli

Understanding the basic science and technology behind expert opinions requires you to know some math, not only for building your case, but also for taking on your opponent's. While your experts will handle most of this, you cannot completely abdicate numerical responsibility if you want to be an effective advocate.

The Critical Role of Math in Science

Math allows the translation of research findings into scientific explanations and predictions about the future. This not only is an important part of what scientists do, but simultaneously serves the law's intent to protect society and promote stability. Math also is definitional and can shape legal critical thinking about the meaning of words with mathematical implications. What does "more likely than not" mean quantitatively? Is it the same as "preponderance of the evidence"?

Figure 24-1. Lawyers must be number crunchers too.

The development of mathematics goes back to the beginning of Western civilization with the ancient Greeks. The foundation on which both algebra and geometry rest has proved durable across time and culture:

> [The] Pythagorean theorem … means the same thing to everyone today as it meant 2,500 years ago, and will mean the same thing to everyone a thousand years from now—no matter what advances occur in technology or what new evidence emerges. Mathematical knowledge is unlike any other knowledge. Its truths are objective, necessary and timeless.[1]

Euclid's *Elements* from 300 B.C. shares many similarities with Sir Isaac Newton's revolutionary 1687 work *Principia Mathematica*. Most scientists believe that if Euclid was called from the grave and shown the evolution of geometry since his time, he would not be at a complete loss.

The Challenges Math Presents to Lawyers

Mathematical ability is on a spectrum. To understand statistics and statistical inference, you have to be fairly high up on the bell curve. Even within the sciences, math is tricky. Professor Michael Townsend of the University of Washington compares the challenges of hitting a baseball to teaching lawyers about numbers:

> When a pitcher throws a ball at 92 mph, it is the batter's job to hit it. We can see it happen and visualize it. We can probably even imagine ourselves doing it. It's a very simple concept, hitting a ball being thrown at you with a stick. But even though this is easy to conceptualize, it is hard to accomplish. You need a certain set of physical skills to be able to do it. It's the same with science, especially science that depends on math to establish validity. This is not to say no one can do it, but it's not easy.[2]

Lawyers in business and finance-related areas seem to understand the basic mathematics involved well enough, and are able to handle concepts like present value. In trust and estate matters, we can do simple fractions, per capita and per stirpes. Truly understanding the math behind expert opinions requires both time and aptitude. However, many of us do not readily grasp either statistical evidence or how to make effective arguments around it. For example, few in the general population understand the question, "How many parts per million of a toxic substance should be permitted in our water supply?" We sidestep this problem by declaring a general policy in favor of clean air and water, assigning the technical details to specialized agencies such as the EPA.

There is a basic difference between the degrees of precision required in math and in law. Math problems usually have a right and wrong answer. Students know there is supposed to be one answer and develop some intuition when they don't know how to get it. Legal analysis is filled with shades of gray. In a law exam, virtually anything you write will get you some points.

Math Is Hard

Both math and science go to the weak side of a lawyer's education, training and aptitude. Most of us can think back to that time in school when the math suddenly got tougher. We struggled to have the same sense of mastery as we did with words, limping through the required college prep math and science courses, relying on tutors and SAT prep classes to squeak by. Largely free of science and math, the law seemed much better adapted to our success. Once safely in college, we looked for the easiest way to satisfy our science or math group requirements, making diligent inquiry of what athletes took, "rocks for jocks" type classes. Under the principle of use it or lose it, whatever understanding we had of science or math quickly faded.

The adversary system is not really the problem here. Math and science are intrinsically hard, with some areas more difficult than others. This difficulty is compounded by the debates about the validity of statistical methods. Even medical doctors and social scientists have trouble with statistics. It is not just a matter of coming to the conclusion, was this done correctly? People argue about how to handle missing data. These are highly technical arguments. As a mathematician, Professor Townsend is skeptical of the capacity of most lawyers to understand technical information:

> Most of us do not have the training or aptitude to make an independent assessment of the validity of science or numbers. We just throw facts out there and hope that the judge or jury does the right things with them.[3]

Statistics Are the Basis for Proving Causal Relationships

In looking at data for patterns and causal relationships, the possible has to be separated from the probable. Statistics and probability terms are used when something is not absolutely certain, but more than a chance occurrence. The study of probabilities came out of the gambling dens of 17th-century France, trying to identify successful betting strategies. The initial focus was on dice and what number might be more likely to come up on a particular roll.

The analysis was simple enough for any non-mathematician to grasp. Each die has six sides, containing numbers 1 through 6. There are six potential outcomes from a single roll. The chances of getting any of the six numbers are the same, 1/6, or 16 2/3%. The second throw has no relationship to the first. Flipping a coin is even easier to understand, as there are only two possible outcomes, heads or tails. While most of us have a hunch, based on prior flips, the odds of getting one outcome or the other remains unchanged at 50%. Whether it is dice or a coin, the probability of an independent event does not depend on what happened in the past, remaining the same.

There are games of chance, such as blackjack, where the outcome depends on what already has happened. For a time, wily mathematicians with sporting blood figured out card-counting strategies to inform betting decisions (promptly defeated by casinos adding multiple decks). Deciding whether to stand pat or take another card depended on what cards had been dealt in prior hands. If only one ace had been seen prior, the chances of drawing one of the other three improves with each round.

The probability from dice rolls and coin flips is based on a very simple formula. To calculate the odds of the outcome you want, you put the total number of outcomes in the denominator (e.g., 6 for a die and 2 for a coin) and the number of ways you can win in the numerator (e.g., 1 for either rolling a die or flipping a coin), turning it into a percentage.

The Applications of Mathematical Probability

The basic ideas of probability can be applied to many situations, including forensics. It often comes into public discussions, such as the risks from one form of travel versus another or the dangers of something like nuclear power. Engineers use the fault-tree analysis method to try to identify all the ways that something bad might happen and then figure out the probability of each.

The potential gain from any decision is offset by the risk, which is the probability something bad will happen multiplied by the probable loss if it does. This is how insurance companies calculate premiums for casualty losses, determining the probability of a house fire or car crash, multiplying this against the likely cost associated with such an event.

Any one of us may not have an adverse casualty loss. Risk focuses on the average across a specific population. Statisticians assume that individual events are random and unpredictable, even if the average risk can be calculated. Averages can be fine tuned within specific categories of individuals. Most auto insurers differentiate between males and females, as well as age categories. Young adult males are at a higher risk to get into an auto accident and carry higher rates. Good students are safer drivers overall than indifferent or bad ones, getting a discount on their premiums.

Predictions through 20/20 Hindsight

A recurrent problem with the use of statistics and probability is 20/20 hindsight, where a causal relationship is advanced after an event has occurred. While the prediction would have been most unlikely prior to the event, it somehow becomes plausible in the light of what happened. A classic example of this is a story widely circulated in the press after the assassination of John F. Kennedy in 1963. A series of parallels were drawn between President Kennedy's circumstances and that of Abraham Lincoln a century earlier. These included the following:

1. Lincoln was elected in 1860 and Kennedy in 1960.

2. Both were shot on a Friday in the presence of their wives.

3. Lincoln was shot in Ford's Theater and Kennedy in a Ford Lincoln Continental.

4. The vice presidents of both had the last name of Johnson, each a Southern Democrat.

5. Andrew Johnson was born in 1808 and Lyndon Johnson in 1908.

The critical difference here is the timing. If any of us sit down and think about it, we always can identify points of similarity between two persons or situations. But science seeks to identify valid causational relationships and make predictions in advance. That is why, even though the parallels between the Lincoln and Kennedy assassinations may provide some morbid fascination, they have no scientific use or validity. The same may occur in the opinions of forensic experts in legal cases.

The Ultimate Forensic Use of Statistics: DNA Testimony

The peak for the prosecution in presenting the direct testimony of a DNA forensic expert is the final probability statistic. No matter what form it takes, the basic question is, "What is the probability of having the same genetic profile in the general population?" It's that last number that everyone is waiting for, the probability statistic everybody can understand. The ability of an expert to come in and say, "The probability is 1 in 10 million that this came from somebody other than the defendant," requires a scientific rigor beyond that in other kinds of forensic evidence. This is where the DNA testimony really leads up to. It is very tough for any nonscientist to argue convincingly against this probability statistic. At this point, it largely is a target that has gone by, as the probabilities have gotten bigger and the percentages of error have gotten smaller.

Some of the scientific techniques in criminal cases offer larger, more robust numbers than others. It all depends on the other evidence available in the case. There are cases where a number like 1 in 100 will be adequate, because of the other evidence. If you know in all likelihood that the defendant touched the shell casing, 1 in 100 can be enough. This is quite different from the stone-cold-stranger case where the defendant is either completely innocent or guilty of some horrible crime. Those cases allow more opportunity for the defense to make statistical challenges. "What else did the prosecutor tell you that's not right here?" This gives an opening to exploit and attack the reliability of the science involved, introducing some doubt.

Despite the general benefit of DNA analysis in criminal cases, Professor Townsend is not convinced that the current mechanism for presenting this testimony is quite right:

> There are very strong arguments on how to present DNA evidence statistically. The courts have not gotten to that. They don't typically allow the statisticians to present any inferential or decision-making guidance. Courts will allow talk about the random match probability, to explain what that means in terms of the population generation model, but that is the extent of it.[4]

Measurement of Individual Differences in Social Science

Moving from basic statistics and probability to scientific research studies, the social sciences try to measure individual differences in populations of interest. For example, in psychological studies, researchers look at facets of human behavior, taking measurements of performance or responses to stimulus. The sample selected for a study

must be random, a matter of chance. If the question is to determine whether two populations are different from one another, such as in drug product research, the subjects
are divided into an experimental and a control group. These must be just two random
samples from the same population.

Sampling error is a significant threat to the reliability of research findings. One of
the classic examples of this was the poll taken by the *Literary Digest* in the 1936 presidential election. The poll results showed Republican candidate Alf Landon beating
Franklin D. Roosevelt in a landslide, when the actual election was a mirror image. The
sampling error was that the readers of the *Literary Digest* were not representative of the
electorate as a whole, tending to be wealthy Republicans who had no love lost for FDR.

Once research data is collected, it is analyzed to see what might be related. Individuals are compared to a defined group according to specified units of measurement (e.g.,
IQ scores). Norm tables put individual scores into context, taking factors such as gender, age and education into account.

Using the Statistical References of Mean, Median or Mode

A standardized norm or percentile score is determined and the individual is placed
in reference to the entire group. The average score, a point on a scale, can be calculated in one of three basic ways: the mean, median or mode.

The mean is the middle score, often the statistic of choice, using all the available information. All the scores in a population are added up and divided by the total number of scores. The median is a somewhat better measure in that it is the middle score,
less influenced by the extremes at either end. The mode is a measure of what comes up
with the greatest frequency. A chi-square analysis compares the frequency of scores.
The standard deviation is a measure of variability, the extent to which the individual
scores deviate from the average.

Correlation: Does a Causal Relationship Exist?

Does a causal relationship exists between two sets of numbers or is it just random?
If there is a relationship, how strong is it? A critical aspect of research findings is the
statistical level of confidence. Are the results 100% sure or something less than that?

Correlation is a term used in all forms of science, referring to the relationship between one thing and another. The coefficient of correlation takes it to the next step and
determines the quality of that relationship, from a positive or a negative angle. The
correlation matrix includes multiple coefficients, with a table broken down into rows,
with columns of numbers.

While you likely will not be able to answer these questions intelligently on your own,
they should be asked of your own experts until you feel comfortable with the body of
research that applies to your case:

    1. How were the sample populations determined?

2. How were the measurements taken?

3. What formulas were used to calculate the data?

4. How do the measurements compare to one another?

5. How significant are the differences between categories?

6. Is there a pattern that goes beyond mere randomness?

7. Can it be shown visually on either a graph or a chart?

8. If so, what is the shape (e.g., bell-shaped curve)?

9. What causal relationship or concepts are revealed?

10. How strong is the correlation?

11. What confidence interval applies to the results?

12. Are there other equally plausible explanations for the outcome, either in whole or in part?

13. Are there other studies which either came to a different outcome or are inconsistent with the findings?

Peer-Review Studies Often Get It Wrong

Even with well-established scientific and mathematical protocols for conducting research studies, the findings often have significant flaws. It is of some comfort to us in the math-avoiding lawyer multitude that even those who are so good with numbers still manage to get it wrong. How much of the time does bad research pass through the peer-review screening, published as scientific truth?

A 2005 article in the *Journal of the American Medical Association*, the medical publication with the greatest total circulation, indicated this happens one-third of the time.[5] The author reported that 45 articles on the efficacy of medical treatments in major medical journals between 1990 and 2003 were wrong in whole or in part. The claims that a particular treatment worked were completely wrong 16% of the time and partially wrong in another 16% of the sample. This is particularly noteworthy in that these articles were very influential, cited at least 1,000 times over the period studied. The lesson for us in all this is that while peer-review literature is an important indicator of quality, by no means is it a guarantee of infallibility.

The reliability of research is more than just a statistical issue. A variety of alternative scenarios could explain the outcome. There could be something else provoking the variable that you believe is causative. Instrumental variables are a statistical way to deal with this problem in nonexperimental sciences. You can reduce these to a graph.

For example, the authors of an article on the relationship between race riots and economic decline found a cause that was totally unrelated to economic factors.[6] It was precipitation that had a strong correlation with the incidence of race riots. Did it rain on the day that Martin Luther King Jr. was assassinated? Or the following day? If it

Figure 24-2. Experts must show their calculations are accurate.

rained, it turns out that a race riot was much less likely. People didn't go outside and assemble in the street when it was raining.

Getting Up to Speed on the Math

Our task as lawyers using science and technology in cases is broken into two basic parts. In the first instance, we have to get up to speed and understand that which applies to our facts, both pro and con. Once that is accomplished, we have to figure out how to get the science across to our audience, both judge and jury. Scientific literature with data is hard. What does the data show? Numbers always carry the underlying danger of unscrupulous use, contained in the well-known saying by Charles H. Grosvenor, "Figures won't lie, but liars will figure." You have to be careful in working with mathematics with experts, always keeping your eye on the basics.

If you know the math, you can take an expert through various hypotheticals in a case, making certain assumptions. If you run the numbers, you know what all the answers are going to be. You can put the assumptions up and show why they are mathematically sound.

Keep It Simple: Show Pictures, Not Figures

A fundamental rule is to keep your case as simple as possible, forgetting the math and showing the pictures based on it. After cause-and-effect relationships are established with the math, translate these into visuals.

Take the data out of books and put it into a chart, using different colors or shapes to explain the general principles involved. Explore the best way to present information with a graphic designer. Whenever your expert is testifying, have a visual to work with.

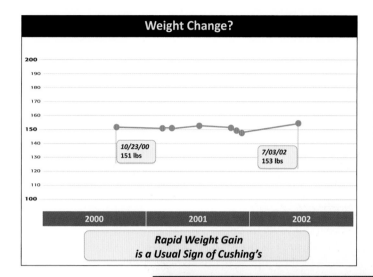

Figure 24-3(a). Critical diagnostic sign was not present.

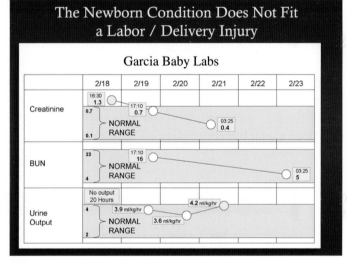

Figure 24-3(b). Visual display of laboratory results, showing all in normal range.

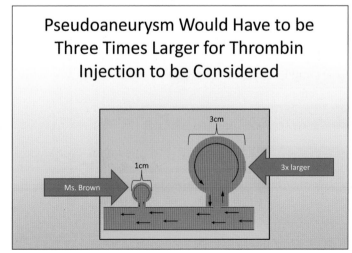

Figure 24-3(c). Showing proper size of artery to begin aneurysm injection.

This always makes it easier to follow along, particularly when the testimony involves an article or a textbook.

Pie charts and graphs are the best way to make statistical issues understandable to nonscientists and nonmathematicians. They magically turn numbers into user-friendly form. Even statisticians prefer the use of graphs because it makes clear the strength of the causal relationship. If you are trying to prove a connection between two things, like smoking and lung cancer, you can plot this relationship on a graph.

Even an audience with the dimmest perceptions of math and science gets visuals illustrating a research conclusion (e.g., the more you smoke, the more likely you are to get lung cancer). Graphs also can help the audience to understand concepts such as dosage or threshold limit value.

The data used in the reconstructions of motor vehicle accidents involves mathematical formulas, with variables such as position, acceleration or deceleration, and stopping distance. But rather than showing the mathematical equations, the results can be visualized in pictures for the expert to comment upon. Though the expert needs to know about the underlying calculations, it is not necessary to use them with the jury.

An accident reconstruction expert never has to discuss the actual equation while testifying. It is more along the lines of, "This is an accepted scientific principle." Rather than equations, the focus is on the end result, giving the numbers for perception-reaction time.

Explanations are given on how to tell from a skid mark what a car's speed was before the brakes were applied. "If you have a skid mark of this length, it will correlate with deceleration at this rate of speed. We know this is the range of speed the driver had to be going prior to braking." Both sides generally will agree on this part.

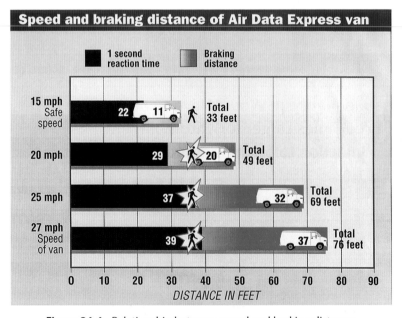

Figure 24-4. Relationship between speed and braking distance.

Vehicle specifications

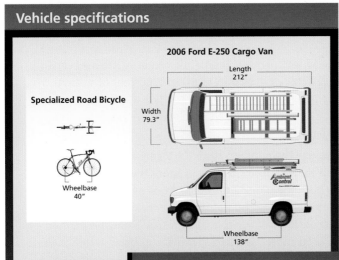

2006 Ford E-250 Cargo Van

Specialized Road Bicycle

Length 212"

Width 79.3"

Wheelbase 40"

Wheelbase 138"

Van proceeding into tight turn

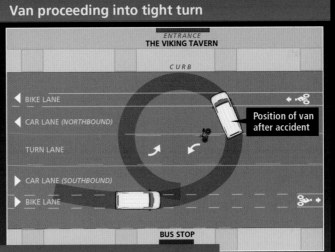

ENTRANCE
THE VIKING TAVERN

CURB

BIKE LANE

CAR LANE *(NORTHBOUND)*

Position of van after accident

TURN LANE

CAR LANE *(SOUTHBOUND)*

BIKE LANE

BUS STOP

Overview of accident

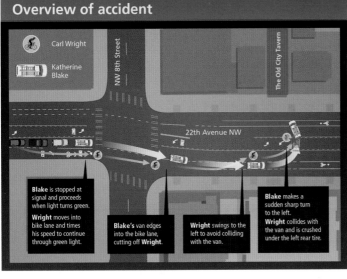

Carl Wright

Katherine Blake

NW 8th Street

The Old City Tavern

22th Avenue NW

Blake is stopped at signal and proceeds when light turns green.

Wright moves into bike lane and times his speed to continue through green light.

Blake's van edges into the bike lane, cutting off **Wright**.

Wright swings to the left to avoid colliding with the van.

Blake makes a sudden sharp turn to the left.

Wright collides with the van and is crushed under the left rear tire.

Figure 24-5(a)–(c).
Use of calculations to reconstruct movement of car and bicycle.

Medical tests are a factor in many cases and frequently involve many numbers, comparing the patient's test results to a normal range. This can be very difficult for the jury to absorb.

> **Example:** A plaintiff in a serious personal injury case had impaired lung capacity. The tests for this are all data, expressed in terms of a percent of normal. His attorney illustrated the conditions under which the test was done, showing a person blowing into the device. Then he showed the scores visually, comparing them to the normal range.
>
> The expert went through the numbers from the plaintiff's pulmonary function test and explained their significance. Even more than the illustrations, what really stuck with both the judge and the jury was when the medical expert said, "After the injury, he has the pulmonary capacity of an 80- to 90-year-old man. As he gets older, just from the aging process alone, his pulmonary capacity will go down even more." It was a great way to bring home the raw numbers, first visualizing and then humanizing them.[7]

The lesson here is clear: We must take our most critical scientific cause-and-effect figures and turn them into pictures.

Economists and the Assumptions They Make

Economic experts make assumptions that form the basis of their testimony. If these assumptions come from information which is widely accepted in their field, and that can be documented, it is going to enhance credibility. Jurors sort out these numbers by applying common sense and real life experience to determine what seems most reasonable. If the jurors conclude that the economic testimony is fuzzy and does not apply to today's economic realities, they will not accept it. Cross-examination of opposing economists and statisticians plays to this, going after the assumptions. The discount rate is a good example of this. Historically this is between 1% and 2%. This is the difference between inflation and what you can make in a safe investment. People understand that.

Beyond just the numbers themselves, there are background credibility issues to explore with economic experts. For example, with annuities, there always is the question of whether it is guaranteed by the United States government. Most of the time, it is not. "What if the company goes under, what then?"

Another area where experts plug numbers into a formula involves the value of a home in a divorce case. Typically there is a battle between the appraisers on each side, who bring in comparable sales to support their value assessment. They purport to use a scientific method in arriving at a dollar figure, but then typically add a number of assumptions into the mix: "The real estate market now is not what it was 5 years ago. I think it has declined by half percent per month over that time." Of course, the other appraiser disagrees, "This is a prime lot. The location is far more desirable than the other comparables." This forces the judge to rely on her own general knowledge as a homeowner in the community, interpreting the numbers in that light.

Takeaways — Using Data, Statistics and Probability

1. Mathematics is critical to an understanding of science and technology.

2. Math is definitional and can be used to shape ways of thinking about the law.

3. You have to be careful in working with mathematics with experts, always keeping your eye on the basics, explaining the general principles and keeping it simple.

4. Science and math go to the weak side of a lawyer's education, training and aptitude.

5. Math problems have a right and wrong answer, while legal analysis is filled with shades of gray.

6. The foundation of any expert opinion relying on mathematics is a potential area to be explored by a skilled advocate.

7. Most lawyers don't understand statistical evidence and can't develop an effective argument against it.

8. Mathematics can be traced back to the ancient Greeks, who provided the foundation on which both algebra and geometry rest. This has proved durable across time and culture.

9. Mathematical ability is on a spectrum. To understand statistics and statistical inference, you have to be fairly high up on the bell curve.

10. Scientific research uses statistics and probability when we can't say something is absolutely certain, but know that it is more than a chance occurrence.

11. The basic ideas of probability can be applied to many situations.

12. Statisticians assume that individual events are random and unpredictable, even if the average risk can be calculated.

13. A recurrent problem with the use of statistics and probability is 20/20 hindsight, where a causal relationship is advanced after an event has occurred.

14. The peak for the prosecution in presenting the direct testimony of a DNA forensic expert is the final probability statistic.

15. Some of the scientific techniques in criminal cases offer larger, more robust numbers than others.

16. Social sciences try to measure individual differences in populations of interest.

17. The sample that is selected for a study must be random.

18. Once research data is collected, it is analyzed to see what might be related.

19. A critical aspect of research findings is the statistical level of confidence.

20. Correlation is a term used in all forms of science, referring to the relationship between one thing and another.

21. Even with well-established scientific and mathematical protocols for conducting research studies, the findings often have significant flaws.

22. The reliability of research is more than just a statistical issue. A variety of alternative scenarios could explain the outcome.

23. After cause-and-effect relationships are established with the math, you need visual representations of them.

24. Pie charts and graphs are the best way to make statistical issues understandable to nonscientists and nonmathematicians.

25. Graphs also can help the audience to understand concepts such as dosage or threshold limit value.

26. The data used in accident reconstruction involves a mathematical formula, with the variables of position, acceleration or deceleration, and stopping distances.

27. Though the expert needs to know about the quantitative calculations, it is not necessary to use those with the jury.

28. Economic experts make assumptions that form the basis of their testimony.

29. Jurors sort out numbers by applying common sense and real-life experience to determine what seems most reasonable.

Chapter 25

Direct Examination

A good director creates an environment that gives the actor the encouragement to fly.

—Kevin Bacon

Much of the work fashioning the direct examination must be done outside of the courtroom, far in advance of a trial. You need to be able to ask all the right questions so that the expert's testimony makes sense. Developing that kind of sensitivity requires much thought, planning and experience. Too many attorneys don't know how.

> It is not my job as an expert to ask questions. Attorneys may not know how to ask the ones I need to answer. It is important to me as a scientist to give my answers in a step-by-step fashion, showing the jury how I reached my opinions. The foundation for my opinions often is not covered as well as it should be. It always surprises me how fundamental things can be left out in presenting my direct testimony, even with lawyers I have worked with before.[1]

What's Your Expert Mix?

No one expert can give you everything you need to prevail in a case. Create a balance in the experts you use. You can't have all academic types. There has to be a mix. You want both clinicians and people who teach at the university level. It's the same as planning a dinner party. Do you have a good mix of genders, ages and personality types? You don't want your group of experts to be seen as a narrow Fox News demographic.

A Good Direct Examination Is Like a Play

The preparation of an expert's direct examination is like writing the script of a play, knowing what questions you will ask and the answers they will elicit. The best lawyers focus on effective communication with their experts:

> The attorneys presenting my testimony want to be clear on all my opinions before I set foot in the courtroom. They don't want to get surprised by any-

Figure 25-1. Direct examination has elements of theater.

thing I say. If they don't understand something during our prep sessions, they will ask me more questions until it is clear.[2]

Just like a good play, the questions and answers should flow with spontaneous energy, not seeming wooden, canned or contrived.

Preparation Is Critical

Expert preparation is critical to a successful direct examination. Make sure that your experts are not hung out to dry. Give them all the information that they need to render an opinion in the case. Nothing is worse than having your expert asked about some key piece of data that they:

1. Don't have, or

2. Haven't read, when you assumed they had, or

3. Haven't remembered or incorporated into their thinking about the case.

Whatever the reason, it makes them look incompetent.

Preparation of an expert out in the hallway of the courtroom never works well. An expert about to testify is like an actor in the green room getting ready to go on stage, anxious and nervous. This is not a good time for major new input. Nobody absorbs much in that mind-set. There only is so much room in the brain. Anything else becomes white noise.

Finding the Comfort Zone through Face Time

Face time with experts is critical in preparing for their direct examination, particularly ones that you have not worked with before. It's important to find a comfort zone with each expert, so that you can maximize their strengths in relaying information to the judge and jury. It is a challenge to make them interesting and likeable without being too obvious about it.

Spending time with the experts is necessary to a thorough understanding of what is going on in your case. They are a great resource that we don't always use to best advantage.

> I will meet with my experts over and over, coming up with excuse after excuse why we need to get together. I need to work that face time and that relationship. They have to develop a comfort zone with me. I make it clear that I am trying to learn from them and will not abuse their trust in any way. They are vital to the case as a teacher of the jury and the judge, who cannot make the right decision without them.[3]

Effective paralegals can be critical in scheduling face time, particularly with reluctant experts. Treating physicians don't want anything to do with the legal system and are notoriously hard to get in to see. They often don't understand why they have to go to court when they just treated the patient. "Why can't you just use my records? Why can't you just settle this case? Can't I just give a deposition? Isn't that declaration I did enough?"

> With treating physicians, I always tell them, "The jury wants to hear from you. They're going to believe a treating physician much more than any expert either side brings in. You weren't picked by anybody for litigation purposes. You are the person the patient picked to help get them better."[4]

Vignettes and Stories

Vignettes are compelling and memorable, conveying the core message of a case. These can transform direct examination into a powerful and persuasive experience for the jury. It takes much time and effort to uncover the personal stories of experts. The best way to find these is to meet your experts outside an office setting, over lunch or dinner. Informality leads to an easier flow of information and gives you a much greater sense of the person.

"Teach Me"

In preparing the direct of the experts in your case, approach them as a student and say, "Teach me." This will better equip you to give the jury a well-rounded picture of the background science, not only on direct examination, but in the case as a whole. The more you know about the subject, the better your ability to make it simple. Too many lawyers cannot seem to reduce complex things to more understandable components. You must be able to present complex scientific concepts in a simple, understandable way. For example, though DNA science is very complex, prosecutors focus their questions on the bottom line—the numbers in favor of a match.

Use Visuals

Have your experts use graphics to explain any research study that is important to your case. Illustrate key findings, asking the expert to use them to explain what the study was trying to accomplish. How did they put it together? What did they find? How did it get verified? What is the peer-review process? Why is it important in this case?

> **Example:** If opposing counsel is relying on a study that doesn't help them as much as they think, develop ways to have your expert explain this visually to the jury.
>
> In complex cases with a great deal of terminology, put together a glossary for the jury, focusing on definitions. Use your experts to interpret and explain these things as they come up, so the jury tracks with the testimony. Stop your experts when these terms are used, "Okay, then this means … ?"[5]

Visual aids are a necessary part of the choreography of expert testimony. It is quite important to develop visuals that will educate the jury. No expert can testify effectively without them. The expert must have seen them in advance, be comfortable with them, and know exactly how they are going to use them. Rely on your experts to help identify these, telling them to imagine the jury as a class or a group of residents.

> I want a variety of media in working with expert testimony. Some of my visuals will be on good old-fashioned foam-core boards. One kind that I always use contains a short summary of the key elements of my case. This helps cue me, making sure that every area gets covered as the experts testify. It serves as a big outline for me, the expert and the jury. I don't want to miss anything.[6]

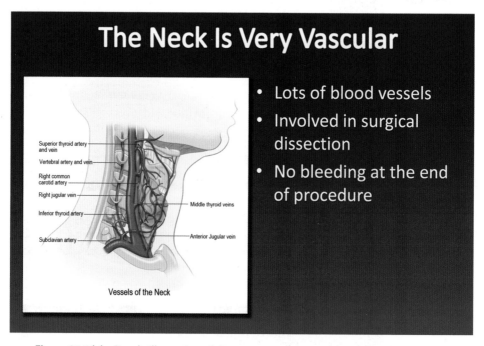

Figure 25-2(a). Simple illustration of the anatomy of the neck to explain disc surgery.

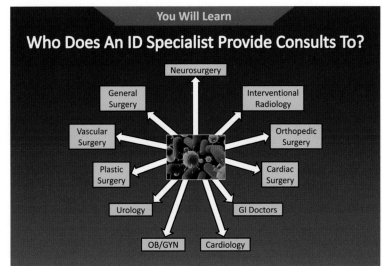

Figure 25-2(b).
Showing hospital
protocol and
relationship
between
different medical
specialists.

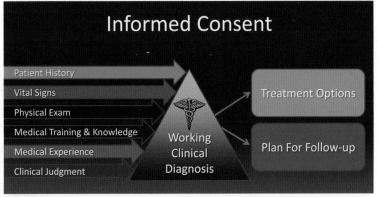

Figure 25-2(c).
Explaining work-
ing diagnosis,
informed consent
and follow-up
care.

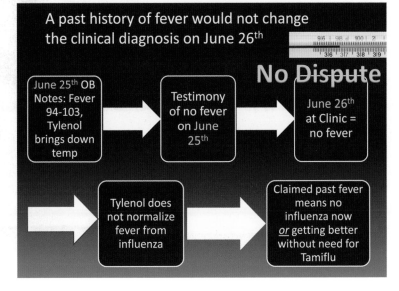

Figure 25-2(d).
Basic flowchart
showing history
of events.

Be resourceful in your approach to visuals, getting a mix of photos, models, illustrations and exemplars. Show jurors the physical evidence relating to an expert's opinions, using props whenever you can. If the design of a car bumper is part of the case, go out to a dealership, buy one and bring it to the courtroom.

Getting Direct off on the Right Foot

A good direct examination of an expert is much harder than cross-examination. It is very important to orient the jury at the outset of a case. Get off on the right foot, crafting your direct with the jurors' point of view in mind, answering the questions you know they have: Who is this person? How do they fit into this case? What are they going to talk about? How will they be helpful to my decision? The jury wants to hear the critical information up front, when they are most interested and receptive. What is going to be most helpful to them in making a decision?

Expert Credentials: A Little Bit Goes a Long Way

Presenting expert credentials often does more harm than good, particularly when considerable time is spent on it. The CV of an expert is not critically important. All the degrees and honors on the résumé are not all that helpful. If you present experts in a linear fashion, starting with reading their résumé, then doing the same with their report, you quickly will lose your audience. Jurors hate expert testimony to start with a lengthy list of qualifications. Who wants to listen to someone read pages of a lengthy

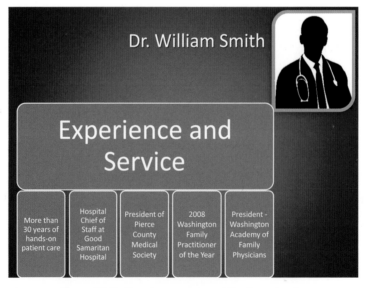

Figure 25-3. Keeping expert qualifications simple.

CV? They will shut down after the first paragraph. This only gets worse as one expert after another is presented in the same way.

Effective qualification of an expert requires a delicate balance. Restraint is always more effective, using subtlety and indirection. A little bit of résumé goes a long way. The goal is to establish credibility without coming off as superior or bragging. Showing the expert's knowledge and independence of thought matters more. Keep things fresh by making subtle shifts in presenting your experts. There is an element of, "I know it when I see it" here. Jurors have an image of what they expect a great surgeon to be like. How will your expert compare to this mental checklist?

Maximizing the Jurors' Learning Capabilities

Try to make the direct compact, energetic, interesting and informational, matching it to the jurors' learning capabilities.

> The best lawyers frame expert examinations by bringing out the key points right up front. This is followed by a little backfill, supporting how those conclusions were reached. This approach is tremendously effective, making the jury receptive to what an expert has to say.[7]

Short opening questions work best. At the beginning of the direct, frame jury orientation questions like, "What were you asked to do?" "What was your conclusion?" Make clear to the jury what each expert will address. That way, the jury understands up front how each expert fits into the case. Limit the points each expert covers, making sure not to attempt too much.

> My rule of thumb is that an expert should not be on the stand for more than an hour. For good points to be remembered by the jury, they can't be buried in a mass of details. They are more likely to get lost the longer you keep the expert on the stand.

> The challenge for the lawyers is not to overdo it, putting in too much technical or confusing language, or questions that are duplicative, overlapping or not precisely on point. Avoid throwing in anything marginal. It is far better to be selective and say, "Here is the one area that is really important." Jurors will understand and retain this.[8]

Tight Succession and Credibility Building

Present the expert's opinions in tight succession, supported by just the right amount of credibility-building detail with questions like, "How did you get there?" You get to repeat the expert's conclusions as you go through the direct examination.

Admit and Explain Any Weaknesses

Prepare your experts to go over and explain the weaknesses in your position. You have to defuse any potential time bombs before the other side can set them off. This applies to all witnesses, expert or otherwise. "You say this, doctor, but another study comes to a different conclusion. How do you explain that?" Then the jury will say during cross-examination, "We've already heard this. So what? Don't you have anything else?" If the bad stuff comes out on cross for the first time, the jury immediately looks over and asks silently, "Why didn't this come out on direct? Why did you only tell us the good things?"

Enhancing Persuasion

The persuasiveness of an expert often is a matter of personal charisma. Is the expert genuinely likeable, motivated by a genuine desire to help the jury? The more humility, the better an expert sells. Some will be a bit of a challenge on this dimension, requiring a certain creativity, spontaneity and lightheartedness on your part, alert to opportunities that come up during the direct examination.

> **Example:** In a case involving a child with spina bifida and cognitive delay, the defense pediatric neurologist had a tendency to give long, detailed and convoluted answers. At one point, the expert said, "The nature of this child's cognitive impairment is such that he would not be able to see the animated film *Finding Nemo* as a story of redemption." Defense counsel's response was incredulous, in a good-natured way: "That's what the film is about?" The jury cracked up. During final argument, counsel put pictures of all her experts up on a foam-core board. She substituted Nemo's picture for her neurologist. She said to the jury, "I thought *Finding Nemo* was a story about a fish. I am glad that our expert cleared this up, that it really is about loss and redemption." This neutralized the expert's verbosity and made him seem more humble and human.[9]

Authenticity is another important key to persuasion. Jurors are very adept at sniffing out phoniness. There always are background stories that will help humanize your experts if you dig around a bit.

> It always is better if you can get the witness to tell a story about why they decided to study in the particular field. If you take the time to look for it, there usually is a human-interest angle in the expert's background.[10]

Ask your experts, "How did you get into this field?" Invariably, the answers will help humanize your expert and inject spontaneity.

> **Example:** Defending a colon and rectal surgeon in a medical malpractice case, his lawyer started by asking: "Doctor, no offense, but what on earth made you decide to focus your career in this area?" The jury immediately cracked up, providing a great authentic moment in the trial. [11]

Objectivity is by far the most important quality in an expert and jurors pick up on it right away. Experts who are advocates end up with far less respect and trust. True experts are scientists, not advocates.

> **Example:** If you've got a good solid expert whose opinions can be well-documented to the jury through visual aids, you are in really good shape. But if you have an expert that looks like an advocate who doesn't make a particularly impressive appearance in the courtroom, then you're in trouble.[12]

Keep Scientific Literature to a Minimum

Never use too much scientific literature in presenting the direct testimony of experts. How much information is enough? You don't want to overdo it. If you have a study that is right on point, spend some time on it if it is crisp and clean, written in black and white terms. Often this will not be the case, as academic papers tend simultaneously to give and take away, leaving doubt. Literature of this kind only will confuse the jury.

National Standards

Jurors like national standards that apply to what happened in the case. They also get an instruction at the end of the case that deviation from a standard or a regulation may be considered as evidence of negligence. The agencies or regulatory bodies that promulgate such standards don't really have a dog in the fight.

Conclusion

Judge Robert S. Lasnik ties together the qualities of good expert direct examination in the same compact manner that we should be using in presenting them:

> The best practices for presenting expert testimony are the same as for the case as a whole. Give the expert the opportunity to tell their story in a way that the trier of fact will understand. Don't get too technical, repeat yourself too much, or go on too long. Use illustrations whenever possible. Prepare the trier of fact for the worst, most vulnerable parts of your position during direct examination. Don't wait for the other side to bring it out on cross.[13]

Takeaways — Direct Examination

1. Much of the work fashioning the direct examination has to be done outside of the courtroom, far in advance of a trial.

2. You need to be able to ask the right questions so that the expert's testimony makes sense.

3. Create a balance in the mix of experts you use.

4. Direct examination of an expert is like writing the script of a play, knowing what questions you will ask and the answers they will elicit.

5. Like the actors in a good play, the interaction between lawyer and expert should flow with spontaneous energy.

6. Expert preparation is critical. Make sure that your expert has been given all the information he or she needs to render solid opinions in the case.

7. Face time with experts is a very important step in preparing for their direct examination.

8. The best way to find good stories is to meet your experts outside an office setting, as informality leads to an easier flow of information.

9. Approach your experts as a student, saying, "Teach me."

10. Visual aids are a necessary part of the choreography of expert testimony. It is quite important to develop visuals that will educate the jury.

11. Have your experts use graphics to explain any research important to the case.

12. In complex cases with a great deal of terminology, put together a glossary for the jury, focusing on definitions.

13. Present complex scientific concepts in a simple, understandable way.

14. It is very important to orient the jury at the outset of a case. Get off on the right foot, crafting your direct with the jurors' point of view in mind, answering the questions you know they have.

15. Presenting expert credentials often does more harm than good. Effective qualification of an expert requires a delicate balance.

16. Vignettes or stories involving an expert are compelling and memorable, often humanizing the expert and conveying a core message of the case.

17. The jury wants to hear the critical information up front, when they are most interested and receptive.

18. Make the direct compact, energetic, interesting and informational, matching it to the jurors' learning capabilities.

19. Present the expert's opinions in tight succession, supported by just the right amount of credibility-building detail.

20. Prepare your experts to go over and explain the weaknesses in your position.

21. Keep things fresh by making subtle shifts in your presentation approach from one expert to the next.

22. The more humility, the better an expert sells.

23. Authenticity is an important key to persuasion.

24. Objectivity is critical to an expert's credibility and jurors pick up on it right away.

25. Never use too much scientific literature in presenting the direct testimony of experts.

26. Use active listening, stopping your experts whenever technical jargon is used, having them explaining these terms in a nontechnical manner.

27. Jurors like national standards that reference what happened in the case.

Chapter 26

Cross-Examination of Experts

Challenging an expert and questioning his expertise is the lifeblood of our legal system ... it is the only way a judge or jury can decide whom to trust.
—Judge David L. Bazelon

A skilled opposing expert is a very dangerous person. If allowed to go unchallenged, experts create doubt about your case. This can be particularly lethal to the side with the burden of proof. No matter how effective a final argument, experts may have caused irreversible damage by then, putting a cloud of doubt around your case. If they do, you have a significant chance of losing.

A Realistic View of Cross-Examination

The overriding goal on cross is to try to advance your case and help win it. This is done in an incremental brick-by-brick fashion, not in a huge drama where you sit down in triumph afterward, feeling, "Oh my God, I really smoked that witness." You never will make your case with the other side's experts and it is foolish to ever think so.

How Aggressive Should You Be with an Opposing Expert?

The adversary system always has given trials a theatrical flavor. Nowhere is the sense of dramatic tension greater than when you square off against an opposing expert. But cross-examination style has evolved over the years, with a change in purpose and technique. It now is more important to promote the story of your case than just to try to tear down opposing experts and make them look bad.

The potential of cross-examining an expert to influence the jury depends heavily on how you go about it. If done in personal terms, it will put the jury off. It is more persuasive to go after the opinion itself, rather than focus on whether the expert is a good or bad person. The basic gestalt of cross comes down to whether there is credible authority contrary to the expert's opinion. Is he/she in the mainstream or an outlier?

Skilled cross-examiners focus on exploiting real vulnerabilities, recognizing that total conquest of the opposing expert is not likely. It is all about scoring points:

243

Figure 26-1. Cross-examination should combine both soft and hard elements.

I am not going to get an opposing expert to change their mind, saying, "Oh, you're right. I am totally wrong." They are never going to do that. The art of the possible is to poke a few holes and get out. I establish the bias of witnesses who advocate for the other side, focusing on where they are stretching their opinions beyond common sense. Otherwise, you end up flailing around, allowing experts to reinforce what they have already said on direct. Why would you want to do that?[1]

In-Depth Understanding of the Science or Discipline

Effective cross-examination of experts requires an in-depth understanding of the science or discipline involved. Even though you may not use much of it in cross, you must have a working knowledge of the narrow issues in order to get anywhere. It often is helpful to sit down with your own expert for tutoring until you reach a basic comfort level. Otherwise, you will be treading on thin ice.

Identifying the Weak Spots

Cross-examination of experts must focus on any weak spots or vulnerabilities in their opinions or foundation. This must be done in a compact, concise and engaging way, so that the jury continues to pay attention. Then sit down. If you can, simplify expert or technical information to the lowest common denominator for the jury and say, "Here's a guy that was trying to put one over on you." You will be much better off with this approach.

The Element of Surprise

Just like in warfare, your big advantage is the element of surprise: "I've got the plan and you don't." This can make all the difference to the outcome. You know where you

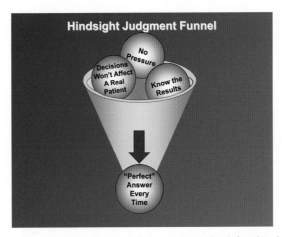

Figure 26-2. Visualization of a weak link, used to help defeat hindsight bias.

are going, with the backup to get there. You don't have to show any of it to the witness until you are ready to spring it on them.

Get In and Get Out

The basic rule is to get in and get out, hit them on the bias, but don't try to take them on in their own field.

> I always try to have my crosses be brief. They're very surgical. It's in and out. When I'm preparing, I constantly cut. It has to be tight, every question meaningful and nothing more.[2]

Trial judges confirm that many of the cross examinations of experts they see are fundamentally flawed. One of the frequent criticisms is that lawyers try to do too much, as noted by federal Judge Robert S. Lasnik, who has presided over hundreds of jury trials in state and federal court:

> I have not seen much good cross-examination of experts in my time on the bench. Most lawyers are not in a position to have a fair fight with an expert over the science involved in an opinion. You are already on dangerous ground as the expert knows far more about his/her field than you do.[3]

Lawyers always get into trouble trying to make a frontal assault on an expert's opinions. No matter how diligently you prepare, the expert always knows more. This method is almost certain to go badly, with the lawyer getting flailed around and losing control of the examination. It usually doesn't feel to the jury like any points are being scored, which is the whole purpose of cross to begin with.

Remember that unless an expert has crossed the line and become an advocate, the jury always will side with the expert, not you. Go in with the small number of points you need to make clearly in mind. You've got to pick your battles carefully, limiting yourself to the ones that you can win. Smart trial lawyers are very selective on what points they pursue on cross.

I look for the parts of their testimony that don't pass the smell test. Experts who are advocates stretch the truth and end up getting in trouble on the assumptions behind their opinions. If their foundation is a push, I pounce on them. I won't go after life care planners on the cost of basic medical supplies. But I will attack inflated costs of future care: "Has the plaintiff received good care up to now?" "Yes." "Okay, this is what it has cost so far. Why are your figures so much higher than this?"[4]

Bring out those things that are helpful to you before the jury and then sit down. You can prove prior agreement with these from the expert's deposition if you need to. Don't try to match wits or convince the expert that he was wrong, getting him to change his opinion on the witness stand in front of the jury. It's not going to happen. If you get in the mud with experts and fight over their field, you are going to lose. Yet, lawyers are very slow to pick up on this.

The baseline tolerance level for most jurors is one hour for the expert's direct and fifteen minutes for the cross-examination. Most cross-examinations go on too long, hurting the case of the lawyer asking the questions:

Whatever the motivation, lengthy cross-examinations of experts are a waste of time and energy, resulting in negative consequences for the lawyer. Jurors remember this and punish the lawyer who does it later on.[5]

You Can't Win on Cross but You Can Lose

You can't win a case on cross-examination, but you certainly can lose one, particularly if you get up and act obnoxious, drawing one bad answer after another. Jurors pay more attention during cross than direct, excited by the one-on-one combat. When you get hurt on cross, you damage your case, just as when your own witness goes south on you.

The worst courtroom trap lawyers fall into is overdoing cross-examination. While a legitimate dispute may well exist between the positions of the experts, too many cross-examinations are ego driven, attempting to show an expert who is the boss. This kind of flailing around is completely wrong, meeting neither the theatrical nor fact-finding elements of a trial.

Do not get caught up in this expectation that you need to "put on a big show." It is not about you. Check your ego at the door. Obviously, we'd all like every cross to be a "wow." But the reality is that this usually isn't what is best for the case. The better, more realistic goal is an evenhanded, low-key cross, where you make a few points, get in and get out. Often it is not having a cross that is a "wow," but, rather, one that keeps the jury focused on what is important in your case.

The best lawyers keep telling their client's story throughout the cross-examination of opposing experts. They start by establishing whatever the opposing expert will agree with that is favorable. Then they shift to a limited number of tight questions about what is in dispute, chipping away at the expert before sitting down. The best of all possible worlds is if an opposing expert disagrees with something previously endorsed as reasonable in writing on some other occasion.

How Much Is Enough?

It is always hard to know how much is enough, particularly in the gladiatorial contest of cross-examining experts. Sometimes you can be winning on all the technical points but still lose the battle of impression, which is what counts the most.

> **Example:** The defense expert was an older gentleman, appealing in a grandfatherly way. There were a number of holes in his argument. The plaintiff's lawyer began his cross-examination about 20 minutes before the break. Scoring one point after another, he was very pleased with his progress, thinking, "This expert is a dead man walking."
>
> Opposing counsel used the break to school his expert, telling him to go completely rope-a-dope. "Agree with everything he says, don't fight him. Just be yourself." After the break, the plaintiff's lawyer couldn't land a punch on this expert. He subtly agreed with everything, while not hanging himself.
>
> The plaintiff's lawyer sat down and whispered to his legal assistant, "What happened? It was going so well before the break." "You turned from making him an incompetent into being an embattled nice old man. You were beating up too much on him when he stopped fighting back."[6]

Know when it is time to quit. Get the opposing expert out of the courtroom before any more damage is inflicted. The worst scenario is when the jurors enjoy seeing you get thrashed. Adrenaline control and self-awareness is critical to the realization that, "It is time to stop. This is going nowhere but bad." The combat instinct makes this somewhat counterintuitive, though, making you want to keep on fighting.

Keep the Heat Out

Jurors always favor an expert going in, sensitive to the tone and civility used by the cross-examining lawyer. Unless and until the opposing expert is shown to be an advocate or a liar, keep the heat out of your demeanor and questioning. However, the stressful circumstances of taking on an expert in the courtroom may make it hard to do.

> **Example:** Early in my career, I came up against a well-travelled opposing economic expert for the first time. He was very smooth and slick. I did not like or trust him. When I stood up to cross-examine him, I was instantly angry, on him from the moment I got out of my chair, intent on proving that he was a liar.
>
> My cross-examination almost ended up doing more harm than good. My paralegal said to me, "To the jury, this is just a nice-looking man in a suit. They don't know he's a liar. You can't stand up and be instantly angry. You know his opinions are lies, but until the jury catches up with you, they are going to look at you and say, 'What is your problem? What caused you to get

out on the wrong side of the bed today? Did you drink too much coffee?' They don't see it as the expert's problem until you lay the foundation that he is cooking the books. Before then, he's just a nice looking man in a suit, there to tell them about economics."

This was an eye opener. I now regularly follow the mantra that civil litigation has to be civil, trying to cut the opposing expert legs off more gently.[7]

Use of Emotional Intelligence

So much of cross-examination is based on instinct, using emotional intelligence to assess how it is going over with the jury. Use your peripheral vision and keep the jury in focus at all times. "Are they tracking with what I am doing here?" You have to be able to read them. You can't get hung up on all the points you want to make.

Cross-examination is an art, not a science. Pick up on the jurors' body language and ask yourself what it means: "Is this working? Are they buying it? Are their arms crossed? Is the look of skepticism about me or the witness?" These are all things that you have to try to read, trusting your gut for the answer.

> **Example:** The plaintiff's lawyer in a medical malpractice case was scoring points with an opposing expert, but the body language of the jury told him that they'd had enough. He stopped and sat down even though he had intended to cover other material. He thought the jury was tired and wanted to go home, as the judge had extended court hours past 5 o'clock.
>
> This jury was allowed to ask questions of witnesses and it was then that the plaintiff's lawyer learned what the jurors thought of this expert. They excoriated him with devastating questions. The presumption that the jury just wanted to leave for the day turned out not to be true. They wanted the lawyer to stop asking questions so they could fire their own at the expert.[8]

Primacy and Recency

Primacy and recency matter tremendously in structuring a cross-examination. It is critical to strongly begin and end every cross-examination. In the war of impression, the psychological and emotional underlay can be more important than the content of the questions themselves. Do as much positive cross as you can in the beginning and save the zingers for the end. There are a number of things that opposing experts will say that don't hurt you. In fact, they can help you. Get them to concede all that you can.

What Points Does the Opposing Expert Have to Agree On?

Honest, straightforward opposing experts always will agree on certain basic points in a well-constructed cross-examination. Careful exploitation of things the expert has to admit in order to be credible is always effective.

Example: In a failure-to-diagnose medical malpractice case, the defense experts have to admit that the patient really did have this condition. And, if it had been treated, this patient would've had a different outcome. That's a tough one for the defense. The effective lawyers hit this hard with a series of questions that are somewhat repetitive and ride it on home.[9]

Leaving the things that really attack the credibility of the witness to the end is obviously purposeful. You want to get out all the positives before telling the jury, "Don't listen to this guy." By the time you get to the attack stuff, sometimes they already have reached this conclusion.

It is particularly important to leave your best questions for the end. If you don't have anything really smoking on bias, ask a set of questions that you know will go your way, reinforcing your case themes and theories. With the best questions, you don't even care what the answer is.

Example: In a medical malpractice case alleging a missed diagnosis, the cross of the defendant doctor ended with plaintiff's theory of why she made the mistake—it was the end of the day and she was in a rush to get home. The plaintiff's lawyer walked her through the preliminary foundation questions and then closed with, "What really happened here, doctor, was that you were tired, it was the end of a long shift and you wanted to go home. You didn't know what was wrong with this patient, but he looked young and healthy. You figured he'd be fine if you just kicked him out of your hospital. You gave up on him."

This was a question where the answer didn't matter, setting out the plaintiff's theory of why this outcome had happened. The defendant leaned into the microphone and screamed, "Absolutely not." The feeling it left in the courtroom was, "This case is over." No one wants an emergency room doctor who can't keep her cool. An important part of the cross-examination involved probing whether this doctor met this expectation.[10]

Avoid Direct Challenges

You can assume due diligence by opposing counsel on expert preparation and selection. It is seldom productive to make a direct challenge to the qualifications of an expert. They know more about the science or discipline involved than you and will be able to back up their opinions. But you can attack their conclusions as unsupported by credible evidence.

Read Everything the Expert Has Written

Try to read everything the expert has written, in hopes of finding something that directly contradicts the testimony in the case. Occasionally, there is an opportunity to set up an expert so that the jury concludes he is totally unbelievable. Compare their prior opinions to those in the present case, looking for inconsistencies. Whenever you find significant ones, start thinking out loud on how best to use this for impeachment.

Example: Attorney David Boies conducted a devastating cross-examination of Dean Richard Schmalensee, one of Microsoft's principal experts in the antitrust case brought by the United States government. It reached a dramatic peak when the witness was forced to admit that he had written an article in the *Harvard Law Review* with the exact opposite opinion to that which he was offering in the case:

Q. You have concluded that Microsoft, in your opinion, does not possess monopoly power, correct?

A. Correct....

Q. And have you made any attempt to study whether Microsoft enjoyed persistently high profits?

A. I have not....

Q. Let me show you an article from the *Harvard Law Review* [written by the witness].... "Even if all measurement problems are solved ... persistent excess profits provide a good indication of the long-run power...."

A. I have had a chance to look at it. It, of course, appeared 16 years ago, and my immediate reaction is, "What could I have been thinking?"[11]

However, this does not work many times, as lawyers are not nearly as clever as they think.

Use Learned Treatises Sparingly

Use of learned treatises should be done very carefully. A battle between lawyer and expert over technical details quickly will bore the jury. Quite often, articles have statements going both ways. An expert will counter a sound bite you like with another one they like from the same article. This kind of debate can only hurt you. Besides the risk of boring the jury, the expert can score points by accusing you of taking things out of context.

It is not uncommon for lawyers to read a paragraph to me without identifying where it came from. Then they ask, "Do you agree or disagree with this?" It is important not to allow these things to be taken out of context or misrepresented. Lawyers often want to ignore the parts of a document which are unfavorable, but I always insist on looking at the whole thing.[12]

Avoid Overdoing Bias Questions

Lawyers are hung up on bias and spend a lot of time on it. This is where most of us feel like we have the best chance of scoring points. Opposing experts do have biased points of view and this is fair game. The basic argument is, "These people testify because they always give the other side the answer they want."

Some experts will admit that they never will testify for the side you represent. Not infrequently, their response is: "There are plenty of those who will, just not me." If a witness says that he would never testify for a particular side, no matter what, that will bother most jurors. When you have experts like that, you know you can go after bias and the money they make from testifying. That ends up being pretty clean impeachment, particularly in personal injury field matters.

Most experts are savvy enough not to admit to a refusal to work for the other side, saying, "I am happy to consult with whoever calls me." This requires a shift of approach, adding up all the appearances by an expert for one side, attacking credibility with questions such as, "How often have you testified for this side?" "How much do you make per year from your testimony?" We are more comfortable with this because it easy to do and doesn't involve any science, just simple arithmetic.

Except in those cases where an expert is seen as an advocate, jurors care much less about the bias of an opposing expert than lawyers think.

> If somebody says, "Hey, 95% of the time I testify for the defense, just because that's who happens to call me," I don't think the jurors really care that much about it. It would have to be a guy who says "I never have and I never would represent a plaintiff because I'm philosophically against representing an injured victim."[13]

Trial judges see most bias attacks on experts during cross-examination as counterproductive:

> Most lawyers go after opposing experts on the issue of financial bias, how much money they are making for giving opinions in the case. I've never seen that be terribly effective. If the expert's fee is outrageously high, it might evoke a response. But it is not worth spending too much time on.[14]

Effective cross-examination requires more than a single-minded emphasis on bias. While it fine to have some focus on the money an expert is making, this has limited juror appeal, particularly as it goes on:

> I watched one of our new deputies go after a defense expert on financial bias, a pharmacologist who is a frequent flyer on the defense side. His bottom line always is that if the defendant was unable to remember the events, then he lacked the requisite mental state to commit the crime.
>
> Our deputy was relentless in going after this expert on the financial stuff. She started there and kept at it. "How much did you get paid last year?" "You flew up here today from Oregon?" "And you took a cab to the courthouse from the airport?" She had great material, but the over-breadth denigrated it. Her cross would have been far better if she'd edited it down to a short, tight sequence and then gotten out.[15]

Jurors don't really care that experts get paid. Nobody works for free. Both sides pay their experts. The money an expert makes is not that impressive to jurors anymore. The bias attacks usually fall flat, so much so that some veteran trial lawyers try to agree that neither side go into this: "Our people get paid, their people get paid, so what?"[16]

Experts who testify frequently will have a credible response to accusations of bias, maintaining that their opinions and the science behind them are absolutely solid.

I focus on the science. No matter who pays me, the conclusions will be the same. The money I make as an expert does not change the physical facts of what happened in an accident. If a Chevy Malibu bumper does not have any visible damage, that is a physical fact which supports my biomechanical opinions about the force of a collision.[17]

The opposing lawyer's response to witness bias accusations in closing argument is, "Of course he gets paid. This is an important, well-trained expert, entitled to make money in this case. Nobody is going to come to court and testify for free. The expert is taking time away from his practice and is entitled to be paid." This is followed with the provocative question, "Do you think the other side's experts are testifying for free? They charge the same kind of rates." Invariably, the jury concludes, "The payment of experts works both ways."

Jurors are interested only in hearing about those who testify exclusively for one side or the other, as well as whether they have fudged on their résumés. If you can show this, you are on much more solid ground, as advocates are suspect.

Experienced Experts Know the Cross-Examination Drill and Are Ready for You

There is a basic pattern for cross-examining expert witnesses. Savvy experts know exactly what is coming and usually are ready for it. Dr. Peter M. McGough, a physician and clinic program director who has testified as an expert, exemplifies this kind of battle-conditioned awareness:

Whenever I have been an expert witness in court, it follows a certain basic pattern. The first thing the lawyer does is explore my credibility, which can be done in a lot of different ways.

The fact that I've done previous expert work often is held up as a reason for suspicion, with the suggestion that I'm in it for the money.

From there, the lawyer will go on to ask, "How many cases have you testified in and what is your total income from that?" It helps that I've done it for both sides, plaintiff and defense. But even so, it is very common for the lawyer to go after this the first thing.

The next typical step is to explore any possible variation from anything I've said in other cases. I know that anything I've said on the record can and will be brought up. I try very hard to be consistent. If there is a change in my opinion, there has to be a really good reason, like new evidence. I am on the alert for any suggestion that there is a conflict in my testimony.

The last part of the standard cross-examination is the suggestion that I've been given a story by the attorney I am working with that I have adopted as my own. It is suggested that I am presenting this as my opinion because that is what was sought by the attorney who retained me, as opposed to something I developed independently.[18]

Concession-Based Cross-Examination in Criminal Cases

In criminal cases, the prosecution cross-examination of defense experts often is concession-based, raising what they will have to concede that is favorable to the state's case. The prosecution uses cross as an opportunity to keep putting their theories before the jury. For example, if an eyewitness identification defense is raised and the lighting at the scene is good, the prosecution will use this in the cross: "When the lighting is good, as it was in this case, you would agree that that improves the ability of the witness to make an accurate identification."

Defense Avoids Direct Challenges to Crime Labs

The defense usually does not directly challenge a state crime lab's scientific testing and analysis, instead focusing on reasonable doubt. Defense experts will discuss generally the problems in labs that can come up in analyzing DNA samples. The bottom line to this is not, "This is not the defendant's DNA," but rather, "They haven't proved it beyond a reasonable doubt." This often takes the form of contamination and chain of custody type arguments. In closing arguments, it is typical for defense counsel to attack the scientific evidence on that basis. The issue here isn't that they are wrong or that we have proved them wrong, the issue is: Has it been proved beyond a reasonable doubt?

Foundation Deficiencies

Many times, an expert will lack some piece of the foundation, not getting some key deposition, testimony or medical record. This can be the result of the limited circumstances under which the expert was retained. For example, doctors who perform CR 35 examinations typically only spend a short time with the client. This can make them unaware of some important facts in the case, which can be raised on cross-examination.

Junk-Science Attacks

In certain limited situations, you may be able to go after an expert as a purveyor of junk science.

> **Example:** A medical expert testified against me in a shoulder birth injury case. This doctor had done considerable research, but it was litigation focused, for the purpose of defending doctors in this kind of case. His conclusion was that these kind of shoulder injuries occur in utero, never from the birthing process. This was pure junk science. There was no support for his position elsewhere in the literature.[19]

But it has to be abundantly clear that the expert opinions completely lack foundation, tainted by bias. This often is hard to do. More common is the assertion that the opinions of an expert have gone beyond the recognized boundaries of his field.

Figure 26-3. Use of blow-ups with critical standards.

Use Visual Anchors

Visuals always provide an effective anchor for cross-examination. Photos, charts, drawings and diagrams can shorten preliminary questioning and make exchanges more compact and dramatic. So can pages from learned treatises, industry guidelines or clinical standards. For example, if a doctor or hospital really has violated a clinical guideline in a medical malpractice case, blowing up the language of the rule can be an effective weapon in cross.

Articles in scientific or professional journals can establish an opposing expert as an outlier. After confirming the expert's opinion, a blow-up of a contrary opinion in an article can damage the expert's credibility. The authors of the article effectively are the ones challenging the expert, not you: "Here's what the *New England Journal of Medicine* says. That's the opposite of what you're saying in this case, isn't it, doctor?"

Medical and other records in a case can undercut an expert's position too. For example, if the defense says the plaintiff never had particular symptoms and records show the contrary, documents with call-outs from the records can be effective impeachment.

A visual which summarizes a theme in the cross-examination of the expert can be used in closing argument. For example, in one case, Elizabeth Leedom used the image of the two-headed Roman god Janus: "Their liability expert is two-faced, talking out of both sides of his mouth."

Only Use Good Deposition Q's and A's to Impeach

Effective use of depositions in cross-examination requires more than a rehash in front of the jury. The reason for this is that skilled lawyers always go over deposition questions and answers with their experts prior to trial, anticipating and diffusing all the issues that potentially can come up:

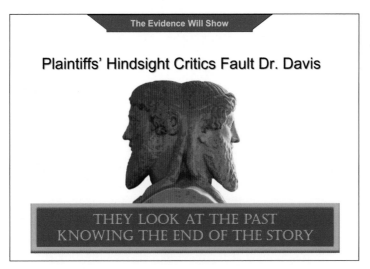

Figure 26-4. Visual metaphor used to show inconsistency.

Example: In medical malpractice cases involving an alleged failure to diagnose, the defense will try to take the sting out of this: "Doctor, we know now that the patient really had this condition, undiagnosed at the time. Can you explain to the jury why this was not a violation of the standard of care? Do good doctors always get the right diagnosis the first time around?"[20]

With these kind of anticipatory explanations, deposition questions can be a "so what" for the jury.

Video Deposition Impeachment

Video has ratcheted up the potential impact of depositions rather significantly. As a matter of timing, depositions often are taken earlier in a case, when the facts may not be fully developed. The circumstances of a deposition also are much less formal than courtroom testimony, which carries with it the greater possibility of unguarded remarks and behaviors. Preserved on video, any significant inconsistency between the expert's opinions or appearance in deposition and in court can be devastating:

Example: Dr. D. L. was an expert for both the defendant hospital and the doctors in a birth injury case. He did not know the facts well enough to understand how badly his general answers would play when superimposed on the facts. At deposition, he was asked some generic questions about the standard of care and what should be done. These were right on target with the allegations against the defendant doctors.

The general nature of the questions caused the expert to miss the implications of his answers.

When asked, "If this happened, would that be below the standard of care," his reply was "Yes." This effectively buried one of the two defendant doctors.

When this expert came to testify at trial, defendant's counsel was looking for a big finish to the day. He took a risk, asking the big question, "Doctor, did any of the physicians attending this patient violate the standard of care?" "Absolutely not." This expert could not walk away from the contradiction between his video deposition and trial testimony. This ended up burying the doctor defendants.[21]

The best trial lawyers are excellent at cleaning up the appearance of their witnesses before bringing them into court. In some cases, it's almost a total makeover. If the video deposition shows a dramatic change in appearance or demeanor, the credibility of the expert can seriously be called into question. The jury likely will believe that both the expert and the lawyer who called them have been putting on a show.

Example: The opposing expert on causation was a well-known doctor. He was extraordinarily arrogant at his video deposition, showing disdain by turning his body sideways, looking at the plaintiff's lawyer only long enough to answer the question and then turning his head away again. The body language was almost like, "I am not going to answer your questions."

When he showed up for trial, this expert turned into Dr. Engaging. None of the arrogant behaviors at the deposition were on display. The jury was shown video clips of the deposition by the plaintiff's lawyer so that they could see the expert's true colors. The difference was dramatic, almost as if the video had been taken by a hidden camera. The jury concluded, "What we are seeing in court is a performance." The jurors changed their attitude toward the expert as soon as they saw the clips. "This guy is really a turkey."[22]

Index Video Depositions and Carve Out Clips

Index every deposition you take of opposing experts. All cross-examination questions should be correlated to page and line references in the expert's deposition. In the alternative, use verbatim language from an exhibit. Once all this is locked in, decide which questions and answers you want backed up with video clips. You have to go and actually review each clip to make sure it is as effective as the transcript makes it seem. Some questions and answers are more effective than they appear on the transcript because of nonverbal behavior or lengthy delays before the witness answers the question.

While it is quite time-consuming, carving out potential impeachment clips from an expert's deposition can pay huge rewards at trial. It is very important to have these ready to show to the jury. Done correctly, this always will allow you to force the witness to say what you want or be thought a liar.

Takeaways — Cross-Examination of Experts

1. If allowed to go unchallenged, opposing experts create doubt about your case.

2. The overriding goal of cross-examination is to advance your case and help win it.

3. You never will make your case with the other side's experts.

4. The potential of a cross-examination to influence the jury depends heavily on how you go after the opposing expert.

5. It all comes down to whether there is some credible authority that is contrary to the opposing expert's testimony.

6. Effective cross-examination of experts requires an in-depth understanding of the science or discipline involved.

7. The best lawyers cross-examine opposing experts on a limited number of points that they will agree with and then sit down.

8. Pick your battles carefully, limiting yourself to the ones that you can win.

9. If you get in the mud with experts and fight over their field, you are going to lose.

10. Do not get caught up in the expectation that "It always is in my client's best interest to put on a big show."

11. Jurors pay more attention during cross than direct, excited by the one-on-one combat.

12. It is time to stop when you know you are getting beaten by the opposing expert.

13. Unless and until the opposing expert is shown to be an advocate or a liar, keep the heat out of your demeanor and questioning.

14. Use emotional intelligence and body language to assess how your cross is going over with the jury, making modifications as necessary.

15. Primacy and recency matter tremendously in structuring a cross-examination.

16. It is critical to strongly begin and end every cross-examination.

17. Do as much positive cross as you can in the beginning and save the zingers for the end.

18. Honest, straightforward opposing experts always will agree on certain basic points in a well-constructed cross-examination.

19. It is seldom productive to make a direct challenge to the qualifications of an expert.

20. Attack the expert's foundation and conclusions as unsupported by credible evidence.

21. Use of learned treatises should be done very carefully. A battle between lawyer and expert over technical details quickly will bore the jury.

22. While it makes sense to go after opposing experts on bias, this is often overdone. Jurors don't care that experts get paid for their testimony. It is only if an expert is shown to be an advocate that this will matter.

23. In criminal cases, the prosecution cross-examination of defense experts often is concession-based.

24. The defense usually does not directly challenge the crime lab analysis, discussing instead the general problems that can come up that impact accuracy.

25. Many times, an expert will lack some piece of the foundation, not getting some key deposition, testimony or medical records.

26. Visuals always provide an effective anchor for cross-examination, often pages from treatises, industry guidelines or clinical standards.

27. Effective use of depositions in cross-examination requires more than a rehash in front of the jury.

28. Video has ratcheted up the potential impact of depositions rather significantly.

29. Preserved on video, any significant inconsistency between the expert's opinions or appearance can be devastating.

30. You must review each clip to make sure it is as effective as the transcript makes it.

Conclusion

There is nothing permanent except change.

—Heraclitus

We live in a world of constant change that is driven by science and technology. Though principles of law remain more steadfast than many other disciplines, their interpretation is subject to what we know about the world around us.

Forensics has given us many more tools in the search for the truth, steadily replacing subjective opinion with greater certainty. The growing limitation we face is our ability to understand and apply what science can tell us, due to our lack of scientific knowledge. The 2009 National Academy of Science report, *Strengthening Forensic Science in the United States: A Path Forward*, clearly outlined these deficits in lawyers who handle criminal cases. A similar pattern exists for those in civil practice.

As the world become more complicated, a great collective burden passes to the legal profession to fairly and efficiently adjudicate disputes. We no longer can accomplish this just by knowing the law. Though he said it more than a century ago, the prophecy of Oliver Wendell Holmes has come to pass. The blackletter lawyer is giving way to one who also knows statistics and science, with technology added to the mix.

Appendix A

Case Problems

Biomechanical Engineering

Bicyclist George Constantine was hit by an SUV driven by Richard Prince, suffering a severe head injury. He died a week later in the hospital. It is unclear whether or not Mr. Constantine was wearing a helmet at the time of the collision.

The personal property inventory in the paramedics report does not state one way or the other whether a helmet was found at the scene. The paramedics treating the bicyclist at the scene provided conflicting testimony. One unequivocally states that she does not believe he had had a helmet on. Another believes that he would have noted the absence of a helmet, remembering a comment about a broken helmet at the scene. The absence of lacerations on the decedent's head and the lack of hair and blood on the SUV of the windshield further indicate to the second paramedic that the decedent likely wore a helmet.

The police investigation did not establish whether Mr. Constantine was wearing a helmet. The principal investigator cannot remember if there was a helmet at the scene. The driver's speed at the time of collision also is in dispute. Mr. Prince remembers driving 20 to 25 miles per hour in the 30 mile per hour zone. The police estimate of Mr. Prince's speed was given a range, between 26 and 36 miles per hour.

The decedent's estate has brought a wrongful death action against the driver. The plaintiff has hired a biomechanical engineer to look at how a helmet could have altered the outcome of this accident. He has calculated and used kinetic energy principles to determine the force the SUV exerted on the decedent at the time of the collision. His conclusion is that the limited protection offered by a standard helmet is insignificant compared to the amount of force applied, making no difference to the fatal outcome.

Assignment: Present the direct testimony of this expert on behalf of the estate. Cross-examine the expert on behalf of the driver.

Computer Forensics

Jason Sindell was a highly placed software developer who had been with Acme Technology for a little over three years. He was working on a sensitive new project involving Acme's proprietary information. On September 5, 2013, Mr. Sindell abruptly resigned from Acme, giving no reason for his departure. A week later, he began working for BV Software, one of Acme's primary competitors.

Alarmed at the possibility for infringement of its intellectual property, Acme asked an expert to examine the company-issued laptop computer used by Mr. Sindell. The computer was delivered to the expert, who specifically was asked to look for any evidence either of copying Acme electronic documents to removable storage or destroying information in the months prior to Mr. Sindell's leaving the company.

The expert made a copy of the computer's hard drive and then reviewed it for unusual activity. He determined that Mr. Sindell had taken steps to destroy electronic data by use of a third-party software utility. This software had overwritten deleted data, making it difficult to perform any recovery of files and user activity in specific areas of the computer's hard drive.

The expert also determined that Mr. Sindell connected removable storage devices to the computer. Files opened on the laptop were stored on these over the same time period when the overwriting of electronic data occurred.

Based on the report of its computer forensics expert, Acme has filed a lawsuit alleging theft and infringement of its proprietary information, naming both BV Software and Mr. Sindell as defendants.

Assignment: Conduct a deposition of Acme's computer forensics expert on behalf of the defendants.

DNA

A young woman sent an email to her sister on New Year's Eve, telling her that she had to rush off to the store to shop for a dinner with friends. Half an hour later, a bearded man in a stocking cap stabbed her to death outside the condominium she recently had purchased.

The fatal attack happened about 7 p.m. as the young woman prepared to re-enter her building. Neighbors heard her screams and rushed to her aid, but the attacker was fleeing from the scene, having inflicted fatal wounds. Police officers who responded to the 911 call found the victim on the sidewalk, bleeding heavily from stab wounds to the chest. She was rushed to the regional trauma center where efforts to revive her were unsuccessful. She was pronounced dead.

Homicide detectives questioned a 48-year-old man who lived in the area as a person of interest. He had a long history of paranoid schizophrenia and was under Department of Corrections supervision at the time. He claimed to have seen the suspect running from the scene of the killing that night. This individual consented to the detectives' request that he provide a DNA swab, which was collected and submitted to the crime laboratory.

The day following the murder, canvassing patrol officers located a knife in some bushes near the scene. Homicide detectives were called to the location and secured this evidence with appropriate protocol, submitting it to the crime laboratory for analysis. It had the victim's DNA on the blade and an unknown male DNA on the handle.

On a chance that there might be a connection between the 48-year-old person of interest and the murder, the swabs from the knife handle and this person were submitted for analysis. A match was made between the two. Now a suspect, the person of interest was brought back in for questioning and confessed to the killing.

Assignment: Conduct a direct and cross-examination of a DNA expert on the match between the DNA on the handle of the knife and the suspect, as well as between the DNA on the blade and the victim.

Economic Loss to Estate — Wrongful Death

The plaintiff has hired an economist to project the loss to the estate of George Constantine from his wrongful death in a car accident. The economist's opinions are based upon the projections of the plaintiff's vocational expert that Mr. Constantine would have earned a professional degree, with much higher lifetime earnings than a graduate of a four-year college. The economist's methodology takes the future earning capacity as outlined by the vocational expert, subtracting the decedent's personal expenses, discounted to present value.

Mr. Constantine died at the age of 22.90 years. His statistical life expectancy at the date of injury was 50.51 years. The economist assumed that Mr. Constantine could have completed a professional degree by age 28. The work-life expectancy of a 28-year-old with fifteen or more years of education is 33.6 years. Assuming continuous labor force participation from degree completion, this implies retirement at age 61.60.

The loss to the estate was measured by the difference between the present value of his projected earnings and expenses. Per the plaintiff's vocational expert, the economist assumed that Mr. Constantine's earnings would be significantly above the average for all workers in the United States. Personal consumption data was subtracted from the projected earnings to determine the present value of the economic loss to the estate.

The economist concluded that the loss to the estate would be $1,184,809, as set forth in Attachment A to her report.

Assignment: Present the direct testimony of the economist on behalf of the estate. Cross-examine her on behalf of the driver who hit Mr. Constantine.

ATTACHMENT A

CONCLUSIONS: PRESENT VALUE SUMMARY OF ECONOMIC LOSS TO THE ESTATE OF GEORGE CONSTANTINE

EARNINGS PERSONAL CONSUMPTION & LOSS TO THE ESTATE BASED ON AVERAGE EARNINGS OF MALES WITH:

MASTER'S DEGREES

EARNINGS:	$2,901,642
PERSONAL CONSUMPTION:	$1,886,067
LOSS TO THE ESTATE:	$1,015,575

PROFESSIONAL DEGREES

EARNINGS:	$3,385,168
PERSONAL CONSUMPTION:	$2,200,359
LOSS TO THE ESTATE:	$1,184,809

Earnings calculation begins at age 28.

Employment Discrimination

Malcolm Greenspan is a 53-year-old who worked for 10 years in an employment-at-will state as a midlevel manager at Technology Solutions International (TSI). Until the last 6 months at TSI, he received consistently strong performance evaluations and regular raises.

Mr. Greenspan alleges that he was forced out of the company for refusing to get rid of a subordinate who had missed considerable work due to the illness of her child. His supervisor complained to him that this subordinate was not pulling her weight, directing that he take steps to force her resignation.

The supervisor suggested specific actions to accomplish this, including negative performance reviews, undesirable assignments and difficult hours. After some thought, Mr. Greenspan refused to follow his supervisor's directions. This led to dramatic change in his own circumstances at TSI. His previously high performance ratings plummeted, with steady deterioration in his working conditions. Ultimately, Mr. Greenspan was forced to resign.

Mr. Greenspan has brought an unlawful termination lawsuit against TSI. His expert opines that he was fired for refusing to do an illegal act, stating that his subordinate was protected under the Family and Medical Leave Act of 1993. His expert also alleges that the defendant failed to follow its own termination policies, which required the involvement of HR. The defendant denies these claims, stating that the plaintiff was an at-will employee who was terminated for declining performance.

Assignment: Take the deposition of the plaintiff's employment practices expert on behalf of the defendant.

Fingerprints

R.J. Henderson is a 39-year-old African-American man who is charged with two counts of first-degree rape. The events started on the morning of October 24, 2013, when the victim, a 69-year-old Caucasian woman, answered a knock on her door. She was confronted with an attacker who forced his way into her home by knifepoint.

The victim later described this intruder as a black male about 6 feet tall, 200 to 225 pounds, about 35 years old, dark-skinned with bushy hair. He sexually assaulted her multiple times, taking off his shirt in the process. He then filled the victim's bathtub with water and forced her to get in, intending to destroy any DNA evidence. After a period of about a half hour, he drained the tub and left.

The victim called the police within minutes of hearing the attacker leave. They were unable to recover a semen sample for DNA testing, but did find a hair on the victim's clothing that was not hers.

The day of the assault, the police showed the victim a photo lineup that included Leon Sanders, who lived in the victim's general neighborhood and had a past criminal history, including several assaults on a female, assault with a deadly weapon and burglary. The victim was unable to identify anyone from these photos.

Two days after the assault, the victim spoke about the assault with a neighbor, Margaret Crockett, who occasionally worked for the police as an informant. After this conversation, the victim later called police and reported for the first time that her attacker had a mole or bump on the side of his face and talked with a lisp, though it might have been because he was drunk.

Ms. Crockett also called the police that same day, suggesting that R.J. Henderson fit the victim's description of her attacker, including the mole on his face. Police then went back to the victim's home and showed her a photo lineup that included Mr. Henderson. The victim identified him as the attacker, though she said his hair was longer.

Mr. Henderson's only prior violations were two drunken driving convictions and a trespassing charge. When he heard that the police had come by his house looking for him, Mr. Henderson walked down to police headquarters with his girlfriend. He stated that he had no idea why the police wanted to arrest him and immediately offered to take a lie-detector test when he found out he was the suspect in a rape case.

The police declined his offer, charging him with the crime on the basis of the photo lineup identification by the victim and a hair found on the victim's clothing, which the crime lab determined was that of an African-American male.

Mr. Henderson told police that he had met the victim only once, about a month before the incident. He had asked to use her phone to report a disturbance at the home of his friend, the victim's neighbor, involving a man named Leon Sanders. The victim had not allowed him in the house, but had called the police for him.

Mr. Henderson said that he was at a house with friends more than two miles away at the time of the incident, all of whom confirmed his presence, saying that he could not have committed the crime. The police and prosecution deemed these alibi witnesses not to be credible.

Defendant's counsel served a demand under *United States v. Brady* for all evidence in this case in the possession of the police and prosecution. It was only then that counsel received several fingerprints that were recovered by the police from a banana in the victim's kitchen. The police stated that these were not considered as there was no proof that the attacker ever entered the victim's kitchen.

Assignment: Conduct a direct and cross-examination of the fingerprint expert called by R.J. Henderson.

Forensic Anthropology

Amy Pitts (White female, age 34, 5 feet 4 inches tall) was reported missing by her husband, Jim Pitts, on January 8, 2013. She was last known alive when she left work on January 4, 2013, at 5 p.m. Co-workers reported to the police that Ms. Pitts had expressed concern for her safety, stating that her husband was violent, regularly threatening to harm her. On September 5, 2013, a hunter in a rural, wooded area discovered human remains wrapped in a carpet. These were identified subsequently as Amy Pitts. The manner of death is homicide.

A forensic anthropologist was retained by the county to examine the remains and make a positive identification. The resulting biological profile indicated a Caucasian female with an age range of 26–42 years with a stature of 5 feet 3 inches, plus or minus 3 inches.

The determination of sex was based on the width of the subpubic angle and sciatic notch, cranial morphology and relative gracility of the supra-orbital tori, mastoid process and nuchal crest.

The determination of race is based on the long, rounded cranium, narrow nasal aperture, sharp nasal sill and receding molars. In addition, Carabelli's cusp is noted bilaterally on the first maxillary molars.

The determination of age is based on the sternal end of the fourth ribs (Iscan phase 4/5) and morphology of the pubic symphyses (Suchey/Brooks Phase IV). The iliac crest and medial clavicle are fully fused.

The following measurements were taken to determine stature, using the formulae of Trotter and Gleser (1952) for White females. Right femur: 42.9 cm. Left femur: 43.0 cm.

On September 14, 2013, the forensic anthropologist compared anterior/posterior radiographs of Amy Pitts from her medical records with the skeletal remains recovered by the county sheriff's office. The results of this comparison were that the person known as Amy Pitts and the skeletal remains recovered are the same individual.

Assignment: Conduct a direct examination of the forensic anthropologist on behalf of the prosecution and a cross-examination of behalf of the defendant.

Insanity Defense

Defendant James Pearson is a 28-year-old single male charged with the murder of Andrea Giannelli on the evening of April 20, 2013. He inflicted the fatal wounds in a random knife attack on the victim in the fast-food restaurant where she worked.

At the time of the incident, Pearson was living at home with his parents, unable to function independently because of a combination of chronic mental illness and mild retardation, with an IQ range of 65–70. His chief diagnosis was schizophrenia, chronic undifferentiated type, with prominent paranoid delusions. Defendant was taking medications to help control the symptoms of his mental illness.

Defendant had very negative feelings toward women in general, with a criminal history of two prior sex offenses. He left his home that evening with the intention to "hurt a female," as he later told police. The defendant was carrying a hidden 6-inch kitchen knife. He walked a short distance to a nearby commercial area. He spotted a woman on the street who seemed a likely assault target, but the presence of her children caused him to change his mind. He kept going, entering a fast-food restaurant.

Once inside, he saw the victim sitting by herself, back toward him. Defendant plunged the knife into the victim's upper left back. She screamed, jumped up and then collapsed. Due to the length of the blade, it penetrated her upper chest wall and lacerated the right lower ventricle of her heart, causing almost instantaneous massive bleeding.

After the attack, the defendant fled the scene, knife in hand, followed by coworkers of the victim. He threw the knife into a field a short distance away. He was captured quickly, with the victim's blood all over his clothing. The defendant later told the police, "I should have stayed home with my stuffed animals. This is all evil stuff I've done. It is too much."

The psychologist examining the defendant for the prosecution concluded that he acted with intent, by initially concealing the knife, and knew he was stabbing a human being; appreciating the wrongfulness of his act when he fled the scene and discarded the knife.

Assignment: As counsel for the defendant, take the deposition of the prosecution's forensic psychologist, exploring the competence of the defendant, his ability to tell right from wrong and to appreciate the nature and consequences of his actions.

Insurance Claims Practices

A Homeowners Association ("HOA") is pursuing a construction defect claim against various contractors, including a framing subcontractor, ABC Framing and its owner, Mike Hammer. XYZ Insurance Company had insured ABC Framing and Mr. Hammer. The HOA's expert has opined that XYZ Insurance violated its duties of good faith toward Mr. Hammer and ABC.

In the fall of 20012, the HOA initiated an arbitration proceeding against Mr. Hammer and several other subcontractors. XYZ Insurance agreed to defend Mr. Hammer pursuant to a reservation of rights, and retained attorney Kenneth Crook. Mr. Crook appeared, conducted an investigation, and filed several pre-hearing motions to dismiss on behalf of his clients, Mr. Hammer and ABC.

In a June 26, 2013, letter, Mr. Crook informed the HOA's attorneys of his clients' Chapter 7 bankruptcy discharge, and asked that the plaintiffs dismiss their claims against Mr. Hammer. Shortly thereafter, the HOA's attorneys notified Mr. Crook that they were proceeding against Mr. Hammer for purposes of recovering against XYZ as Mr. Hammer's insurer.

Mr. Crook then filed a motion requesting that the claims against Mr. Hammer be dismissed due to the bankruptcy. The arbitrator apparently accepted this argument, ruling that "(t)he amount awarded against Mr. Hammer may only be applied to insurance proceeds."

On November 14, 2013, the arbitrator entered an interim award finding Mr. Hammer liable to the HOA for $783,798. A few days later, Mr. Crook sent an email to XYZ containing legal advice about how much of the award was covered by Mr. Hammer's insurance. When Mr. Hammer found out about this email and questioned Crook about it, Crook told Mr. Hammer that "even though you're technically my client, you're now judgment proof so my real client is XYZ." Crook eventually told XYZ's adjuster that he estimated the covered portions of the arbitration award at $500,000.

XYZ Insurance disclaimed coverage for significant portions of the award due to a "your work" exclusion. This is a common issue in construction coverage matters, where the cost to repair the contractor's own defective work generally is not covered, but damage to other property caused by construction defects generally is.

On November 27, 20013, XYZ Insurance offered the HOA $100,000 to settle its claims against Mr. Hammer. The HOA demanded full payment. XYZ Insurance increased its offer to $125,000. On February 1, 2014, the arbitrator entered a final award against Mr. Hammer for $893,648.

On March 19, 2014, the HOA filed suit against XYZ Insurance, asserting breach of contract and various extra-contractual claims. Mr. Hammer assigned its rights against XYZ Insurance to the HOA on July 7, 2014, and the HOA subsequently amended its complaint to assert the assigned claims as well as claims by the HOA in its own right.

1. <u>Claims handling issues prior to August 6, 2013</u>

a. <u>ABC's initial investigation</u>. The HOA's expert opines that ABC failed to conduct a timely initial investigation. The demand was dated June 6, 2012. However, ABC's internal file notes indicate that it was not received until December 7, 2012.

ABC assigned claims adjuster Lou S. Cannon to the case on October 18, 2012. On November 10, 2012, Mr. Cannon sent an initial letter regarding coverage and regarding ABC's reservation of rights. According to ABC's notes, Mr. Cannon spoke with the attorneys for the claimant, the HOA, sometime prior to November 22, 2012. After ABC received the arbitration demand, Mr. Cannon retained counsel, Mr. Ken Crook, to defend Mr. Hammer. On December 18, 2012, Crook filed a notice of appearance and agreed to use the arbitrator suggested by the HOA's attorneys.

b. <u>Policy information</u>. XYZ's November 10, 2012, reservation of rights letter stated that the applicable policy limits were $300,000 per occurrence, $600,000 aggregate. The letter also referenced a "multi-unit" exclusion as a potential bar to coverage. These statements were inaccurate because the relevant policy had limits of $1 million per occurrence and $1 million aggregate and no "multi-unit" exclusion.

The HOA's expert found "no evidence" that the correct policy information was ever subsequently conveyed, and that this falls below the applicable standard of care.

c. <u>Representation By Mr. Crook</u>. XYZ retained Mr. Crook to defend Mr. Hammer. He works for a law firm that consists only of XYZ employees and represents only XYZ insureds. The HOA's expert states that the very fact of his employment creates an issue about compliance with the duty of an insurer to defend its insured.

2. <u>Claims handling issues subsequent to August 6, 2013</u>

On August 6, 2013, the HOA indicated that it would not pursue a claim against Mr. Hammer's personal assets.

Assignment: Conduct a direct and cross-examination of the insurance practices expert for the Homeowners Association.

Medical Malpractice

A 76-year-old male had a medical history of diabetes, hypertension and obesity. He took prescription medications on a daily basis to manage his diabetes and blood pressure, as well as aspirin that he purchased over the counter from the pharmacy. He had no prior medical history of a stroke.

The patient was watching television at home with his wife at around 9:00 p.m. when the onset of stroke symptoms occurred. His speech was garbled and he couldn't move his right side.

The patient's wife called 911 immediately and an EMT unit arrived within 10 to 15 minutes. It was an obvious stroke and the patient was taken to a smaller outlying hospital nearby. A head CT scan was performed there, which initially was not enhanced with a contrast medium. The results were negative for the presence of blood on the brain. A second CT scan followed, this time contrast enhanced, which showed a blockage of the right middle cerebral artery.

The acute onset and early diagnosis of this event was unusual. Most strokes take longer to present, with greater resulting devastation at the time the diagnosis is made. This patient's brain was still viable. The sooner the blockage was opened, the better.

There are two basic treatment options for a patient in this situation. The first is systemic, administering blood clot dissolving medical lytics by IV. The second is to have an interventional radiologist insert a catheter into the patient to dissolve the clot. The second option is not available at smaller hospitals and required the patient to be transported.

The attending hospitalist in the ER called an interventional radiologist for a consulting opinion on how best to manage the patient's care. IV (systemic) lytics then were given at the local ER instead of the 90-minute transport to the city for intra-arterial, catheter directed lytics and other measures. The patient experienced a large hemorrhage after the IV and died.

The decedent's family has brought a medical malpractice case against the hospitalist and the consulting interventional radiologist, claiming that the administration of systemic lytics caused the brain to bleed. The plaintiffs allege that the patient should have been airlifted to the medical referral center, where the clot could have been dissolved by an arterial catheter, with fewer risks.

Assignment: Conduct a direct and cross-examination of the medical liability expert testifying on behalf of the hospitalist and consulting interventional radiologist that the standard of care was not breached in this situation.

Structural Engineering

On June 22, 2013, Capital Development applied for a building permit for an 11-story office building. The permit was issued on July 25, 2013, requiring that this structure conform with applicable rules and the Uniform Building Code. The general contractor for the project was Hurst Construction.

ACS Engineering prepared structural plans that specified the fabrication and placement of the steel rebar in the concrete slabs of this building. Subsequent to completion of construction, the building exhibited significant cracking over the beam support and excessive mid-span vertical deflection.

Once this was discovered, county building inspectors examined photos taken during construction and noted that the contractor had only put one-half of the reinforcing steel into the beam supports that had been specified by the structural engineer. The county then issued a notice to vacate and demolish the building.

Hurst Construction brought an action to enjoin the county from enforcing the notice to vacate and demolish the building. The contractor has hired a licensed professional engineer to support its assertion that the building is safe.

The engineer studied the site photos and performed structural analysis calculations related to the slab capacity. Two typical reinforced concrete slabs, 6 inches and 6.5 inches thick, were studied with respect to the anticipated design loads. Using yield line theory, the engineer determined that the ultimate load capacities of the slabs are in excess of the design loads, with a minimum factor of safety of 1.15. Based on this, it is the engineer's conclusion that the structure does not pose a dangerous condition and should not be demolished.

Assignment: Conduct a deposition of Hurst Construction's engineering expert on behalf of the county.

Toxicology

On November 12, 2013, shortly before 10:30 p.m., Peter Fabian was returning home on a familiar two-lane arterial street. There was a double yellow line down the middle and a parking lane on both sides. Suddenly, he noticed headlights coming right toward him in his lane. He swerved and jammed on his brakes, but the oncoming vehicle hit him with great force. The driver was Jerry Cartwright, a 32-year-old construction worker. He just had left the Gasoline Lounge, a mile away, where he had been drinking for hours. He was a regular there, going 2–3 times a week.

Mr. Cartwright arrived at the bar at 6:00 p.m. that night. He was by himself and drank double scotches, followed by beer chasers. Eyewitnesses at the scene observed Mr. Cartwright get out of his truck and fall on the ground. The responding police officers found that he could not say the alphabet correctly, and kept trying to sing it. He could not stand without losing his balance. His speech was slurred and slow. A blood draw was done within two hours of the collision, with a blood alcohol level of .19 g/100 ml.

Mr. Fabian sued the Gasoline Lounge for over-serving Mr. Cartwright. He has retained a toxicologist. Based on the fact that the human body burns off .015 g/100 ml. of alcohol per hour, the toxicologist opined that Mr. Cartwright would have had an even higher blood alcohol level at the time of the collision, appearing even more intoxicated before he left the Gasoline Lounge than he was at the scene of the collision.

Assignment: Conduct a deposition of the toxicologist on behalf of the Gasoline Lounge, focusing on the obvious intoxication question.

Vocational Assessment — Loss to Estate

George Constantine was a 22-year-old single male who was hit and killed in a crosswalk while working as a bicycle messenger. He was the youngest of three children in his family. His father is an airline pilot and his mother is a homemaker. The decedent's older sister received her law degree and works at a large corporate firm. His older brother obtained his degree in civil engineering and is employed by an environmental consulting firm.

The decedent attended college for four years with a 3.23 GPA as an arts and sciences major. Mr. Constantine was 4 credits short of receiving his bachelor's degree. Though he expressed a strong interest to family members in following his sister's path to law school and the LSAT study guide his sister gave him was by his bedside table when he died, Mr. Constantine had taken no active steps to apply to law school or complete the remaining credits for his undergraduate degree.

Mr. Constantine had been working at Mercury Messenger Service for two years at the time of his death. He had grown out his hair, gotten tattoos, smoked marijuana and embraced Eastern religious thought. Before his death, he wrote a personal essay in his journal titled the "Dharma Manifesto." This extolled the virtues of "living in the now" and lamented the tendency of people to look at life through "mechanical, robot, industry-stifled, pollution-encrusted, prejudiced eyes."

The decedent's family has filed a wrongful death action against the driver who struck him in the crosswalk. They have retained the services of a certified vocational counselor who has opined that if he had not died in this accident, Mr. Constantine would have gone on to get a graduate degree in some field, earning significantly higher income than those with a four-year college degree.

You represent the driver in this matter. Your vocational expert takes issue with the plaintiff's claims, finding no indication of any definite career path in decedent's academic or employment records.

Assignment: Take the deposition of the decedent's vocational expert.

Report of Plaintiff's Vocational Expert: *Constantine v. Prince*

1. As a career counselor, I look at people's backgrounds and determine what their capacities are.

2. Had he not died in this accident, Mr. Constantine would have gone on to get a graduate degree in some field.

3. When I interviewed several close friends and his sister, all indicated that Mr. Constantine had stated a strong preference for becoming a lawyer.

4. The fact that he was taking a break from school at the time he was killed did not make Mr. Constantine less likely to return to graduate school at a later time.

5. The parents and siblings of George Constantine are successful professionals. This is a good indication of his future achievement level.

6. George Constantine tested well, was goal oriented and performed at a high level in school.

7. Student academic performance in college is positively associated with applying, being accepted and enrolling in graduate school.

8. George Constantine's GPA and record of doing well on standardized admission tests made him likely to get into law school.

9. The National Center for Education Statistics reports that a large majority (85%) of bachelor degree recipients in Mr. Constantine's age group expected to earn a graduate or professional degree.

10. Of the college graduates in this group, 83% of those who applied for an advanced degree were accepted and enrolled in a program.

11. There is no evidence in any of the materials I reviewed which would indicate that George Constantine used recreational drugs to an extent that would impair his earning capacity. Many successful professionals smoke marijuana with no apparent ill effects on their career.

Report of Defendant's Vocational Expert: *Constantine v. Prince*

1. Vocational counselors have to make judgment calls on job candidates' level of motivation and life direction in order to determine their likelihood of career success in the competitive labor market. My training and experience allows me to make an assessment of the future prospects of George Constantine.

2. Mr. Constantine had the intelligence to engage in a variety of occupations, including the pursuit of an advanced degree.

3. There is no indication of any definite career path in any of his academic or employment records.

4. While Mr. Constantine had the ability to pursue a law degree, it would be sheer speculation to conclude that he in fact would have gone in this direction. Mr. Constantine was 4 credits short of the 180 required to graduate from the University of Washington. He had no plan to complete those and had not even applied to take the LSAT.

5. Mr. Constantine's performance in college was uneven. He was able to maintain a respectable GPA only by taking a number of fairly easy classes.

6. No vocational expert can say on a more probable than not basis what Mr. Constantine would have done in the future. He had been a bicycle messenger for more than two years at the time he died, which did not prepare him for any kind of professional job.

7. Even if we presume that Mr. Constantine would have gone on to law school and graduated, incomes earned by lawyers are all over the map. Some make six-figure incomes right out of school and others remain unable to get any employment in the legal profession.

8. The plaintiff's reliance on family background information to predict the future occupational success of Mr. Constantine is not valid. The fact that his sister works for a big law firm and is successful has no bearing on whether Mr. Constantine would have been able to achieve the same status.

9. Marijuana use tends to decrease one's motivation and academic performance. It is a definite possibility that this explains why Mr. Constantine seemed to have lost his prior level of ambition.

10. Mr. Constantine's alternative appearance and philosophical attitudes would have limited his vocational options.

Appendix B

Cross-Examination of an Opposing Medical Expert

Background Facts

In *Cody v. Grant*, a negligent motorist hit the plaintiff as he stood by his truck in a parking lot. Plaintiff suffered multiple orthopedic injuries and required several surgeries, with residual pain and physical limitations. In the trial of the tort action, the defense relied heavily on the testimony of its forensic medical expert, orthopedist William B. Grimm.

A skilled forensic witness with an impressive résumé, Dr. Grimm steadily had shifted from orthopedic surgery to medical assessments for insurance companies. Dr. Grimm concluded in the Cody case that the plaintiff should have recovered fully from his injuries, with any remaining physical complaints either psychosomatic or due to lack of diligence in rehabilitation.

Plaintiff's counsel, C. Steven Fury, of Seattle, Washington, had a well-thought-out, systematic plan to undermine Dr. Grimm's credibility through a storytelling method of cross-examination. Experience has taught Mr. Fury the limitations of the traditional impeachment method of cross-examination. Even if you succeed in destroying a witness, this does not necessarily solidify your trial story:

> The goal of cross-examination is not so much combat as it is moving your case forward.

Mr. Fury was both an actor and director in the cross-examination of Dr. Grimm, demonstrating that the expert was an advocate by the way he responded to tightly drawn questions. A contrast was made between Dr. Grimm's role as a medical advocate for one side and the plaintiff's unbiased treating physicians.

General Strategic Approach

Mr. Fury did not just accept Dr. Grimm's report at face value, instead forming a plan of collateral attack. He collected considerable information about this expert from other lawyers, including depositions, trial transcripts and his reports in other cases. Without ever having met this expert, all this information gave Mr. Fury a good idea of how he would respond to questions. He received a trial transcript where Dr. Grimm had refused to testify about his income. His testimony was stricken and a mistrial was declared.

Applying the observer effect, that you can't measure something without changing it, Mr. Fury decided not to take Dr. Grimm's deposition prior to trial:

> A deposition will help an expert better withstand my cross-examination, educating him as to where I'm going. I prefer to gather enough information from other sources.

The information Mr. Fury received from other attorneys about Dr. Grimm's forensic income opened a rich potential vein of vulnerability, making a deposition less important:

> This expert's refusal to answer question about his income told me that he was arrogant enough to refuse a judge's order. It also told me was that this was an extremely sore spot for him and he likely would react to it in the same way in my case. This reaction would heighten the issue of how much he was paid for doing this kind of work for one side, making it both more important and damaging to his credibility.

In that Dr. Grimm was willing to testify about his hourly rate and how many cases he handled, Mr. Fury opted for a simple multiplication and common-sense approach to financial bias.

Sequencing

The sequence of the questions in cross-examination is critical. Many experts line up on one side or the other. Attacking the jury's presumption of the neutrality of a medical expert is the most important primary target.

Dr. Grimm worked only for the defense in civil cases. However, Mr. Fury knew that the standard lawyer approach of starting out with money questions would not work. The jury knows that everyone involved in a case is being paid.

A more effective cross-examination of an opposing expert begins with educating the jury why the money matters. Once bias is established, the money becomes the explanation for the expert's one-sidedness:

> The financial bias of an expert witness must come late in the cross-examination. Everybody knows that all the players in a trial are earning a living. This is not an altruistic venture. If you immediately leap upon the doctor for being paid, it's a so what. Being paid a lot may just mean that they're good at it, an effective doctor who can examine people well and knows what he/she is doing, rather than being biased. You have to demonstrate the bias of the witness first before you give the money as their explanation for it.

The Contrast Method of Cross-Examination

The contrast method of cross-examining an expert starts with an analysis of the preconceived attitudes that jurors may have. As a general matter, jurors always start out on the side of the witness, not the lawyer:

> Most jurors will feel sorry for the witness who is being made to look bad. This is not the emotion you want the jury to feel. You want your jury to say, "I like the story, it makes sense to me. This witness's testimony doesn't."

Polling data shows that doctors are highly respected and well-liked by the public, as they treat patients and help make them better. Lawyers suffer by comparison, on the low end of the public approval list:

> I'm a few points behind when I first stand up to cross-examine the doctor. I've got to even the playing field and try to remove the patina of credibility that doctors have, based upon their humanitarian role.

Unless given good reasons why the usual presumption should not apply, a medical expert is viewed as far more credible than the lawyer who cross-examines him/her. This imbalance in baseline professional goodwill presents a serious challenge:

> In cross-examination, every question or every series of questions comes down to a credibility balance between the lawyer and the witness. Who's winning in this tennis game of back and forth questions? Medical experts invariability claim "I'm independent and fair, just calling them as I see them. Therefore, you should believe me." They make it even tougher by adding the "I'm a doctor and I know best" rubric.

In the *Cody* case, Mr. Fury sought to undermine the credibility of Dr. Grimm by contrasting his work as a paid medical expert with the elevated public image of doctors who treat patients. He educated the jury about the differences that occur when physicians work as paid forensic experts. They do not see patients for purposes of providing care and treatment, causing a fundamental shift of attitude and role.

A great advantage of cross-examination is that you get to choose the subjects. The challenge with an opposing medical expert is to win the war of impression by focusing on areas of true vulnerability, leaving the rest alone:

> There are subjects on which questions can only help you. If the witness avoids talking about those subjects, they look like an advocate. You can talk about the differences between a forensic medical examiner and a treating doctor for a long time without getting hurt.

A forensic medical expert always knows what it is like to be a treating doctor. This then becomes a reference point for showing how different the role of a professional medical witness is, showing him/her to be an advocate by talking about what this means.

In the first part of his cross-examination, Mr. Fury had Dr. Grimm talk about his own role as a treating doctor, addressing all the elements of providing patient care: "A treating doctor is…," filling in the blanks. This brought out the qualities that jurors see in their own treating doctors, explaining why they are well liked. This establishes the foundation needed for the next phase, where the forensic medical expert's role is distinguished as advocacy rather than patient care. The ultimate goal is to show that the testifying medical expert is not entitled to the usual halo extended to doctors.

Cross-Examination — William B. Grimm, M.D.

BY MR. FURY:

Q. Dr. Grimm, do you treat patients?

A. Yes, I do.

Q. But, you're not here today as a treating doctor?

A. That's correct.

Q. A treating doctor needs to listen to his patient's problems?

A. I think that would be advisable.

Q. He uses the patient's reports of symptoms in making a diagnosis?

A. We all do that.

Q. That's what a treating doctor does.

A. I think every doctor does that.

Q. And he gets to know the patient as a person?

A. That may happen.

Q. Does that happen over time?

A. Generally, yes.

Q. And getting to know them over time can help in evaluating their symptoms?

A. I'm not sure that those two are related.

Q. A treating doctor develops an ongoing relationship with the patient?

A. He does that.

Q. And wants to establish the patient's trust?

A. I think he probably does.

Q. Well, you certainly want your patients to trust you.

A. That's correct.

Q. A treating doctor takes responsibility for the patient's care?

A. He does.

Q. And educating the patient about their health?

A. I would recommend he do that.

Q. In fact, a treating doctor has an ethical responsibility to make the patient's interests paramount?

A. Yes.

Q. And the goal of the treating doctor is to make the patient better?

A. Yes.

Q. In fact, if the patient doesn't get better, a treating doctor will be concerned.

A. I'm sure that's true.

Q. And if the treating doctor makes a mistake, he's got to live with those mistakes and try to fix them?

A. Every mistake we make, we have to live with.

The Underlying Theme: Forensic Medical Experts Are Advocates

The theme of Mr. Fury's cross-examination story was that Dr. Grimm was an advocate. All of his questions were carefully designed to demonstrate to the jury why this was true, bringing out these qualities in the witness. After establishing what treating doctors do, he shifted to forensic medical experts. Using the term "professional witness," his questions reflected how a doctor in this role differs from a treating physician. With the implicit premise of an opinion for hire, the professional witness term is meant to sting, often drawing an emotional response.

Unlike the traditional cross-examination of tight control, only asking leading questions, the contrast method seeks to get the expert to talk as much as possible:

> My questions tell the story. I didn't care what his answers were. I wanted to get him to talk as much as possible. When he disagreed with me and wanted to go on for a paragraph, I just stood there and let him. It was extremely uncomfortable to listen to these speeches, unresponsive to the question, slanted in his favor. But I didn't interrupt, try to stop him or force him to answer my question. I just let him go. That was purposeful. His answers prove that a real physician expert witness should not be an advocate.

The cross-examination was designed to turn Dr. Grimm into an advocate for the other side, so much so that it might as well be opposing counsel testifying. The more an expert fights the professional witness label, the more it proves the accuracy of the description. The bottom line is that a treating doctor cares about the patient's outcome and a professional witness does not.

Q. You're here today, however, not as a treating doctor, but as a professional witness, right?

A. I'm an expert witness who's paid for my time.

Q. You were picked by the defense lawyer?

A. I'm not sure how she came to hire me.

Q. But she's the one who hired you?

A. The letter is from her.

Q. A professional witness is professionally skeptical about what a patient might tell him?

A. My goal is to reach the truth. If that means being skeptical about what I hear or see, then that would be correct. I'm looking for the truth.

Q. You look for inconsistencies in the record?

A. If there are inconsistencies, we should all know about them, yes.

Q. You focus on objective findings?

A. I think all physicians should do that.

Q. Do you dismiss the subjective symptoms of pain?

A. That is not correct. Doctors make diagnosis 80 percent of the time based on the patient's history and subjective complaints. We understand the natural history of the disease process. If the clinical course is different from what would be expected, then it's appropriate to question the initial diagnosis.

Q. So, you see your job as questioning the subjective symptoms of your patient?

A. I think that's true of every doctor.

Q. It's different when you see an individual for a forensic examination like in this case, then you've become a professional witness.

A. I object to your use of the word professional witness. I'm an expert witness here, and I am paid for my time.

Q. You're a professional?

A. Baseball players are professional when they're paid. If that's the definition of a professional, then that's what I am. If we just accept that I am being paid for my time, then I am a professional.

Q. So, you see my client here as a case.

A. And when I see my patient, they are a case.

Q. Not a person?

A. One of the interesting things doctors do is they deal with the patient first. They take the history and examine the patient before they look at the records and the X-rays. That's what I can do here, too.

Q. You saw my client just one time?

A. Yes. Usually people like you do not allow me to see them again. I have seen people on more than one occasion when the plaintiff has waived that right or the court has ordered it to be the case. Otherwise, I see them only once.

Q. For a matter of minutes?

A. I see them for as long as it takes. It's scheduled for an hour. Some people take longer, some take less.

Q. This was less, wasn't it?

A. I don't know. Your client gave a pretty long history, and he had multiple problem areas. I don't time them. All I can say is it takes as long as necessary for me to get the information I need. I do the exam that I need to do.

Q. And a professional witness like you doesn't care if the patient trusts you, do you?

A. Whether he trusts me or not is not my concern, that's correct.

Q. You have no responsibility for the patient in these circumstances.

A. I think I have a responsibility to tell the truth. I think we all benefit from the truth.

Q. You have no responsibility to a patient like my client, do you?

A. My evaluation is in his best interests. If he were to take it to heart, he would be better off.

Q. You have no responsibility for his care?

A. I'm not a treating physician for him, that's correct.

Q. No responsibility for patient education?

A. Correct. They very rarely ask me any questions, so—

Q. And you don't take it upon yourself to explain things to them, do you?

A. If they ask, I will talk to them. Most of the time, people don't ask.

Q. You make no effort to help the patient get better?

A. That's not correct. The truth is in everybody's best interests. I believe what I've said here today is the truth. It is supported by the medical record. If your client is ready, willing, and able to take my advice, he'll be better off.

Q. Nothing to do with my client ever keeps you awake at night?

A. That's true. I've not lost any sleep over him.

Q. And as a professional witness, you can walk away from your mistakes and without any consequences?

A. I don't believe there are any mistakes. I take what I do seriously. I believe my opinions are supported by the evidence. I'm willing to argue about them here today. And if there's been a mistake made, I think we should identify and fess up.

Q. You do have some ethical duties as a professional witness though, don't you?

A. I think it's to the truth; it's to be honest.

Using Professional Ethical Standards

Simply using the word "ethics" with a forensic expert often will touch a nerve. Witnesses do not like this and their visceral discomfort shows. If the witness indeed is selling his/her opinion to the highest bidder, down deep, it troubles the conscience.

In addition, most professions have ethical rules and standards, particularly for testifying in court. Comparing these with the reality of what a forensic witness does often is very useful in cross-examination. Medical ethical rules explicitly state that doctors should not be advocates or offer opinions without adequate information. If there are unanswered questions, a doctor should resolve those before offering an opinion:

> These standards are written by peers and cannot be easily dismissed. This is particularly true with explicit prohibitions against being an advocate. They are being paid a lot of money for this and feel uncomfortable about it. Whether they admit it to themselves or not, many physicians who do frequent forensic work feel somewhere down deep that it's dirty. It just doesn't square with a physician's oath to help others and do no harm.

Q. Are you familiar with the American Academy of Orthopedic Surgeons?

A. Yes.

Q. The academy says the ethical duties of a witness are to not adopt an advocacy or partisan position. Do you agree with that?

A. Sure.

Q. The American Medical Association also says that a doctor who's a witness should never be an advocate, giving only testimony that will enlighten the court or jury, not impress or prejudice. Do you agree with that?

A. Yes.

Q. Medical authorities have written that a physician who relies on the remuneration received for insurance, medical exams, or testifying as an expert has an inherent conflict of interest. Physicians who author reports that are consistently unfavorable to an insurance company will often find themselves unemployed as evaluators. Do you agree with that?

A. No.

Q. Some physicians are corrupted and write opinions as zealous advocates for the attorney that employ them. The American Academy of Orthopedic Surgeons has recognized this problem, and that's why they have these ethical rules, right?

A. Probably there are some people who write inappropriate opinions.

Q. A busy orthopedist usually avoids doing high volumes of insurance medical exams, and legal testimony?

A. Most people don't do what I do.

The jury doesn't come into court with a standard for determining whether a medical expert is an advocate. The foundation questions in cross-examination give them everything they need to make this determination, establishing the differences between a real doctor and a professional medical witness. When this point was reached, Dr. Grimm understood the extent that his credibility had been impeached, reacting in a highly emotional manner.

Q. Now, we could recognize someone who is an advocate, couldn't we, doctor? Someone who doesn't want to answer straightforward, yes-or-no questions with a yes or no acts as an advocate, right?

A. I don't believe so. I think it's important to explain the question. Attorneys are able to phrase questions for yes and no, when actually a yes-or-no answer is not appropriate. The question itself can be slanted and would lead to the wrong opinion with just a yes or no. I think the witness who explains himself is a witness who you should believe.

Q. An advocate would be someone who wants to express opinions only on one side of the case?

A. I'm your witness now, counselor. If you want to bring out some information for your side, I'm perfectly willing to explain the medical facts. The same integrity that went into my examination is available to you now.

Q. An advocate would be someone who would give long answers to short questions.

A. This counselor is attempting to impugn my integrity. I greatly object to that. He'll find nothing anyplace where I have not told the truth or where my opinions are not supported by evidence. Nothing he will say today indicates that my opinion is not supported by the evidence. If you attempt to impugn me, Mr. Fury, then I'm going to answer directly to the jury, and they will decide.

Q. And that would be what an advocate would do.

A. I believe that's somebody who is defending their integrity.

The Expert's Report

The opposing expert's report is in his/her area of comfort, applying familiar scientific or technical principles to the case. You never will know this field better than the expert, who has years of education and experience in it. The art of the possible here is to chip away at the expert's report, showing where the foundation is lacking or where the conclusions don't make sense:

> Whatever I may think personally of the ethics, credibility and bias of the opposing expert medical witness, the jury doesn't necessarily go there. I will lose any direct challenge to the expert based on the report. However, hit-and-run guerilla tactics can help to win the war of impression against an opposing expert.

Once he took the medical credibility patina away from Dr. Grimm, establishing that he was a medical advocate, Mr. Fury moved on to inflict whatever damage he could on the opinions in his report:

> I did want to talk some about the medical issues in this case, if only to demonstrate to the jury that I didn't want to run away from them. I don't have to address every opinion, just focusing on selected issues that I can deal with. The obvious one is the bias that comes from the expert being paid.

Q. You talked about headaches in this case.

A. Yes.

Q. These are not migraines? These are not post-concussive headaches?

A. I don't believe so, no.

Q. Headaches like these can come from trauma, can't they?

A. Yes, but as the trauma subsides, that pain should subside too.

Q. My client's pain could be caused by some other serious underlying condition, right?

A. Yes.

Q. You didn't tell him that there was any possibility of another problem, did you?

A. No.

Q. You didn't really examine any other underlying condition, did you?

A. No.

Q. You didn't do anything to try to help him get better.

A. I'm not his treating physician and your client asked me no questions.

Q. You did conclude he had a shoulder injury in this crash.

A. Yes.

Q. Caused from the crash?

A. Yes.

Q. All right. With regard to his elbow, you've seen his treating orthopedist's declaration that this was causally related to this crash?

A. Yes.

Q. And this surgeon actually performed the operation on his elbow?

A. Yes.

Q. You disagree with my client's treating surgeon?

A. I do.

Q. Now, you do agree that my client has an impairment from his injuries?

A. No.

Q. He has no impairment from the injuries?

A. He has no impairment from the physical injuries in this accident.

Q. You're familiar with the American Medical Association Guide for permanent impairment?

A. Yes.

Q. These would indicate that there is impairment here, right?

A. His limited motion is temporary, not permanent. I think he is deconditioned. There's no physical reason why he couldn't move the shoulder again and likely will again. It's not a ratable permanent impairment.

Q. You've had patients with shoulder problems before, haven't you?

A. Yes.

Q. And one of the problems, if you've got a shoulder injury, is that working overhead can be a challenge?

A. Yes.

Q. Well, let's move on to this arthritis issue. Arthritis is a degenerative change, correct?

A. It's an inflammation, the result of degenerative change.

Q. Degenerative changes come on over time?

A. Correct.

Q. Happens to people who get old, as they get older.

A. Yes.

Q. Sort of like me losing my hair and yours turning gray.

A. Yes.

Q. Or wrinkles or what's happened to my eyes, so that I've got to use my glasses. These all would be degenerative changes, correct?

A. The eyes get less accommodating as we get older. We get stiffer.

Q. Would it surprise you if I had some degenerative changes in my neck?

A. It would not surprise me.

Q. But it wouldn't surprise you that it doesn't hurt, either, would it?

A. That's correct.

Q. A lot of people have degenerative changes that don't cause any symptoms.

A. Yes.

Q. Many of your patients have that?

A. Yes.

Q. You might have it yourself?

A. I'm sure I do.

Q. These degenerative changes can make someone more susceptible to having symptoms from an injury.

A. That's correct.

Q. And they can be symptomatic after an injury?

A. That's correct.

Q. In my client's first shoulder surgery, they took out some bone, didn't they?

A. Yes.

Q. Now, the second surgery, you said, was for arthritis, right?

A. In part, that's correct.

Q. Why didn't the surgeon note this in his report?

A. He wasn't looking at the joint.

Q. You would expect him to note it if he had seen it?

A. I would expect him to note what he saw.

Q. You have another conclusion about my client's failure to rehabilitate himself. You've repeated that many times, right?

A. Yes.

Q. Is there any reference to this in my client's medical records?

A. Not that I recall.

Q. Did the lawyer that hired you ever tell you that she found anything anywhere that my client didn't cooperate?

A. I don't know.

Q. If my client was not following his doctor's advice, wouldn't that be noted in his records?

A. Sometimes doctors do, sometimes they don't.

Q. If a physical therapist sees lack of effort by a patient, they'll make a note of it?

A. I don't know.

Q. Did the physical therapist ever note that here?

A. Not that I know of.

Q. Did you see here where it says "compliance with treatment plan, good"?

A. No.

Q. You didn't write that in your report, did you?

A. No.

Q. This note indicates that he is doing everything he's supposed to, doesn't it?

A. That's what the therapist said.

Q. And did you see the various places where the surgeon recorded he's working on his home exercises?

A. I probably did.

Q. That indicates he is doing what he's supposed to be doing, right?

A. If that's what they say.

Q. So, there is no evidence in the medical record that my client ever failed to do as he was told?

A. Not that I know of.

Q. My client's supervisor at work has said he was very consistent in working to try to come back to work. That would indicate good motivation, wouldn't it, doctor?

A. He does seem to be motivated to get back to work.

Q. Have you ever had a bad result in surgery?

A. Yes.

Q. Where the patient didn't get better as you hoped?

A. Yes.

Q. Where you knew the patient was trying everything they could?

A. I don't think I've had a bad result from a patient's failure to rehabilitate themselves, only for other reasons.

Q. And you don't blame yourself for the bad result, do you?

A. I did the best I could, and it doesn't always work out.

Q. And the patient, you know, is doing the best they can?

A. When my patients do the best they can, they succeed.

Q. So, sometimes you have a bad result that you just can't blame on the patient?

A. Not because of failure to rehabilitate.

Opinions Beyond the Expertise of a Witness

By attacking the credibility of the plaintiff's report of symptoms and motivation, Dr. Grimm essentially made a psychiatric diagnosis. As an orthopedist, this raised the question of whether he had stepped outside his area of expertise. If he was treating this patient, would he have paid attention to the symptoms the patient reported, or offered an opinion that this was all psychosomatic? Either way, this required Mr. Fury to use his client's medical records, showing the lack of foundation for this opinion.

Q. One of the things you diagnosed here is a chronic pain syndrome, right?

A. Yes.

Q. That's a psychological or psychiatric diagnosis?

A. That's a psychosomatic condition.

Q. And it's a psychiatric diagnosis.

A. There is a psychiatric component.

Q. You don't practice psychiatry?

A. No.

Q. You don't treat chronic pain patients, do you?

A. That's correct.

Q. You would refer a patient like this to somebody else?

A. That's correct.

Q. There are doctors who focus on chronic pain, right?

A. Yes.

Q. Now, this psychiatric diagnosis you made on my client …

A. Excuse me, I didn't make a psychiatric diagnosis. I made an orthopedic diagnosis that has psychiatric overtones.

Q. You finished?

A. I am.

Q. A psychiatric diagnosis of chronic pain syndrome requires that specific criteria are met.

A. I did not make a psychiatric diagnosis. Please don't misquote me.

Q. You're not qualified to make a psychiatric diagnosis?

A. That's correct.

Q. And that one of the criteria for such a diagnosis is that the pain must cause significant distress, right?

A. I don't know what the criteria are.

Q. You do know that chronic pain is a personal and individual experience for an individual?

A. Yes, it is.

Q. That pain is invisible.

A. It is.

Q. But that it's there as a constant companion for someone if they have it.

A. If a person says they have pain, then that's what they have.

Q. You have no reason to disbelieve that my client has the pain he says?

A. If he says he has it, then he has it.

Q. It's real to him?

A. Yes.

Q. And it affects him every day?

A. That's what he says.

Q. In everything he does?

A. It's what he says.

Q. You've had patients with ongoing pain, haven't you?

A. Yes.

Q. And it can make them feel helpless?

A. Some people get depressed.

Q. Nobody else understands them?

A. That's part of depression.

Q. Anxious.

A. Again, that's a part of depression.

Q. Frustrated?

A. That can happen.

Q. Do you tell your patients with serious, chronic pain that it's all in their heads?

A. People are not very receptive to being told that it's in their heads. What we can do is evaluate them, and we can find that there's no physical cause for the pain. We can try not to make them worse by doing needless surgeries and by doing treatments that don't help. Ultimately, if the problem is psychiatric, the only thing that helps is to lead them to the truth, that the problem is psychiatric, not physical.

Q. Do you recall my question, Doctor?

A. Actually, I don't.

Q. My question was, do you tell your patients who have pain that interferes with their life that it's all in their head?

A. I think I answered that. People don't like to hear that. By and large, I don't tell people things that offend them. So no, I don't do that.

Q. Inappropriately treated pain seriously compromises a patient's quality of life and causes emotional suffering?

A. Yes.

Q. Each physician bears the responsibility to evaluate and treat persistent pain as a serious medical problem.

A. Yes.

Q. Physicians should approach each patient with respect and urgency with regard to their pain.

A. Of course.

Q. Doctor, this isn't the first time you've offered a medical-legal diagnosis of chronic pain syndrome, is it?

A. No.

Q. That's a common diagnosis for you to make with people you examine, isn't it?

A. I think, when it's the correct diagnosis, it's appropriate to make it, and that's what I do.

Q. It's common for you to do that, isn't it?

A. Whether it's common or not depends on the nature of the patient that's sent to me for these exams.

Q. Well, do you remember seeing a Ms. P. in March of last year?

A. Of course not.

Q. You diagnosed her as having chronic pain syndrome, using the words "learned and patterned behavioral response," didn't you?

A. I think what we should do is look at that record, her complaints and her findings. Going through reports in other cases I've done is misleading. The sun will come up tomorrow, because it comes up every day. If you send me chronic pain patients every day, it's appropriate for me to make that diagnosis every day.

Q. And you always use the same exact words "learned and patterned behavioral response," in your reports, don't you?

A. That's what it is.

Q. You have no idea how many times you've made that diagnosis in people who you have examined?

A. I don't keep track.

If Dr. Grimm had been fair and objective in his assessment, he would have reached a different conclusion, as none of the treating physicians had concluded that the plaintiff had failed to follow their recommendations. Mr. Fury used this as a part of his story of Dr. Grimm's customary behavior as a paid expert:

> "You diagnose everybody the same way, using the same language." He'd been such an advocate in all his answers up to that point that simply raising it and asking him to agree with it was good enough. His answer didn't matter. I didn't need to force him to agree that I was right.

Follow the Money

Having established that Dr. Grimm was a medical advocate, it now was time for Mr. Fury to explain why—he did it for the money:

> I knew that I could get his forensic income to the magic number of $1,000,000 a year by simple math, based on information gathered from other lawyers. I also knew from his past testimony that he wouldn't admit to it. Not only did his refusal make him look bad, but also his lie that he didn't know how much his income was. The combination of the refusal, the lie and the $1,000,000 together are worse for him than if he had just acknowledged the true amount.

Q. You testified today that one half of what you do is forensic medical work?

A. Yes.

Q. That's an increase over the last year from 40 percent to a half, right?

A. I have gradually done more, that's correct.

Q. You are looking forward to retirement?

A. At some point, I will retire.

Q. And you are looking forward to that probably happening sooner rather than later?

A. It's not decided when that will happen.

Q. You still do some surgery?

A. I do.

Q. How many surgeries did you do last year?

A. I think I did 75.

Q. This is much less than the number of forensic exams you do now, isn't it?

A. Yes.

Q. How many exams did you do, doctor?

A. I might do anywhere from seven to eight and a half, nine and a half exams in a week.

Q. And you have testified recently you do about 450 to 475 examinations a year?

A. That's probably in the right range.

Q. And in addition to that, you do some records reviews, where you didn't see the person?

A. Yes.

Q. You do another 50 or so of those?

A. Probably a little less than that.

Q. 35?

A. It could be that.

Q. So, between the two, you are over 500 or in the neighborhood of 500 cases?

A. Looking at 500 different cases?

Q. Yes.

A. That could be.

Q. And these are almost entirely, 99 percent, for the defense, right?

A. That's correct.

Q. Now, you said you get $360 an hour for reviewing records, right?

A. Yes.

Q. And you do reports in addition to the exam?

A. Yes.

Q. And you charge by your time for that?

A. Yes.

Q. And virtually always it will be a long report like you did here, 10, 12 pages?

A. Depends on the records.

Q. And you also testify at depositions?

A. Yes.

Q. And you do a number of those every year?

A. Yes.

Q. And you get $468 for that?

A. Yes, per hour.

Q. And then you testify here, and you're charging a bit more than that, right? $636?

A. Yes, that's correct, per hour.

Q. When you add all of that up, you are probably up to a couple thousand dollars per case, on average, because you've charged more than $2,000 for all your work in this case, haven't you?

A. That's probably true.

Q. Do you have any idea how much it is?

A. No.

Q. Probably $10,000 here?

A. I don't know what it is.

Q. So, if you've got $2,000 per case, 500 cases, that's pushing a million dollars every year for this work you do almost exclusively for defendants, right?

A. Are you asking me if I bill that much?

Q. That's what it comes up to, isn't it?

A. What? What comes up to that?

Q. Pushing a million dollars yearly that you bill out for doing these examinations.

A. No.

Q. The American Medical Association says that it's an appropriate area of inquiry to ask a physician witness, such as you, how much you make from testifying, don't they?

A. I don't know.

Q. In the past, you've been ordered by the court to say how much it is you make annually from testifying, haven't you?

A. I don't believe so.

Q. How much do you make from working half time just for defendants, 500 cases a year, doctor?

A. I don't separate the income, and I don't know how.

Q. Well, you make half your income doing that.

A. I probably do.

Q. So, what's half your income?

A. I'm not willing to have my personal income become a part of the public record.

Q. We're entitled to know the extent of how much money you are making testifying just for defendants.

A. I'm not willing to say what my income is.

THE COURT: The witness can estimate how much he makes with regard to his work as an expert witness. He doesn't have to give his personal income.

THE WITNESS: I'm unable to do that. The money I make here is paid to my medical group. I do know what my personal income is.

Q. And about half of that would be associated with testifying?

A. I have other sources of income.

Q. Well, can you tell us about how much of it is for testifying?

A. I don't know what that amount is.

Q. Can you estimate?

A. No.

Q. It's that much?

A. I don't think it makes a difference how much it is. I'm not willing to have my personal affairs become a part of the public record. I think that's an invasion of my privacy. It's not necessary. If you want to ask how much I get paid per hour, that's fine. You can add it up, multiply it however you want, but my private affairs are mine. It's not a part of the contract for me to come in and expose my personal affairs.

THE COURT: Thank you, doctor. We are running out of time here.

BY MR. FURY:

Q. Doctor, you have testified for the defendants over a hundred times in the last few years, haven't you?

A. Oh, yes.

Q. And every time you come in and testify, it would be just like here; you say the treating doctor was wrong?

A. That's not correct, I don't always do this.

Q. Not talking about here, doctor. I'm talking about all that hundred times you've testified. You come in and you say the treating doctor was wrong each time.

A. That, again, is incorrect. By the time we get to trial, there is always somebody on both sides.

Q. And usually it's the treating doctor for the plaintiff?

A. Sometimes it is, and sometimes they get a new treating physician.

Q. And sometimes, you are saying, the treating physician is wrong, just like the surgeon here.

A. All I can say is that the surgeon's opinion here doesn't sit with the facts and I disagree with that.

Q. In each of these hundred times you've testified, you disagreed with the treating doctor in some way, didn't you?

A. In some way; you're very good at couching that. It's not as if I disagree with everybody, but when we get to trial, there's always somebody on the other side. Otherwise, there's no trial, so I disagree with them.

The Outcome

Mr. Fury's cross-examination of Dr. Grimm played a critical role in convincing the jury of the validity of his client's case. Not only did the jury disbelieve Dr. Grimm's testimony, but it also concluded that both Mr. Fury and the plaintiff's case story were entirely credible, awarding the exact amount of money damages to the plaintiff asked for in closing argument.

Appendix C

Creation of Computer Animation Illustrating Engineering Expert's Opinion

Facts — *Roger v. Property Development Associates*

Plaintiff Michael Roger was a 35-year-old skilled carpenter who was working on the rehabilitation of a historic building. The project ended up being far more expensive and complicated than the developers anticipated, causing them to make various economy moves. One such was the failure to keep the old freight elevator in the building properly maintained.

The elevator failed every safety inspection for the several years prior to Mr. Roger's serious industrial accident. The violations included inoperable alarms, burned out lighting and poor ventilation. The developers did not have the elevator regularly serviced under a scheduled maintenance contract. A number of unauthorized modifications were made on the safety gate, including cutting a large hole in it to accommodate a new beam on the top floor

On the day Mr. Roger was injured, the lights in the elevator were burned out and the safety switches also were improperly aligned, causing it to stop and start unpredictably in between floors. Workers were required to look into the shaft to try to determine where the elevator was, calling out to one another.

Mr. Roger was on the third floor on the day he was injured. A worker on the first floor was unsuccessful in trying to call the elevator. He yelled up the shaft to see if anybody could assist him. Mr. Roger walked over to the darkened gate and called back down. When he brushed against the gate, it re-engaged the safety switch and the elevator suddenly started up again. Mr. Roger's head was caught between the gate and the elevator floor, about to be decapitated. He pushed with all his strength to pull his body free of the gate. When space was temporarily created after his jaw broke in multiple places, Mr. Roger was able to pull free. However, he still suffered serious injuries.

The Need for Expert Consultation

Co-author William S. Bailey represented Mr. Roger against defendant Property Development Associates. The tort claim was based upon the failure of the defendant to maintain a safe elevator, complying with all the applicable code requirements. The testimony of an elevator expert would be critical to establishing the danger presented by the freight elevator and how defendant's failure to maintain it properly led directly to what occurred.

However, there was a high probability of significant comparative fault being assessed to Mr. Roger for voluntarily putting his head inside the hole that defendant had cut in the safety gate. In order to minimize the chances of this, plaintiff would have to show that the conditions on this jobsite required him to act in the way he did on the day he was injured. In order for the jury to understand this, it was going to be necessary to put them in the shoes of the plaintiff, taking them to the scene of the event, re-creating what happened.

Finding the Right Expert

Mr. Bailey did jury verdict and settlement research on all elevator cases in his jurisdiction over a 10-year period. He called another plaintiff's counsel who had successfully handled a similar case several years prior, inquiring about the experts used in the case. The other counsel told him that the elevator expert used by the defense in his case, T.L. Davis, was by far the better of the two, concluding, "I wished I'd had him on my side." Mr. Davis was a licensed engineer who had considerable experience in the industry and had consulted in litigation cases on an occasional basis, more for the defense than the plaintiff. When contacted, Mr. Davis agreed to serve as an expert for the plaintiff in this case.

Collecting Background Material

The site of the accident had changed significantly since the event, with the freight elevator being removed as unsafe and the remodeling largely completed. Mr. Davis would not be able to make an in-person inspection, relying instead on the reports, inspections and photographs of others. The city licensing agency maintained a file on this freight elevator, a copy of which was obtained through subpoena. The architect for this project had plans and drawings of the project, as well as photographs of the building interior as the work progressed. Copies of all of this material were gathered by another subpoena. The state industrial safety agency provided photos taken of the freight elevator and safety gate after Mr. Roger's injury.

Plaintiff's counsel determined that a computer animation showing the multiple safety defects would be the best way to maximize the liability case. Job photographs in the architect's file showed that the lighting inside the building was poor. Most jurors would not be familiar with a situation like this. Since plaintiff had the burden of proof, this barrier would have to be overcome. Showing documents of inspection violations would not be enough to address the comparative fault argument. However, whether or not an animation would help on this aspect depended on the findings, conclusions and opinions of Mr. Davis.

The Elevator Expert's Findings

The plaintiff's expert found that the owners of the elevator failed to meet industry safety requirements designed to protect workers like the plaintiff from the danger of injury. He opined that the owners knew of the numerous problems with the elevator that could cause injury or death, receiving safety violation notices from the city in each of the three years leading up to plaintiff's injury. The defendant owners knew of the large section improperly cut out of the safety gate, as this was done at their request. This modification was dangerous, greatly increasing the chance of injury or death. Defendant owners did nothing to warn or guard against this harm, allowing these violations of the city code and unsafe conditions to persist. They clearly violated the common carrier duty of care with this dangerous, nonconforming freight elevator.

Building the Foundation for the Animation

With the elevator expert's report in hand, plaintiff's counsel engaged a computer animator to re-create the events that led up to Mr. Roger's serious injuries. The animator was provided with all the photographs and diagrams of the scene. These included the photographs taken by the architect, the industrial accident investigator and the city's inspection file on the elevator. Plaintiff also had his client draw where he was standing at various points in the process, as well as how he was caught in the elevator.

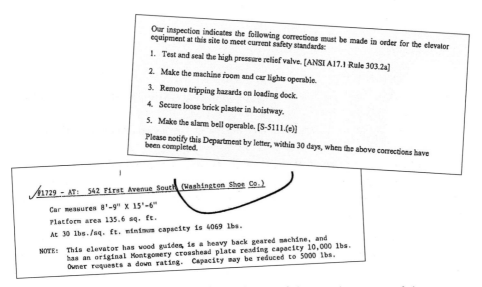

Figures C-1 and C-2. Inspection safety violations of elevator; dimensions of elevator.

Figure C-3. Photo of the safety gate, showing the notch illegally cut in it.

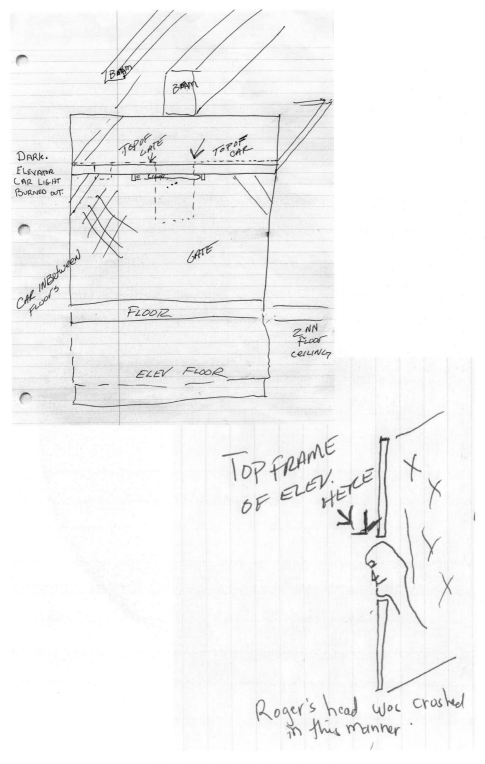

Figure C-4. Client drawings of events.

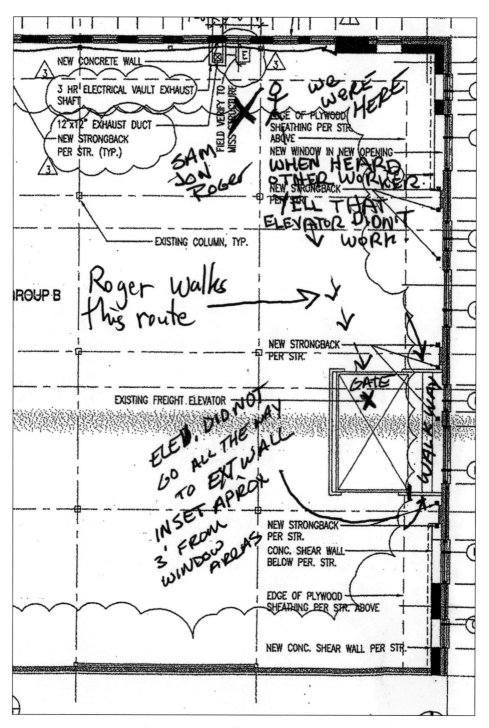

Figure C-5. Plaintiff route to elevator gate.

Figure C-6. Architect's photo showing interior lighting conditions.

Exam: Contrast enhanced Maxillofacial CT scan.

Comparison: None.

Clinical history: Person verses object

Technique: Axial 2.5 mm images were obtained from the top of the lateral ventricles through the C1 vertebral body. This was followed by acquisition of direct coronal 1.25 mm images from the tip of the nose through the sphenoid sinuses. Data is displayed in soft tissue and bone algorithms.

Findings:

There is comminuted mandibular symphysis fracture.

There are also comminuted and displaced bilateral fractures of the mandible at the junction of the ramus and condyles. No evidence of subluxation or dislocation.

There is mildly depressed nasal bone fracture.

Figure C-7. Results of the CT scan.

Expert's Comments on Animation Drafts

The animator consulted with both counsel and the elevator expert on a regular basis throughout the creation of the animation. The expert gave detailed input to the animator, so that the final product would accurately reflect what occurred that day and his analysis as to what had caused this event. The following is one such critique of an animation draft by the expert:

Comments on Animation

Floor indicator shown at approximately 2:00 min. Locate this above the alarm buzzer speaker so that it is at eye level or higher but not higher than 8'-0".

Should indicate improper modifications to gate. <u>Not done by a licensed elevator technician</u>, <u>No permit applied for.</u>

Typically, elevators used for construction, as this one was, would have an intercom system so the operator could communicate with people on the various floors and visa versa. In addition to an Alarm buzzer or in place of perhaps you could show a speaker box with a "push to talk" button near the alarm buzzer. Persons wishing to summon the elevator would speak into the speaker box and talk to the elevator operator requesting that he pick them up.

At 2:20 minutes into the animation you show the elevator going down and the top (dome) of the elevator striking the gate. Typically the elevator would strike the gate on the way up and lift the gate slightly, causing the gate switch or interlock to open and stop the elevator. Alternatively, as the elevator would go down the gate on the car would strike something and lift up slightly causing the gate switch on that gate to open and stop the elevator. Co-worker stated in his declaration that this occurred while the elevator was traveling <u>upward</u>. You may want to show the elevator coming up to the floor and hitting the gate, causing it to move upward slightly and the elevator stopping.

Early in the animation you show that there is a gate on the car with a portion of that gate showing through the "notch" cut in the protection gate. This same gate is not shown later in the animation when you show how Mr. Roger was injured around 3:30 minutes.

Reviewed by T.L. Davis

Final Version of Animation

After multiple drafts, the client, an eyewitness and the liability expert all approved the final version as fair and accurate. It was done without sound, to avoid any hearsay issue, set up so the elevator expert could narrate it from the witness stand, stopping at various points to discuss both the safety requirements and the violations of this elevator. The animation also accurately re-created the poor lighting inside the building, which was a causal factor in plaintiff's injury.

Figure C-8(a). Computer animations can be used to illustrate an expert's opinions.

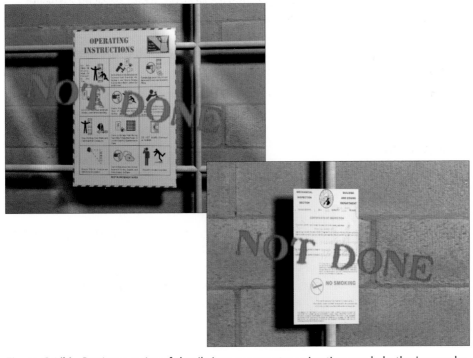

Figure C-8(b). Putting a series of details into a computer animation can help the jury understand expert conclusions on the overall pattern.

Notes

Chapter 1

1. Frederick Lewis Allen, *Only Yesterday: An Informal History of the 1920's* (New York: Harper and Rowe, 1931), 164.
2. Ronald W. Clark, *Einstein: The Life and Times* (New York: World Publishing, 1971), 295–96.
3. Ann McFeatters, "In American Politics, It's Still Science vs. Religion," *McClatchy-Tribune News Service*, February 14, 2014.
4. *Id.*
5. 127 S. Ct. 1438 (2007).
6. Interview of Judge Robert S. Lasnik by William S. Bailey, June 15, 2012.
7. Interview of Judge Ronald Kessler by William S. Bailey, March 19, 2012.
8. William Shakespeare, *Julius Caesar* (I, ii, 140–141).

Chapter 2

1. Interview of Judge William L. Downing by William S. Bailey, June 8, 2012.
2. Interview of Todd W. Gardner by William S. Bailey, April 27, 2012.
3. Interview of Elizabeth A. Leedom by William S. Bailey, April 10, 2012.
4. Malcolm Gladwell, *The Tipping Point: How Little Things Can Make A Big Difference* (New York: Little Brown, 2000).
5. Carl Iver Hovland, Arthur A. Lumsdaine and Fred D. Sheffield, *Experiments on Mass Communication* (Princeton: Princeton University Press, 1949).
6. Carl Iver Hovland, Irving L. Janis and Harold H. Kelley, *Communication and Persuasion: Psychological Studies of Opinion Change* (New Haven: Yale University Press, 1953).
7. *See, e.g.,* Theodore H. White, *The Making The President 1960* (New York: Atheneum Publishers, 1961).
8. J.B. Engelmann, C.M. Capra, C. Noussiar, and G.S. Berns, "Expert Financial Advice Neurobiologically 'Offloads' Financial Decision-Making under Risk." PLoS ONE 4(3): e4957. Doi:10.1371/journal.pone.0004957.
9. News Release, Woodruff Health Sciences Center News, Emory University, March 24, 2009.
10. *Id.*
11. Interview of Judge William L. Downing by William S. Bailey, June 8, 2012.
12. Interview of Judge William L. Downing by William S. Bailey, June 8, 2012.
13. Interview of Judge William L. Downing by William S. Bailey, June 8, 2012.
14. Interview of Todd W. Gardner by William S. Bailey, April 27, 2012.
15. Interview of Elizabeth A. Leedom by William S. Bailey, April 10, 2012.
16. Interview of Ralph J. Brindley by William S. Bailey, May 30, 2012.
17. Interview of Todd W. Gardner by William S. Bailey, April 27, 2012.

18. Interview of Todd W. Gardner by William S. Bailey, April 27, 2012.

19. Interview of Todd W. Gardner by William S. Bailey, April 27, 2012.

Chapter 3

1. 509 U.S. 579 (1993).

2. *Id.* at 588 (describing *Frye's* test as "rigid," "austere," and "at odds with the liberal thrust of the Federal Rules and their general approach of relaxing the traditional barriers to opinion testimony.") (Internal quotation marks omitted). Here and elsewhere, the Court impliedly describes its new standard as more liberal than the preceding one, an irony, considering how the decision was interpreted thereafter.

3. Lloyd Dixon & Brian Gill, *Changes in the Standards for Admitting Expert Evidence in Federal Civil Cases Since the Daubert Decision*, RAND Institute for Civil Justice (2001), available at http://www.rand.org/content/dam/rand/pubs/monograph reports/2005/MR1439.pdf.

4. *Id.* at xvii.

5. Price Waterhouse Coopers, *Daubert Challenges to Financial Experts: A Yearly Study of Trends and Outcomes* (2011), available at http://www.pwc.com/enUS/us/forensic-services/publications/assets/daubert-study-2011.pdf.

6. Andrew Jurs & Scott DeVitto, *The Stricter Standard: An Empirical Assessment of Daubert's Effect on Civil Defendants*, 62 Cath. U. L. Rev. 675 (2013).

7. *See* Edward K. Cheng & Albert H. Yoon, *Does* Frye or Daubert *Matter? A Study of Scientific Admissibility Standards*, 91 Va. L. Rev. 471, 503 (2005) (finding that *Daubert* had no significant impact on removal rates). Jurs and DeVitto, *supra*, note 6, found fault with Cheng and Yoon's methodology, thus explaining their different result.

8. Carol Kafka et al., *Judge and Attorney Experiences, Practices, and Concerns Regarding Expert Testimony in Federal Civil Trials*, 8 Psychol. Pub. Pol'y & L. 309 (2002).

9. *Id.* at 329.

10. *Id.* at 443.

11. FRE 702, *Comment to 2000 Amendments*.

12. Both the RAND and Price Waterhouse Coopers studies support this notion. So too do Jurs and DeVitto; presumably, civil defendants are fleeing to *Daubert* jurisdictions in order to make *Daubert* motions.

13. *See General Electric Co. v. Joiner*, 522 U.S. 136 (1997).

14. *See Kumho Tire v. Carmichael*, 526 U.S. 137 (1999).

15. James F. Rogers et al., *Changes in the Reference Manual on Scientific Evidence* (3d Ed.), 80 Def. Couns. J. 287, 295 (2013) (citing RMSE 3d at 36).

16. FRE 702, *Comment to 2000 Amendments* ("When a trial court, applying this amendment, rules that an expert's testimony is reliable, this does not necessarily mean that contradictory expert testimony is unreliable.").

17. *See Daubert, supra*, note 2.

18. *Ruiz-Troche v. Pepsi Cola*, 161 F.3d 77, 85 (1st Cir. 1998).

19. *Holbrook v. Lykes Bros. S.S. Co., Inc.*, 80 F.3d 777, 784 (3d Cir. 1996).

20. *In re Paoli R.R. Yard PCB Litigation*, 35 F.3d 717, 744 (3d Cir. 1994).

21. *See, e.g.,* Ronald J. Allen, *Expertise and the* Daubert *Decision*, 84 J. Crim. L. & Criminology 1157, 1159 (1994) (arguing that jurors can assess scientific merit competently if they receive proper instruction).

22. *See* Ronald L. Carlson, *The Curious Case of Differing Literary Emphases: The Contract Between the Use of Scientific Publications at Pretrial Daubert Hearings and at Trial*, 47 Ga. L. Rev. 837 (2013).

23. *Id.* (citing *Wells v. SmithKline Beecham Corp.*, 601 F.3d 375, 381 (5th Cir. 2010)).

24. *See id.* (citing *Hendrix ex rel. G.P. v. Evenflo Co.*, 609 F.3d 1183 (11th Cir. 2010) (rejecting expert's theory that cranial trauma causes autism for lack of supporting medical literature)).

25. Edward J. Imwinkelried, *The Epistemological Trend in the Evolution of the Law of Expert Tes-*

timony: A Scrutiny at Once Broader, Narrower, and Deeper, 47 Ga. L. Rev. 863, 870 (2013).

26. *Rider v. Sandoz Pharm. Corp.*, 295 F.3d 1194, 1198–99 (2002) ("best evidence of causation" but "lack thereof is not fatal," citing cases to this effect).

27. *Id.*

28. *Id.* at 1202 ("In the absence of epidemiology … plaintiffs simply have not provided reliable evidence to support their conclusions.").

29. 252 F.3d 986 (8th Cir. 2001).

30. *See id.* at 992.

31. *See, e.g.*, Peter J. Neufeld, *The (Near) Irrelevance of* Daubert *to Criminal Justice and Some Suggestions for Reform*, 95 Am. J. Pub. Health 107 (2005); Paul C. Giannelli, Daubert *and Criminal Prosecutions*, 26-Fall Crim. Just. 61 (2011).

32. Erica Beecher-Monas, *Blinded by Science: How Judges Avoid the Science in Scientific Evidence*, 71 Temp. L. Rev. 55, 56–57 (1998).

33. National Academy of Sciences, *Strengthening Forensic Science in the United States: A Path Forward*, at 11 (2009), available at http://www.nap.edu/catalog.php?record id=12589 (emphasis in original).

34. Jennifer L. Groscup et al., *The Effects of* Daubert *on the Admissibility of Expert Testimony in State and Federal Criminal Cases*, 8 Psychol. Pub. Pol'y & L. 339, 363 (2002).

35. *See, e.g.*, *U.S. v. Sherwood*, 98 F.3d 402, 408 (9th Cir. 1996) (admitting fingerprint analysis despite the trial court's failure to conduct a *Daubert* hearing). This case was later described in *U.S. v. Havvard* as a "brief [opinion] asserting that the reliability of fingerprint comparisons cannot be questioned." 260 F.3d 597, 600 (7th Cir. 2001). *See also U.S. v. Cline*, 188 F. Supp. 2d 1287, 1294 (D. Kan. 2002) (agreeing with several other opinions that "recognized that evidentiary *Daubert* hearings were unnecessary as the reliability of [fingerprint identification] methods could be properly taken for granted").

36. *See, e.g.*, *U.S. v. Joseph*, 2001 WL 515213 at *1 (E.D. La. 2001) (admitting evidence because "fingerprint analysis has been tested and proven to be a reliable science over decades of use for judicial purposes"). *See also U.S. v. Turner*, 285 F.3d 909, 913 (10th Cir. 2002) (opting not to disturb or question the lower court's conclusion that fingerprint evidence "has always been upheld as reliable and appropriate" and was therefore not the proper subject of a *Daubert* hearing).

37. For a discussion of how *Daubert* has affected specific substantive areas, *see* Paul C. Giannelli, Daubert *and Criminal Prosecutions*, 26-Fall Crim. Just. 61 (2011) (criminal prosecution generally); George Vallas, *A Survey of Federal and State Standards for the Admission of Expert Testimony on the Reliability of Eyewitnesses*, 39 Am. J. Crim. L. 97 (2011) (eyewitness experts); Price Waterhouse Coopers, *supra*, note 5 (financial experts generally); Jonathan M. Dunitz & Nancy J. Fannon, Daubert *and the Financial Damages Expert*, 26 Me. B.J. 62 (2011) (damages experts); Gregory G. Wrobel & Ellen Meriwether, *Economic Experts: the Challenges of Gatekeepers and Complexity*, 25-SUM Antitrust 8 (2011) (antitrust); Lucinda Finley, *Guarding the Gate to the Courthouse: How Trial Judges Are Using Their Evidentiary Screening Role to Remake Tort Causation Rules*, 49 DePaul L. Rev. 335 (1999) (torts).

38. *See supra*, notes 10–11.

39. *Daubert*, 509 U.S. at 594.

40. Sarah Jane Gillet et al., *The* Daubert *Challenge and Hearing: Defending Your Expert Against a* Daubert *Challenge, in* Litigators on Experts, 194, 197 (Wendy Gerwick Couture and Allyson Haynes, 2010).

41. *Id.* (citing Jennifer Wolsing, Daubert's *Erie Problem*, 82 Ind. L.J. 183, 183–84, 210 (2007)).

42. *Id.* (citing *Larson v. Kemper*, 414 F.3d 936 (8th Cir. 2005)).

43. *Id.*

44. 526 U.S. at 141.

45. FRE 702, *Comment to 2000 Amendments.*

46. Gillet, *supra*, note 41.

47. Alice B. Lustre, *Post–*Daubert *Standards for Admissibility of Scientific and Other Expert Evidence in State Courts*, 90 A.L.R. 5th 453 (Updated 2013).

48. *See id.*

49. David E. Bernstein, *Frye, Frye Again: The Past, Present, and Future of the General Acceptance*

Test, 41 Jurimetrics J. 385 (2001) (arguing that, at least as of 2001 when there were several more *Frye* jurisdictions than there are today, those jurisdictions had begun adopting aspects of *Daubert* implicitly without adopting it explicitly).

Chapter 4

1. Quoted in Katherine Long, "UW Professor Wins Big Prize for Ecology Work," *The Seattle Times*, July 30, 2013.

2. Interview of Allan F. Tencer, Ph.D by William S. Bailey, June 20, 2012.

3. C. Glenn Begley and Lee M. Ellis, "Drug Development: Raise Standards for Preclinical Cancer Research," *Nature*, 483, 531–533 (March 29, 2012).

4. Michael Suk-Young Chwe, "Scientific Pride and Prejudice," *The New York Times*, February 2, 2014.

5. Eryn Brown, "Why Time Is Spent Proving the Obvious," *The Los Angeles Times*, June 3, 2011.

6. Quoted in Pam Belluck, "Health Risks Lower for the Slightly Overweight," *The New York Times*, January 1, 2013.

7. *Id.*

8. Craig Welch, "WSU Prof Was Right: Mastodon Weapon Older Than Thought," *The Seattle Times*, October 30, 2011.

9. Quoted in Brian Vastag, "Downside of Drugs Kept Quiet, Report Finds," *The Washington Post*, March 21, 2012.

10. Michael Suk-Young Chwe, "Scientific Pride and Prejudice," *The New York Times*, February 2, 2014.

11. Quoted in Eryn Brown, "Why Time Is Spent Proving the Obvious," *The Los Angeles Times*, June 3, 2011.

12. Quoted in Clifton Leaf, "Do Clinical Trials Work?," *The New York Times*, July 14, 2013.

13. Gary Taubes, "Why Nutrition Is So Confusing," *The New York Times*, February 8, 2014.

14. Quoted in Sarah Zhang, "Study Ties Medication to Breast Cancer," *The Seattle Times*, August 6, 2013; Results published online by JAMA Internal Medicine, August 8, 2013.

15. Sarah Zhang, "Study Ties Medication to Breast Cancer," *The Seattle Times*, August 6, 2013.

16. 522 U.S. 136, fn 6 (1997) (Stevens, J., concurring in part and dissenting in part) ("An example of 'junk science' that should be excluded under *Daubert* as too unreliable would be the testimony of a phrenologist who would purport to prove a defendant's future dangerousness based on the contours of the defendant's skull.").

17. Quoted in Steve Lohr, "The Age of Big Data," *The New York Times*, February 12, 2012.

18. Quoted in Jeff Sommer, "A Skeptic of 'People Who Look Impressive,'" *The New York Times*, October 20, 2013.

19. Sarah Zhang, "Higher Prostate-Cancer Risk Linked to Fish Oils, Study Says," *The Seattle Times*, July 11, 2013.

20. Carol M. Ostrom, "Baby's Birth Day Can Be Risky If Rushed, Hospitals Are Told," *The Seattle Times*, January 1, 2013.

21. Committee on Identifying the Needs of the Forensic Sciences Community, National Research Council, *Strengthening Forensic Science In The United States: A Path Forward* (Washington, D.C., August, 2009).

Chapter 5

1. Interview of Judge Robert S. Lasnik by William S. Bailey, June 15, 2012.

2. Elizabeth F. Loftus, "The Malleability of Human Memory," 67 *American Scientist* 312–320, May-June, 1979.

3. *State v. Larry R. Henderson*, 27 A.3d 872 (N.J. 2011).

4. Thomas McGarity and Wendy Wagner, *Bending Science: How Special Interests Corrupt Public Health Research*, (Cambridge: Harvard University Press, 2012).

5. Interview of Judge Robert S. Lasnik by William S. Bailey, June 15, 2012.

6. Linda Geddes, "Miscarriages of Justice Will Occur," *New Science*, February 11, 2012.

7. The 2009 Task Force Report of the National Academy of Sciences, *Strengthening Forensic Science in the United States: A Path Forward*, is a prime example.

8. David Stout, "Report Faults F.B.I.'s Fingerprint Scrutiny in Arrest of Lawyer," *The New York Times*, November 17, 2004.

9. Alex B. Berezow, "Order in the Court, Science Does Matter," *USA Today*, March 8, 2011.

Chapter 6

1. Comment of Hannah Osul, "Difference Between Hard Science and Soft Science," available at http://chemistry.about.com/b/2013/02/18/difference-between-hard-science-and-soft-science.htm.

2. Quoted in Tamar Lewin, "As Interest Fades in the Humanities, Colleges Worry," *The New York Times*, October 30, 2013.

3. *Id.*

4. *Id.*

5. Interview of Allan F. Tencer, Ph.D, by William S. Bailey, June 20, 2012.

6. Interview of Professor Michael Townsend by William S. Bailey, May 4, 2012.

7. Interview of Ralph J. Brindley, by William S. Bailey, May 30, 2012.

8. Interview of Judge Ronald Kessler by William S. Bailey, March 19, 2012.

9. Interview of Judge Ronald Kessler by William S. Bailey, March 19, 2012.

10. Interview of Judge Ronald Kessler by William S. Bailey, March 19, 2012.

11. Interview of Judge Ronald Kessler by William S. Bailey, March 19, 2012.

12. Interview of Judge Robert S. Lasnik by William S. Bailey, June 15, 2012.

13. Interview of Mark R. Larson by William S. Bailey, March 12, 2012.

14. Interview of Judge William L. Downing by William S. Bailey, June 8, 2012.

15. Interview of Judge Robert S. Lasnik by William S. Bailey, June 15, 2012.

16. Interview of Erin Ehlert, by William S. Bailey, March 12, 2012.

Chapter 7

1. Yin Xiao-hu, "'Feng Zhen Shi' and Ancient Forensic Science," *Chinese Journal of Forensic Sciences* 63–64, Issue 2, 2005.

2. Giles, H.A., "'*His Yuan Lu*' or '*Instructions to Coroners*,'" Proceedings of the Royal Society of Medicine 59–107, 1924.

3. Scientific Working Group on Friction Ridge Analysis, Study and Technology (SWGFAST), et al., *The Fingerprint Sourcebook*, (National Institute of Justice. 2011).

4. H. Faulds, "On the Skin—Furrows of the Hand." *Nature*, 22 605. 1880.

5. Alphonse Bertillon, *Signaletic Instructions Including the Theory and Practice of Anthropometrical Identification*, (Chicago: The Werner Company, 1896).

6. S. A. Cole, *Suspect Identities: A History of Fingerprinting and Criminal Identification*, (Cambridge, MA: Harvard University Press. 2001).

7. Max M. Houck, Frank Crispino and Terry McAdam, *The Science of Crime Scenes*, (Academic Press; Elsevier, 2012).

8. American Academy of Forensic Science, 2013, available at www.aafs.org/what-do-forensic-scientists-do, (October 3, 2013). Last accessed October 3, 2013.

9. U.S. Department of Labor, 2011, Occupational Employment and Wages, Forensic Science

Technicians, 19-4092. Bureau of Labor Statistics, available at http://www.bls.gov/oes/current/oes 194092.htm.

10. Amelia Bizzaro, "Challenging the Admission of Forensic Evidence," *Wisconsin Lawyer*, Vol. 83, No. 9, 2010.

11. Committee, Science and Technology, *Forensic Science on Trial*. House of Commons, 2005.

12. *Ibid.*

13. Committee on Identifying the Needs of the Forensic Sciences Committee, National Research Council, *Strengthening Forensic Science in the United States: A Path Forward*, (Washington D.C.: The National Academies Press, 2009).

14. *Ibid.*

15. *Ibid.*

Chapter 8

1. Andrea M. Burch, Matthew R. Durose, Kelly A. Walsh, *Census of Publicly Funded Crime Laboratories 2009*, (Bureau of Justice Statistics, August 2012).

2. Committee on Identifying the Needs of the Forensic Sciences Community, National Research Council, *Strengthening Forensic Science in the United States: A Path Forward*, (Washington D.C.: National Academies Press 2009).

3. Max M. Houck, Frank Crispino, and Terry McAdam, *The Science of Crime Scenes*, (Academic Press, Elsevier, 2012).

4. FBI, available at www.fbi.gov/about-us/cjis/fingerprints/biometrics/iafis 2013.

5. Max M. Houck, Frank Crispino, and Terry McAdam, *The Science of Crime Scenes*, (Academic Press, Elsevier, 2012).

Chapter 9

1. P. Buscemi and W. Washington, "Collection and Handling of Physical Evidence for a Forensic Laboratory. Sampling, Standards, and Homogeneity." *American Society for Testing and Materials*, 1973, ASTM STP 540: 37–44.

2. Max M. Houck, Frank Crispino, and Terry McAdam, *The Science of Crime Scenes*, (Academic Press; Elsevier, 2012).

3. *Id.*

4. *Crime Scene Investigation: A Guide for Law Enforcement*. Office of Justice Programs, U.S. Department of Justice, 2013.

5. Max M. Houck, Frank Crispino, and Terry McAdam, *The Science of Crime Scenes*, (Academic Press, Elsevier, 2012).

6. Cunningham, Michael, "The Numbers Don't Lie," *Evidence Technology Magazine*, March-April 2014: 20–23.

7. C.R. Swanson, N.C. Chamelin & L. Territo, *Criminal Investigation*, 8th ed., (McGraw-Hill, 2003).

Chapter 11

1. National Institute of Justice, *The Fingerprint Sourcebook*, Washington D.C., 2011.

2. M. Kucker and A.C. Newell, "Fingerprint Formation," *Journal of Theoretical Biology*, 235 (Elsevier, 2005).

3. R.M. Lavker, P. Zheng, and G. Dong, "Morphology of Aged Skin," *Journal of Geriatric Dermatology* 5, No. 1 (1989).

4. C. Champod, "Edmond Locard—Numerical Standards and 'Probable' Identifications," *Journal of Forensic Idenification*, 45, No. 2, (1995).

5. I. Evett and R. L. Williams, "A Review of the Sixteen Points Fingerprint Standard in England and Wales," *Journal of Forensic Identification* 46, No. 1 (1996).

6. Committee, IAI Standardization, *Identification News*, (August 1973).

7. National Institute of Justice, *The Fingerprint Sourcebook*, (Washington D.C. 2011).

8. National Research Council, *Strengthening Forensic Science in the United States: A Path Forward*, (Washington, D.C.: National Academies Press 2009).

9. *Id.*

10. B.T. Ulery, R.A. Hicklin, J. Buscaglia, and M.A. Roberts, "Accuracy and Reliability of Forensic Latent Fingerprint Decisions," (Proceedings of the National Academy of Science 2011).

11. *Daubert v. Merrell Dow Pharmaceuticals, Inc.*, 509 U.S. 579 (1993).

12. *Kumho Tire Co. v. Carmichael*, 526 U.S. 137 (1999).

13. *Frye v. United States* 293 F. 1013 (D.C. Cir. 1923).

14. *United States v. Mitchell*, 199 F. Supp. 2d 262 (E.D. Pa. 2002).

15. *United States v Mitchell*, 365 F.3d 215 (3d Cir. 2004) *cert. denied*, 125 S. Ct. 446 (2004).

Chapter 12

1. SWGGUN "Admissibility Resource Kit," available at www.swggun.org (October 2013).

2. J.E. Murdock, "A General Discussion of Gun Barrel Individuality and an Empirical Assessment of the Individuality of Consecutively Button Rifled .22 Caliber Rifle Barrels," *AFTE Journal* 13, No. 3 (1981); J.E. Hamby, D.J. Brundag, J.W. Thorpe, "The Identification of Bullets Fired from 10 Consecutively Rifled 9mm Ruger Pistol Barrels," *AFTE Journal* 41, No. 2 (2009).

3. "Comparison of 10,000 Consecutively Fired Cartridge Cases from a Model 22 Glock .40 S&W Caliber Semiautomatic Pistol." *AFTE Journal* 40, No. 1 (2008); S.G. Bunch and D. Murphy, "A Comprehensive Validity Study for the Forensic Examination of Cartridge Cases," *AFTE Journal* 35, No. 2 (2003).

4. E. Smith, "Cartridge Case and Bullet Comparison Validation Study with Firearms Submitted in Casework," *AFTE Journal* 37, No. 2 (2005).

5. T.G. Fadul, et al., *An Empirical Study to Improve the Scientific Foundation of Forensic Firearm and Tool Mark Identification Utilizing 10 Consecutively Manufactured Slides*, National Institute of Justice, Office of Justice Programs (2009).

6. AFTE Criteria for Identification Committee, "Theory of Identification, Range of Striae Comparison Reports and Modified Glossary Definitions—an AFTE Criteria for Identification Committee Report," *AFTE Journal* 24, No. 2 (1992).

7. J. Griffin, J. and D. Lamagna, "*Daubert* Challenges to Forensic Evidence: Ballistics Next on the Firing Line," *The Champion* (September/October 2002); A. Schwarz, "A Systemic Challenge to the Reliability and Admissibility of Firearms and Toolmark Identification," *The Columbia, Science and Technology Law Review* VI (2005).

Chapter 13

1. S.S. Tobe, N. Watson and N.N. Daéžid., "Evaluation of Six Presumptive Tests for Blood, Their Specificity, Sensitivity, and Effect on High Molecular-Weight DNA," 52 *Journal of Forensic Science* 1, 102–109 (2007).

2. R.E. Gaensslen, "Blood Identification—Crystal Tests," *Sourcebook in Forensic Serology, Immunology, and Biochemistry*, 73–100, University of Michigan Library (1983).

3. *DNA for the Defense Bar*, National Institute of Justice, 2012.

4. Center, National Forensic Science Technology, 2014, available at http://www.forensic-

sciencesimplified.org, last accessed April 20, 2014.

5. *Id.*

6. Committee On Identifying the Needs of the Forensic Science Community, *Strengthening Forensic Science in the United States: A Path Forward*, (Washington D.C.: National Research Council 2009).

7. *Id.*

8. *People v. Castro* 545 N.Y.S.2d 985 (N.Y. Sup. Ct. 1989).

9. D.E. Shelton, "Twenty-First Century Forensic Science Challenges for Trial judges in Criminal Cases: Where the 'Polybutadiene' Meets the 'Bitumen,'" 18 *Widener Law Journal* 309 (2009).

10. W.C. Thompson, F. Taroni and C.G.G. Aitken, "How the Probability of a False Positive Affects the Value of DNA Evidence." 48 *Journal of Forensic Sciences* 1 (2003).

Chapter 14

1. Carina A. Wasko, Christine L. Mackley, Leonard C. Sperling, Dave Mauger, and Jeffrey J. Miller, "Standardizing the 60-Second Hair Count." 144 No. 6 *Archives of Dermatoogy.*, 759–762 (2008).

2. Siegel, Jay A., *Forensic Science: The Basics*, 2d ed., (Boca Raton: CRC Press, 2010).

3. Committee On Identifying the Needs of the Forensic Science Community, *Strengthening Forensic Science in the United States: A Path Forward*, (Washington, D.C.: National Academies Press 2009).

4. Maureen Bottrell, "Forensic Glass Comparison: Background Information Used in Data Interpretation." *Forensic Science Communications*, Volume 11, No. 2 (April 2009).

5. D.F. Nelson and B. C.Revell, "Backward Fragmentation from Breaking Glass," 17 *Journal of the Forensic Science Society* 58–61 (1967).

6. C.I. Petterd, J. Hamshere, S. Stewart, K. Brinch, T. Masi, and C. Roux, "Glass Particles in the Clothing of Members of the Public in South-Eastern Australia—A survey," 103 *Forensic Science International*, 93–98 (1999).

7. J.M. Curran, T.N. Hicks and J.S. Buckleton, *Forensic Interpretation of Glass Evidence,* (Boca Raton, Florida.: CRC Press 2000).

8. Robert W. Fitzpatrick and Mark D. Raven, "How Pedology and Mineralogy Helped Solve a Double Murder Case: Using Forensics to Inspire Future Generations of Soil Scientists," *Soil Horizons* (2012).

9. John D. DeHaan, *Kirk's Fire Investigation*, (Upper Saddle River, New Jersey: Pearson Education, Inc. 2007).

10. *Id.*

11. Committee On Identifying the Needs of the Forensic Science Community, *Strengthening Forensic Science in the United States: A Path Forward*, (Washington, D.C.: National Academies Press 2009).

Chapter 15

1. The Comprehensive Drug Abuse Prevention and Control Act of 1970 21 USC § 801 et seq.; 21 (1970).

2. SWGDRUG, *The Scientific Working Group for the Analysis of Seized Drugs (SWGDRUG) Recommendations, Revision 6.* U. S. Dept. of Justice, Drug Enforcement Administration (2011).

3. Committee On Identifying the Needs of the Forensic Science Community, *Strengthening Forensic Science in the United States: a Path Forward*, (Washington, D. C.: National Academies Press 2009).

4. *Id.*

Chapter 16

1. Interview of Judge Andrea A. Darvas by William S. Bailey, July 6, 2012.

2. Interview of Judge Robert S. Lasnik by William S. Bailey, July 15, 2012.

3. Interview of Judge William L. Downing by William S. Bailey, June 8, 2012.
4. Interview of Judge William L. Downing by William S. Bailey, June 8, 2012.
5. Interview of Judge William L. Downing by William S. Bailey, June 8, 2012.
6. Interview of Judge Robert S. Lasnik by William S. Bailey, July 15, 2012.
7. Interview of Judge Robert S. Lasnik by William S. Bailey, July 15, 2012.
8. Interview of Elizabeth A. Leedom by William S. Bailey, April 10, 2012.
9. Interview of Judge Andrea A. Darvas by William S. Bailey, July 6, 2012.
10. Interview of Judge William L. Downing by William S. Bailey, June 8, 2012.
11. Interview of Judge William L. Downing by William S. Bailey, June 8, 2012.
12. Interview of Judge William L. Downing by William S. Bailey, June 8, 2012.
13. Interview of Judge Ronald Kessler by William S. Bailey, March 19, 2012.
14. John Cloud, "The First Major Murder Trial of the Social Media Age," *Time* (June 27, 2011).
15. Interview of Judge Ronald Kessler by William S. Bailey, March 19, 2012.
16. Interview of Judge Andrea A. Darvas by William S. Bailey, July 6, 2012.
17. Interview of Judge Robert S. Lasnik by William S. Bailey, July 15, 2012.
18. Interview of Judge Ronald Kessler by William S. Bailey, March 19, 2012.
19. Interview of Judge Robert S. Lasnik by William S. Bailey, July 15, 2012.
20. Interview of Judge Andrea A. Darvas by William S. Bailey, July 6, 2012.
21. Interview of Judge William L. Downing by William S. Bailey, June 8, 2012.
22. Interview of Judge William L. Downing by William S. Bailey, June 8, 2012.

Chapter 17

1. Interview of Elizabeth A. Leedom by William S. Bailey, April 10, 2012.
2. Interview of Judge William L. Downing by William S. Bailey, June 8, 2012.
3. Interview of Todd W. Gardner by William S. Bailey, April 27, 2012.
4. Interview of Philip Vogelzang, M.D. by William S. Bailey, November 17, 2010.
5. Interview of Allan F. Tencer, Ph.D by William S. Bailey, June 20, 2012.
6. Interview of Elizabeth A. Leedom by William S. Bailey, April 10, 2012.
7. Interview of Elizabeth A. Leedom by William S. Bailey, April 10, 2012.

Chapter 18

1. *House v. Combined Ins. Co. of Amer.*, 168 F.R.D. 236, 238 (N.D. Iowa 1996).
2. Fed. R. Civ. P. 26, *Committee Notes on Rules—2010 Amendment*.
3. *Id.*
4. *Id.*
5. Several opinions have acknowledged and discussed this split. *See, e.g., R.C. Olmstead, Inc. v. CU Interface*, 657 F. Supp. 2d 899, 904 (N.D. Ohio 2009) ("The cases addressing this precise issue follow two lines of authority."); *Estate of Manship v. U.S.*, 240 F.R.D. 229, 233 (M.D. La. 2006) (finding that courts addressing this issue have "consistently discussed two lines of cases which reached conflicting outcomes …").
6. *Olmstead*, 657 F. Supp. at 902 ("overwhelming majority"); *Davis v. Carmel Clay Schools*, 2013 WL 2159476, at *3 (S.D. Ind. 2013) ("prevailing view," at least until 2009).
7. 136 F.R.D. 638 (N.D. Ill. 1991).
8. *See, e.g., Estate of Manship*, 240 F.R.D. at 234 (stating that these cases "originate from" *Ross*).
9. *Ross*, 136 F.R.D. at 639.
10. *Id.*
11. 727 F.2d 888, 891 (10th Cir. 1984). In *Durflinger*, the court only implicitly addressed the re-designation issue. It held simply that a defendant who had requested and received a report from plain-

tiff's consulting expert violated the FRCP's work product protections, and it held so despite the fact that the expert had previously been designated as a testifying one.

12. 136 F.R.D. at 639.

13. 190 F.R.D. 670, 671 (E.D. Wash. 2000).

14. *Id.* at 672.

15. *Estate of Manship*, 240 F.R.D. at 237.

16. *Id.*

17. *See, e.g., Olmstead*, 657 F. Supp. 2d at 904 (holding that re-designation of testifying expert as non-testifying restores work product protections and accordingly blocking deposition of former testifying expert who had already offered a report); *Callaway Golf Co. v. Dunlop Slazenger Group Americas*, 2002 WL 1906628 (D. Del. 2002) (holding that re-designation as non-testifying insulates expert from discovery regardless of whether opinions were already disclosed and noting that this approach is the "common theme"); *FMC Corp. v. Vendo Co.*, 196 F. Supp .2d 1023, 1046 (E.D. Cal. 2002) (applying the exceptional circumstances standard to attempted discovery of re-designated expert). *See also Fed. Ins. Co. v. St. Paul Fire and Marine Ins. Co.*, 2008 WL 761417, at *3 (N.D. Cal. 2008); *Green v. Nygaard*, 213 Ariz. 460, 143 P.3d 393, 397 (2006); *Dayton–Phoenix Group, Inc. v. Gen. Motors Corp.*, 1997 WL 1764760 (S.D. Ohio 1997).

18. *Employer's Reinsurance Corp. v. Clarendon Nat. Ins. Co.*, 213 F.R.D. 422, 426 (D. Kan. 2003).

19. *Id.*

20. 168 F.R.D. 236 (N.D. Iowa 1996).

21. *Id.* at 245.

22. *Id.* at 246.

23. *See, e.g., Ferguson v. Michael Foods, Inc.*, 189 F.R.D. 408 (D. Minn. 1999) (citing and adopting the approach taken in *House*); *Agron v. Trustees of Columbia Univ.*, 176 F.R.D. 445, 448–50 (S.D.N.Y. 1997) (identification of expert as a witness and disclosure of that expert's report and opinions waived the consultative expert discovery protections).

24. *See, e.g., Olmstead*, 657 F. Supp. 2d at 903; *Callaway Golf Co.,* 2002 WL 1906628 at *3 (describing the opposite approach as the "common theme").

25. 557 F.3d 736, 744 (7th Cir. 2009).

26. *Id.*

27. *See Davis v. Carmel Clay Schools*, 2013 WL 2159476 at *5–7 (S.D. Ind. 2013) (discussing *Koenig*, the Seventh Circuit opinions flowing from it on this issue, and the trend that they reveal).

Chapter 19

1. Benedict Carey, "This Is Your Life," *The New York Times*, May 22, 2007.

2. Interview of Elizabeth A. Leedom by William S. Bailey, April 10, 2012.

3. Interview of Elizabeth A. Leedom by William S. Bailey, April 10, 2012.

4. Richard E. Mayer, ed., *The Cambridge Handbook Of Multi-Media Learning*, 22, (Cambridge: University Press, 2005).

5. Scott McCloud, *Understanding Comics*, 140–41 (Northampton: Kitchen Sink Press, 1993).

6. Allan Paivio, *Mental Representations: A Dual Coding Approach*, (Oxford: University Press, 1966).

7. Mayer, *supra*, at 13.

8. G. A. Miller, "The Magic Number Seven, Plus or Minus Two: Some Limits on Our Capacity for Processing Information," *Psychological Review* 63, 81–97 (1956).

9. L. Peterson and M. Peterson, "Short-Term Retention of Individual Verbal Items," *Journal Of Experimental Psychology* 58, 193–98 (1959).

10. Marshall McLuhan and Quentin Fiore, *The Medium Is the Massage*, 114 (New York: Bantam Books, 1967).

11. *See generally* J. R. Levin & A. M. Lesgold, "On Pictures and Prose," 26 *Communication & Technology*, 233–43 (1978); J. R. Levin, "On Functions of Pictures and Prose," in F. J. Pirozzolo and M.C.

Wittrock (Eds), *Neuropsychological & Cognitive Processes In Reading* (New York: Academic Press, 1981).

12. Sylvie Molitor, et al., *Knowledge Acquisition from Text and Pictures*, Mandl & Levin (Eds), (Amsterdam: Elsevier, 1989).

13. Edward Tufte, "PowerPoint Is Evil—Power Corrupts. PowerPoint Corrupts Absolutely," *Wired*, November, 2009.

14. Lynn Oppenheim, *A Study of the Effects of the Use of Overhead Transparencies on Business Meetings* (Philadelphia: Wharton Applied Research Center, 1981).

15. *Id.*

	CONSENSUS	NO CONSENSUS
NO OVERHEADS	58%	42%
OVERHEADS	79%	21%

16. Douglas R. Vogel, Gary W. Dickson, and John A. Lehman, "Persuasion and the Role of Visual Presentation Support," (June 1986).

17. Mayer, *supra*, n. 4 at 13.

18. William Winn, "The Design & Use of Instructional Graphics," 134, in *Knowledge Acquisition from Text & Pictures,* Mandl & Levin (Eds), (Amsterdam: Elsevier, 1989).

19. *Id.*

20. Mayer, *supra*, n. 4 at 187.

21. Richard E. Mayer, *Multi-Media Learning*, 73–80 (Cambridge: University Press, 2001). Mayer reports the following increases in retention and transfer through the use of multi-media:
   1. Using both words and pictures.
      - Retention + 23%
      - Transfer + 89%
   2. Putting words and pictures close together on a page.
      - Retention + 42%
      - Transfer + 68%
   3. Simultaneous words and pictures.
      - Retention 0%
      - Transfer + 60%
   4. Eliminating unnecessary words and visual information.
      - Retention + 126%
      - Transfer + 82%
   5. Narration rather than on screen text.
      - Retention + 30%
      - Transfer + 80%

22. Molitor, et al., *supra*, n. 12 at 83.

23. D. A. Norman, *Things That Make Us Smart: Defending Human Attributes in the Age of the Machine*, xi (New York: Addison Wesley, 1993).

Chapter 20

1. Interview of Judge William L. Downing by William S. Bailey, June 8, 2012.
2. Interview of Mark R. Larson by William S. Bailey, March 12, 2012.
3. Interview of Todd W. Gardner by William S. Bailey, April 27, 2012.
4. Interview of Mark R. Larson by William S. Bailey, March 12, 2012.
5. Interview of Elizabeth A. Leedom by William S. Bailey, April 10, 2012.
6. Interview of Ralph J. Brindley by William Bailey, May 30, 2012.
7. Interview of Mark R. Larson by William S. Bailey, March 12, 2012.
8. Interview of Ralph J. Brindley by William Bailey, May 30, 2012.
9. Interview of Dr. Allan F. Tencer by William S. Bailey, June 20, 2012.
10. Interview of Judge William L. Downing by William S. Bailey, June 8, 2012.
11. Interview of Dr. Allan F. Tencer by William S. Bailey, June 20, 2012.

12. Interview of Dr. Allan F. Tencer by William S. Bailey, June 20, 2012.
13. Interview of Elizabeth A. Leedom by William S. Bailey, April 10, 2012.
14. Interview of Todd W. Gardner by William S. Bailey, April 27, 2012.
15. Interview of Todd W. Gardner by William S. Bailey, April 27, 2012.
16. Interview of Todd W. Gardner by William S. Bailey, April 27, 2012.
17. Interview of Ralph J. Brindley by William S. Bailey, May 30, 2012.
18. Interview of Todd W. Gardner by William S. Bailey, April 27, 2012.
19. Interview of Dr. Allan F. Tencer by William S. Bailey, June 20, 2012.
20. Interview of Dr. Allan F. Tencer by William S. Bailey, June 20, 2012.
21. Interview of Dr. Allan F. Tencer by William S. Bailey, June 20, 2012.

Chapter 21

1. *Philippides v. Bernard*, Superior Court of Washington for King County, Case No. 01-2-09974-4 SEA (2002).
2. *City of Seattle, LLC v. Professional Basketball Club, LLC*, Case No. 2:2007 CV 01620 (W.D. Wash. 2007).
3. Interview of Todd W. Gardner by William S. Bailey, April 27, 2012.

Chapter 22

1. C. Glenn Begley and Lee M. Ellis, "Drug Development: Raise Standards for Preclinical Cancer Research," *Nature*, 483, 531–33 (March 29, 2012).
2. *Id.* at 531.
3. Interview of Judge William L. Downing by William S. Bailey, June 8, 2012.

Chapter 23

1. Interview of Philip Vogelzang, M.D. by William S. Bailey, November 17, 2010.
2. Interview of Philip Vogelzang, M.D. by William S. Bailey, November 17, 2010.
3. Interview of Philip Vogelzang, M.D. by William S. Bailey, November 17, 2010.
4. Interview of Peter M. McGough, M.D. by William S. Bailey, September 14, 2009.
5. Institute of Medicine, *To Err Is Human: Building a Safer Health System* (Washington, D.C., November, 1999).
6. Department of Health and Human Services, Office of Inspector General, *Adverse Events in Hospitals: National Incidence among Medicare Beneficiarie*s, OEI-06-09-00090 (Washington, D.C., November, 2010).
7. Leah Binder, "Stunning News on Preventable Deaths in Hospitals," *Forbes*, (September 23, 2013) available at http://www.forbes.com/sites/leahbinder/.
8. Interview of Philip Vogelzang, M.D. by William S. Bailey, November 17, 2010.
9. Interview of Philip Vogelzang, M.D. by William S. Bailey, November 17, 2010.
10. Interview of Philip Vogelzang, M.D. by William S. Bailey, November 17, 2010.
11. Interview of Michael S. Wampold by William S. Bailey, April 19, 2011.
12. Interview of Elizabeth A. Leedom by William S. Bailey, April 10, 2012.
13. Interview of Peter M. McGough, M.D. by William S. Bailey, September 14, 2009.
14. Interview of Peter M. McGough, M.D. by William S. Bailey, September 14, 2009.
15. Alice Park, "A New Study Reveals Mammograms May Not Be Doing Much Good," *Time,* February 24, 2014.
16. Interview of Elizabeth A. Leedom by William S. Bailey, April 10, 2012.

Chapter 24

1. Edward Frenkel, "Is the Universe a Simulation?", *The New York Times*, February 16, 2014.

2. Interview of Professor Michael Townsend by William S. Bailey, May 4, 2012.

3. Interview of Professor Michael Townsend by William S. Bailey, May 4, 2012.

4. Interview of Professor Michael Townsend by William S. Bailey, May 4, 2012.

5. John P.A. Ioannidis, "Contradicted and Initially Stronger Effects in Highly Cited Clinical Research," *Journal of the American Medical Association* 294, 218–28 (2005).

6. *The Journal of Economic History*, Vol. 67, p. 849–83 (December, 2007).

7. Interview of Todd W. Gardner by William S. Bailey, April 27, 2012.

Chapter 25

1. Interview of Dr. Allan F. Tencer by William S. Bailey, June 20, 2012.

2. Interview of Dr. Peter M. McGough by William S. Bailey, September 14, 2009.

3. Interview of Todd W. Gardner by William S. Bailey, April 27, 2012.

4. Interview of Todd W. Gardner by William S. Bailey, April 27, 2012.

5. Interview of Judge William L. Downing by William S. Bailey, June 8, 2012.

6. Interview of Todd W. Gardner by William S. Bailey, April 27, 2012.

7. Interview of Judge William L. Downing by William S. Bailey, June 8, 2012.

8. Interview of Judge William L. Downing by William S. Bailey, June 8, 2012.

9. Interview of Elizabeth A. Leedom by William S. Bailey, April 10, 2012.

10. Interview of Judge William L. Downing by William S. Bailey, June 8, 2012.

11. Interview of Elizabeth A. Leedom by William S. Bailey, April 10, 2012.

12. Interview of Judge William L. Downing by William S. Bailey, June 8, 2012.

13. Interview of Judge Robert S. Lasnik by William S. Bailey, June 15, 2012.

Chapter 26

1. Interview of Elizabeth A. Leedom by William S. Bailey, April 10, 2012

2. Interview of Michael S. Wampold by William S. Bailey, April 19, 2011.

3. Interview of Judge Robert S. Lasnik by William S. Bailey, June 15, 2012.

4. Interview of Elizabeth A. Leedom by William S. Bailey, April 10, 2012.

5. Interview of Judge William L. Downing by William S. Bailey, June 8, 2012.

6. Interview of Todd W. Gardner by William S. Bailey, April 27, 2012.

7. Interview of Todd W. Gardner by William S. Bailey, April 27, 2012.

8. Interview of Michael S. Wampold by William S. Bailey, April 19, 2011.

9. Interview of Elizabeth A. Leedom by William S. Bailey, April 10, 2012.

10. Interview of Michael S. Wampold by William S. Bailey, April 19, 2011.

11. *United States v. Microsoft*, trial transcript (January 14, 1999).

12. Interview of Allan F. Tencer, Ph.D, by William S. Bailey, June 20, 2012.

13. Interview of Michael S. Wampold by William S. Bailey, April 19, 2011.

14. Interview of Judge Andrea Darvas by William S. Bailey, July 6, 2012.

15. Interview of Mark R. Larson by William S. Bailey, March 12, 2012.

16. Interview of Elizabeth A. Leedom by William S. Bailey, April 10, 2012.

17. Interview of Allan F. Tencer, Ph.D, by William S. Bailey, June 20, 2012.

18. Interview of Dr. Peter M. McGough by William S. Bailey, September 14, 2009.

19. Interview of Todd W. Gardner by William S. Bailey, April 27, 2012.

20. Interview of Elizabeth A. Leedom by William S. Bailey, April 10, 2012.

21. Interview of Todd W. Gardner by William S. Bailey, April 27, 2012.

22. Interview of Todd W. Gardner by William S. Bailey, April 27, 2012.

Photo and Illustration Credits

The attorney illustrations in the Takeaway sections are by Duane Hoffmann/Hoffmann Legal Design.

Figure	Source
2-1	Duane Hoffmann/Hoffmann Legal Design
2-2	Duane Hoffmann/Hoffmann Legal Design
3-1	Duane Hoffmann/Hoffmann Legal Design
4-1	Duane Hoffmann/Hoffmann Legal Design
4-2	Duane Hoffmann/Hoffmann Legal Design
5-1	Duane Hoffmann/Hoffmann Legal Design
6-1	Duane Hoffmann/Hoffmann Legal Design
7-1	Public Domain
7-2	Public Domain
7-3	Public Domain
7-4	Public Domain
7-5	Terry McAdam
8-1	Terry McAdam
8-2	Terry Franklin
8-3	Caleb Conn
9-1	Ian Goodhew; King County (WA) Sheriff's Office
9-2	Ian Goodhew; King County (WA) Sheriff's Office
9-3	Seattle P.D. CSI Unit
9-4	Seattle P.D. CSI Unit
9-5	Seattle P.D. CSI Unit
9-6	Tony Grissim, Leica Geosystems
9-7	Tony Grissim
9-8	Tony Grissim
9-9	Tony Grissim
9-10	Ian Goodhew; King County (WA) Sheriff's Office
9-11	Ian Goodhew; King County (WA) Sheriff's Office
11-1	Randy Watson & Sarah Trejo
11-2	Randy Watson & Sarah Trejo
11-3	Randy Watson & Sarah Trejo

11-4	Randy Watson & Sarah Trejo
11-5	Randy Watson & Sarah Trejo
11-6	Randy Watson & Sarah Trejo
11-7	Randy Watson & Sarah Trejo
11-8	Randy Watson & Sarah Trejo
11-9	Randy Watson & Sarah Trejo
11-10	Randy Watson & Sarah Trejo
11-11	Randy Watson & Sarah Trejo
11-12	Randy Watson & Sarah Trejo
12-1	Ray Kusumi
12-2	Terry Franklin
12-3	Ray Kusumi
13-1	Hoffmann Legal Design
13-2	Authors (created using Microsoft PowerPoint 2013)
13-3	© Thorstenschmitt	Dreamstime.com
13-4	forensicsciencesimplified.org
13-5	forensicsciencesimplified.org
13-6	forensicsciencesimplified.org
14-1	Ray Kusumi
15-1	Ray Kusumi
15-2	Ray Kusumi
17-1	Duane Hoffmann/Hoffmann Legal Design
17-2	Kevin C. Kealty, Jr.
18-1	Duane Hoffmann/Hoffmann Legal Design
19-1	Duane Hoffmann/Hoffmann Legal Design
19-2	Duane Hoffmann/Hoffmann Legal Design
19-3(a)	David Newman/Cognition Studio
19-3(b)	David Newman/Cognition Studio
19-4	Kevin C. Kealty, Jr.
19-5	Duane Hoffmann/Hoffmann Legal Design
19-6(a)	Duane Hoffmann/Hoffmann Legal Design
19-6(b)	Duane Hoffmann/Hoffmann Legal Design
19-6(c)	Kevin C. Kealty, Jr.
19-7(a)	Duane Hoffmann/Hoffmann Legal Design
19-7(b)	Duane Hoffmann/Hoffmann Legal Design
19-7(c)	Kevin C. Kealty, Jr.
19-8(a)	Aaron Weholt/Legal Media
19-8(b)	Aaron Weholt/Legal Media
19-8(c)	Aaron Weholt/Legal Media
19-8(d)	Kevin C. Kealty, Jr.
19-9(a)	Kevin C. Kealty, Jr.
19-9(b)	Kevin C. Kealty, Jr.
19-9(c)	Duane Hoffmann/Hoffmann Legal Design
19-9(d)	Aaron Weholt/Legal Media
19-9(e)	Duane Hoffmann/Hoffmann Legal Design

19-9(f)	Duane Hoffmann/Hoffmann Legal Design
19-9(g)	Kevin C. Kealty, Jr.
19-10	William S. Bailey
19-11	Duane Hoffmann/Hoffmann Legal Design
20-1	William S. Bailey
20-2	Duane Hoffmann/Hoffmann Legal Design
20-3	David Newman/Cognition Studio
20-4	Duane Hoffmann/Hoffmann Legal Design
20-5	William S. Bailey
20-6	William S. Bailey
20-7	Duane Hoffmann/Hoffmann Legal Design
20-8(a)	Onpoint Productions
20-8(b)	Onpoint Productions
20-8(c)	Onpoint Productions
20-9(a)	Aaron Weholt/Legal Media
20-9(b)	Aaron Weholt/Legal Media
20-9(c)	Aaron Weholt/Legal Media
20-9(d)	Duane Hoffmann/Hoffmann Legal Design
20-10(a)	William S. Bailey
20-10(b)	William S. Bailey
20-11(a)	William S. Bailey
20-11(b)	William S. Bailey
20-11(c)	William S. Bailey
20-11(d)	William S. Bailey
22-1	Duane Hoffmann/Hoffmann Legal Design
22-2(a)	William S. Bailey
22-2(b)	Kathy A. Cochran/Cochran Productions
23-1	Duane Hoffmann/Hoffmann Legal Design
24-1	Duane Hoffmann/Hoffmann Legal Design
24-2	William S. Bailey
24-3(a)	Kevin C. Kealty, Jr.
24-3(b)	Kevin C. Kealty, Jr.
24-3(c)	Kevin C. Kealty, Jr.
24-4	Duane Hoffmann/Hoffmann Legal Design
24-5(a)	Duane Hoffmann/Hoffmann Legal Design
24-5(b)	Duane Hoffmann/Hoffmann Legal Design
24-5(c)	Duane Hoffmann/Hoffmann Legal Design
25-1	Duane Hoffmann/Hoffmann Legal Design
25-2(a)	Kevin C. Kealty, Jr.
25-2(b)	Kevin C. Kealty, Jr.
25-2(c)	Kevin C. Kealty, Jr.
25-2(d)	Kevin C. Kealty, Jr.
25-3	Kevin C. Kealty, Jr.
26-1	Duane Hoffmann/Hoffmann Legal Design
26-2	Kevin C. Kealty, Jr.

26-3   William S. Bailey
26-4   Kevin C. Kealty, Jr.
C-1   City of Seattle
C-2   City of Seattle
C-3   Washington State Department of Labor and Industries
C-4   William S. Bailey
C-5   William S. Bailey
C-6   Mithon, Inc.
C-7   Harborview Medical Center, Radiology Department
C-8(a)   Onpoint Productions
C-8(b)   Onpoint Productions

Index